Imagining and Knowing

Works of fiction are works *of* the imagination and *for* the imagination. Gregory Currie energetically defends the familiar idea that fictions are guides to the imagination, a view which has come under attack in recent years. Responding to a number of challenges to this standpoint, he argues that within the domain of the imagination there lie a number of distinct and not well-recognized capacities which make the connection between fiction and imagination work. Currie then considers the question of whether in guiding the imagination fictions may also guide our beliefs, our outlook, and our habits in directions of learning. It is widely held that fictions very often provide opportunities for the acquisition of knowledge and of skills. Without denying that this sometimes happens, this book explores the difficulties and dangers of too optimistic a picture of learning from fiction. It is easy to exaggerate the connection between fiction and learning, to ignore countervailing tendencies in fiction to create error and ignorance, and to suppose that claims about learning from fiction require no serious empirical support. Currie makes a case for modesty about learning from fiction—reasoning that a lot of what we take to be learning in this area is itself a kind of pretence, that we are too optimistic about the psychological and moral insights of authors, that the case for fiction as a Darwinian adaptation is weak, and that empathy is both hard to acquire and not always morally advantageous.

Gregory Currie is Professor of Philosophy at the University of York. He was educated at the London School of Economics and at the University of California, Berkeley. He has taught at universities in Australia, New Zealand and the UK, and held visiting positions at the Australian National University, the University of Oxford, and the School for Advanced Studies in the Social Sciences (EHESS), Paris. He is a Fellow of the British Academy and of the Australian Academy of the Humanities.

T0355310

Imagining and Knowing

The shape of fiction

GREGORY CURRIE

OXFORD
UNIVERSITY PRESS

OXFORD
UNIVERSITY PRESS

Great Clarendon Street, Oxford, OX2 6DP,
United Kingdom

Oxford University Press is a department of the University of Oxford.
It furthers the University's objective of excellence in research, scholarship,
and education by publishing worldwide. Oxford is a registered trade mark of
Oxford University Press in the UK and in certain other countries

Published in the United States of America by Oxford University Press
198 Madison Avenue, New York, NY 10016, United States of America

British Library Cataloguing in Publication Data
Data available

Library of Congress Cataloging in Publication Data
Data available

ISBN 978-0-19-965661-5 (Hbk.)
ISBN 978-0-19-286468-0 (Pbk.)

To the memory of Alan Leslie Murray (1914–2005)
Head of History, John Ruskin Grammar School

Acknowledgements

Some of the material in this book was given as lectures at L'École des hautes études en sciences sociales, Paris in 2014. I am grateful to those who attended for their comments and criticism and especially to Pascal Engel for arranging my visit, and for the good philosophical company he has been over many years. Other material was given as an Olazabal Lecture at the University of Miami in 2017; I am grateful to Otávio Bueno and his colleagues for their generous hospitality, and their excellent criticism. Parts have been read at colloquia, workshops, and conferences around the world, and many people deserve my thanks for sitting through these talks and for offering helpful and constructive commentary. The fact that I recall only some of these contributions will not prevent me from thanking those I can remember, some of whom were helpful on several occasions: Catharine Abell, Paloma Atencia-Linares, Nancy Bauer, Jan Berofsky, Otávio Bueno, Simon Blackburn, Noel Carroll, Robyn Carston, Josep Corbi, Julien Deonna, Julian Dodd, Anya Farennikova, Owen Flanagan, Roman Frigg, Manuel García-Carpintero, Berys Gaut, Jonathan Gilmore, Peter Goldie, James Helgeson, Robert Hopkins, Matthew Kieran, Amy Kind, Fred Kroon, Peter Lamarque, Jerry Levinson, Bence Nanay, Fiona Macpherson, Tony Marcel, Aaron Meskin, Margaret Moore, Michael Morris, Adam Morton, Paul Noordhof, Catarina Dutilh Novaes, Elisa Paganini, Elizabeth Picciuto, Jesse Prinz, Jon Robson, Nancy Sherman, Natallia Schabner, Susanna Schellenberg, Barry Smith, Joel Smith, Murray Smith, Kathleen Stock, Mauricio Suárez, Adam Toon, Neil van Leeuwen, Tom Stoneham, Molly Wilder, Dawn Wilson, and Deirdre Wilson.

I'm particularly grateful to Terence Cave, whose Balzan-funded project 'Literature as an Object of Knowledge' gave me an ideal group of people to discuss literature and cognition with, including Terence himself; also to Steve Ross, who (literally) went out of his way to argue about the material in Chapter 10. Thanks to Andrew George for helping me understand the *Gilgamesh* epic, to Michael Devitt and Maria Jodłowiec for reading and commenting on Chapter 5, and to Stacie Friend, Paul Harris, and Fiora Salis for discussion of the topics of this book over a number of years. Special thanks are due to my former student Anna Ichino, now at the University of Milan, for many hours of discussion and collaborative work which resulted in two joint essays on which I draw on in Chapters 2 and 9. I am grateful to her generosity in allowing me to use material from these two essays here. Two readers for the Press (David Davies was one) provided extensive and detailed criticisms and suggestions. This may not be a good book and its faults are all my responsibility, but it is a better one for their work. Thanks, as always, to my editor, Peter Momtchiloff, for good advice, and for patience.

Time to work on this book was generously provided through a Leverhulme Foundation research grant (number RPG-2017-365). A collaboration with psychologist Heather Ferguson and philosopher Stacie Friend, this project aims to produce new empirical and philosophical work on the topic of Part III. In 2014 Peter Lamarque and I held a development grant for work on cognitive and aesthetic values in cultural artefacts as part of the AHRC's project 'Culture and Value' (AH/L005719/1). The workshops we held at that time (and all the delightful discussions we have had since then) have been important for shaping my thinking in this book. Finally, my thanks go to the University of York for granting me research leave, and my colleagues in Philosophy for taking on the extra work that such arrangements always involve.

I have incorporated some material from various publications into the book, always in substantially revised form. Those earlier publications are:

'Standing in the last ditch: on the communicative intentions of fiction-makers', *Journal of Aesthetics and Art Criticism* (2014) 72: 351–63.

'Aliefs do not exist', (with A. Ichino), *Analysis* (2010) 72: 788–98.

'Some ways to understand people', *Philosophical Explorations* (2008) 11: 211–18.

'Tragedy', *Analysis* (2010) 70, 1–7.

'Emotions fit for fictions', in S. Roeser and C. Todd (eds) *Emotions and Values*, Oxford University Press, 2014.

'On getting out of the armchair to do aesthetics', in M. Haug (ed.) *Philosophical Methodology: The Armchair or the Laboratory?* Routledge, 2013.

'Literature and theory of mind', in N. Carroll and J. Gibson (eds) *The Routledge Companion to Philosophy and Literature*, Routledge, 2015.

'Truth and trust in fiction', (with A. Ichino), in E. Sullivan-Bissett, H. Bradley, and P. Noordhof (eds) *Art and Belief*, Oxford University Press, 2018.

'Creativity and the insight that literature brings', in E. S. Paul and S. B. Kaufman (eds) *The Philosophy of Creativity*, Oxford University Press, 2014.

'Does fiction make us less empathic?' *Teorema* (2016) 25: 3–23.

I thank the editors and publishers concerned for permission to use this material.

I have dedicated this book to the memory of a teacher to whom I owe a great deal: Alan Murray, musician, Anglican, and democratic socialist. Educated at Cambridge in the 1930s, he taught a now inconceivable A-level history syllabus that ended in 1509. (For relaxation there was a Roman Britain paper, with Collingwood's 1937 work for the *Oxford History of England* as our guide). His teaching made me imagine (that is the only possible word) a career as a mediaevalist, propelling me into the LSE and a degree in mediaeval economic history, another defunct option. It was no loss to historical scholarship that I moved to philosophy and economics. Occasionally irritated by the arrogance of his sixth form, Mr Murray otherwise displayed a cheerful, reflective calm though his life, I came to know, was not easy.

My greatest debt, as always, is to Martha, Gabriel, and Penny.

G. C.

Contents

PART III: FICTION, KNOWLEDGE, AND IGNORANCE

Mr. Little: 'It amazes me that a man as young as you can have been able to plumb human nature so surely to its depths; to play with such an unerring hand on the quivering heart-strings of your reader; to write novels so true, so human, so moving, so vital!'
Wooster: 'Oh, it's just a knack.'

P. G. Wodehouse, *Jeeves in the Springtime*

... it is very important not to take all the examples in one's moral thinking out of fiction, as the young and those who have led sheltered lives are apt to do.

R. M. Hare, *Freedom and Reason*

The project: a geometry of fiction

It is unlikely that this book will attract screaming headlines from the tabloid newspapers. If it does, a typically misleading banner might read 'Imagination, Yes—Knowledge, No.' The first bit is fine, the second is wrong, but a hasty reading and the desire for a simple message may give rise to it. Hoping to avoid such mistakes I will briefly outline the project.

One thing I won't do in this book is to define *fiction*; I won't offer a set of conditions both necessary and sufficient for something to be an actual or possible case of what we intuitively regard as a work of fiction, even allowing as usual for minor deviation from intuition and for vagueness or stipulation about unclear cases. Attempts to do that need not be useless even if they don't succeed—we have learned a good deal about knowledge from the so far inconclusive attempt to define it. But there is, as Edward Craig (1990) has pointed out, another, perhaps complementary way to proceed. Craig (who was focusing on knowledge and not at all concerned with fiction) notes that there are things deeply important to an understanding of an idea that disappear in the ruthless stripping out that the search for necessary and sufficient conditions imposes. Even if we knew what those necessary and sufficient conditions were, we would still like an answer to the question: what role does that concept play in our life?

Craig answers his own question, the one about knowledge, by offering what he calls a 'state of nature explanation', which tells us how practices aimed at determining the reliability of informants might have arisen in response to the need for information. I don't have an explanation of this kind that is helpful for understanding the role of fiction in our lives and there are serious difficulties in the way of getting one. But it is not hard to see that asking the question is going to bring forth responses that appeal to either or both of two things: imagination and knowledge. It will be said that works of fiction are devices for transporting us, by way of the imagination, to 'other worlds' of experience, and that most of us do not have the imaginative and inventive capacities to create entertaining departures from reality; instead we identify and support those with the right kinds of talents to do that for us. So we have authors, and we have audiences. And it will be said that, while fictions certainly are devices of imaginative transport, they are often also the means by which we come to know things, to learn skills, and to sharpen our abilities. Indeed, one of the problems facing simple definitions of fiction in terms of imagination (e.g. 'a work of fiction is a representation the content of which intended to be imagined') is that a lot of what we find in works of fiction

Imagining and Knowing: The Shape of Fiction. Gregory Currie, Oxford University Press (2020). © Gregory Currie.
DOI: 10.1093/oso/9780199656615.001.0001

(stated or implied) is intended to inform or persuade and so to induce or reinforce belief.[1] Some will add that it's unlikely, on scientific grounds, that we would have our unrestrainable enthusiasm for fictions if it did not provide significant opportunities for useful learning of some kind.[2] In pursuing these two aspects of fiction's role in our lives I will come to somewhat different conclusions: first, that the imagination is deeply implicated in any engagement we make with fiction in ways that are, broadly speaking, quite well understood; second, that the idea of learning from fiction is immensely important to us but the nature and extent of that learning is obscure.

Part I deals with the imagination and Parts II and III are devoted to knowledge. While a picture of the role of fiction in our lives needs to account for both these factors—imagination and knowledge—I have sought to keep the arguments as independent from one another as I can, partly because I want to give people the opportunity to agree with me about knowledge without having to buy into sometimes controversial claims about the imagination. Certainly, my discussions of the ways we might get knowledge from fiction focus a good deal on how *imaginative engagement* with fictions might bring knowledge; this is most evident in Chapter 8. But the arguments depend very little on exactly how one conceptualizes imaginative engagement. Why, then, deal with imagination and knowledge between the covers of a single book? I suggest we think in this way: Instead of seeking to define fiction we are trying to describe the *shape* of fiction, and the shape of a thing can be highly significant and go a long way towards explaining our interest in it, without it being an essential property of the thing, let alone being absolutely definitive of it. Think of fiction as a rectangle, and our interest in its role as an interest in the rectangle's shape. Any discussion of shape needs to speak about the length and the breadth of the rectangle, though these are independent: a specification of length is consistent with any specification of breadth and vice versa. But once specified, length and breadth determine shape. That is pretty much how I am thinking about imagination and knowledge: as independent determiners of an important property—the shape of fiction.

Part I begins with a defence, and an elaboration, of this deep, non-definitional connection between fiction and imagination. I start with the idea of a fictive utterance, characterized by the intention to get an audience to imagine something. What we call works of fiction consist by no means exclusively of such utterances, so a definition 'from below' is not in prospect. But a look at our practices of categorizing works as fiction and arguing about whether this or that work is fiction shows how strongly we are guided in our judgements by the fiction/imagination connection. I also argue that a recent attempt to define fiction in other terms is unsatisfactory. A yet more radical proposal to dispense altogether with the idea

---

[1] See below, Section 1.3 for discussion of such cases.   [2] See below Chapter 7.

that there is a distinctive connection between fiction and imagination will also be rejected.

At the same time as people have worried that imagination might be less helpful for understanding fiction than was originally proposed, there has been a comparable tendency towards deflationism about the imagination outside the realm of fiction. Part I also displays some opposition to this tendency. Why? After all, this is a book about fiction, not about human behaviour in general. One reason is suggested by this observation of Tim Williamson:

> If we try to understand the imagination while taking for granted that fiction is its central or typical business, we go as badly wrong as we would if we tried to understand arms and legs while taking for granted that dancing is their central or typical business. (Williamson 2016: 123)

That's why a philosopher of fiction needs to be confident that their claims about imagination's role in the experience of fiction cohere well with what we should say about its role in those activities we can reasonably assume made having an imaginative capacity an advantageous trait, and hence one likely to have emerged in our distant past. In part of Chapter 2 I spend some time arguing for the explanatory power of the imagination in activities distinct from fiction making and fiction consuming.

The rest of Part I goes on the offensive, exploring some rather unfamiliar forms that imaginative engagement with fiction may take. A first thought about these cases might be that they exemplify a general fact about imagination: an imaginative project is able to draw on a range of capacities outside the domain of imagination itself, capacities such as desiring and responding emotionally to things. I'll argue instead that these capacities have their own distinctive imaginative versions; in co-opting these capacities the imagination makes them part of itself. All this is evident, I argue, in our engagement with fictions of various kinds. The connection between fiction and imagination is, therefore, wide as well as deep.

Part II takes up the question of how engagement with fiction affects our mental economy and our behaviour beyond the imaginative realm, how it creates belief and might even lead to knowledge, including practical forms of knowledge such as knowing how to do something, acquiring skills and being able to understand what certain experiences are like. This part is exploratory with a nuanced message the tabloids will never get. But nuance is no excuse for unclarity or evasion so here is a shot at saying where I am going in this part, and why.

I don't say we cannot or do not learn from fictions. That will never, I am sure, be a reasonable conclusion to draw. At best we will be able to say, with some confidence, that learning from fiction is apt/not apt to take place for some people, in some circumstances, for some works of fiction. But I do think that the idea that we learn from fictions of any kinds faces difficulties not well recognized by those who want to argue that fictions are generally or often or sometimes 'educative', though this term suggests a model of learning I shall quickly distance myself from.[3] In pointing to some of these difficulties and trying to estimate their danger I hope I won't be regarded as an enemy of learning from fiction; someone on the *Titanic* looking out for icebergs would not have been labelled 'an enemy of transatlantic travel'.[4]

One reason for a cautious attitude to the idea that we learn from fiction is that we want it to be true. Give us a random sequence of numbers and we will find a pattern in it; look for faces and we find them in clouds and on stones; look for reasons and we find plans and motives in the accidental, a meaning in history, a god in the world. The drive for intelligibility is vastly satisfied in imaginative storytelling, which so often imposes a pattern on events that would never be there in reality. And the belief that reading quality fiction does us some good is almost an article of faith with liberal, educated people; the example of Mr. Gradgrind has made it difficult to question this view without seeming to adopt a particularly soulless form of utilitarianism. While there is some evidence to point to and which we will consider, the situation is best compared to that concerning the effects of children's pretend play, also widely believed to confer all sorts of cognitive and other advantages. While many studies over several decades have claimed that pretend play is crucial to the development of various capacities in children, including understanding mental states, a review by Angeline Lillard and colleagues (2013) concludes that there is after all little real evidence that pretend play aids in the development of this or other capacities. The details of Lillard's conclusions will be tested over time, but her work does suggest that we have been too confident about the positive benefits of pretend play, and too ready to accept questionable evidence in that view's favour. We should be similarly hesitant about the connection between empathy and fiction, especially given that the number of studies claiming a positive effect of fiction on empathy is small by comparison with the number claiming positive effects for pretend play. There is every reason here for caution—even for some healthy scepticism.

With the chapters in Part III I hope in a small way to shift the terms of the debate over learning from fiction. Contrast two kinds of dispute. The first is focused on settling matters of fact, such as whether smoking causes cancer or whether humans and chimpanzees have a common ancestor. Responsible participants, while they may have ethical and emotional investments in one side, try to seek evidence and arguments which support the line they advocate, while trying also to remain sensitive to the merits of their opponents' position. Such debates

---

[3] I regard my earlier self as a pretty bad offender in this regard; see my (1995), (1998).

[4] A reader suggested that my attitude towards learning from fiction is analogous to that of Anne Eaton towards the case against pornography (Eaton, 2007); while my arguments are, as far as I can see, independent of hers, Eaton's paper is certainly a paradigm of reasoned and evidenced re-assessment.

rarely bring about a quick victory for one side or the other, but they do often in the long term bring about a convergence of opinion that either favours the side able to gather the strongest evidence, or finds some rational and lasting compromise between them.

The second kind of dispute involves activity that it is hard to classify as argumentative or evidence-seeking, and is closer to expressive behaviour, exercises in rhetorical speech, and displays of affiliation to a group. The claims made in these sorts of debates often seem deliberately inflated, are hard to associate with the provision of reasons, and display a pervasive insensitivity to evidential issues. Moral and political debate is often of this kind, though I don't claim that this is the essential condition of debate in these domains.

We see disputes of both these kinds concerning the cognitive effects of fiction. But there is an asymmetry in the location of what we might call the positive and the negative cases. The positive case is the case for fiction as cognitive improvement: improvement in belief, in cognitive skills, in emotional sensitivity and regulation, in self-understanding. The negative case is the case for thinking that fictions (only some, of course) bring about cognitive harm, especially where that harm might be violent or anti-social behaviour; these days the focus here is mostly on fictions in visual media.

Note, these are two independent debates, not two opposed sides in a single debate; you can, and probably should, think that fictions have good and bad effects on their audiences. There is, however, a contrast between how these two debates are typically conducted. Arguments about the harm that (some) fictions may cause are, these days at least, expected to be conducted with an eye to the evidence available.[5] Those who condemn various kinds of fiction as leading to ignorance, error, or bad behaviour are rightly challenged to produce evidence for their claims, and the few philosophers who have taken up this cause have generally been careful to seek evidential support for their case.[6] By contrast, we find books extolling the improving powers of fiction which fail to provide, or even consider providing, any evidence.[7] Why is this so little remarked? Part of the answer may be that lack of evidence is disguised by the author managing to suggest that their own manifestly civilized values and demeanor are evidence enough for the claim; few people, by contrast, present themselves as instances of the power of literature to degrade and corrupt.[8]

---

[5] I mean arguments that engage public attention and which have some claim to be the representation of informed opinion; I don't include casual debates in the pub.

[6] See Hurley (2006) and Harold (2005); Eaton (2007) is also relevant here.

[7] See Nussbaum (1990) and Mack (2012); see comments on this issue in Anders Pettersson's (2012) review of Mack.

[8] And there is plenty of evidence that suggests our unreliability when it comes to self-assessment of positive social characteristics. People over-estimate their propensity to donate to charity or to give blood (Goethals 1986). A recent study of prison inmates found that they rated themselves above average in kindliness and morality and average in law-abidingness (Sedikides et al. 2014).

We should not automatically discount people's claims to know that literature has changed them, and changed them for the better, but there are reasons to be careful about such claims.[9] There are general grounds for doubting that people have reliable access to their own inner cognitive processes, of which learning is one; we also know that people are very apt to believe in the positive worth of things they have chosen to invest in.[10] It is quite possible that, rather than reporting realistically on their own development, the advocates of literary learning are persuaded by their own self-supporting but false accounts. And if the philosophical work on literature's positive moral and epistemic value is read mostly by those with a prior commitment to the value of reading, we can expect these accounts to receive a relatively uncritical welcome.

Perhaps this situation reflects a general principle: people are more seriously engaged by threats than they are by prospects of benefit.[11] Threats are up for urgent evaluation and need to be realistically understood if they are to be avoided. Benefits (especially somewhat vague ones unrelated to easily measurable aspects of well-being) lack urgency, sharply focused opposition is hard to find and debates, if any, generally resolve into distinct forms of approval of the activity concerned. It is pleasant to imagine these vaguely specified benefits, irksome to seek evidence that might show them to be illusory. In a literary context, these discussions are also useful occasions for displaying a certain kind of sensibility, a connoisseur's delight in subtlety, and an enlightened opposition to a narrowly scientific view of the world. Within the scope of such activities, manifestations of the claim that literature is good for you tend to be understood as well-meaning expressions of a favourable attitude towards the literary project rather than as serious factual claims urgently in need of evidence no one has yet found. If someone says they learned so much from *Anna Karenina* it seems poor form to ask: 'What exactly did you learn?'

The analogy between commitment to the idea of learning from literature and moral and political commitment goes further. With all three we see, at least in the public media, a quasi-religious asymmetry: while those who believe in the educative power of literature don't often seek evidence relevant to their view they do show some enthusiasm for positive evidence combined with a tendency to ignore or explain away negative evidence. In discussion I've noted a highly predictable degree of hostility to the idea that evidence could weaken the claim that we learn from literature; the effects of literature are too subtle, too pervasive, to be

---

[9] In Chapter 6 I will ask whether this request for evidence of what people have learned is secondary to a deeper, more traditionally philosophical question about what there is to be learned.

[10] On the failures of introspection see Carruthers (2011). For a wealth of evidence on this topic see Doris (2015). In a study about which I say more later, (Kahnaman and Klein 2009) the authors, the second of whom has a generally pro-attitude to expert judgement, agree that one thing that is not predictive of expert competence is the subject's own confidence in their judgement.

[11] This is called loss aversion: see Kahneman and Tversky (1984). But the explanatory power of loss aversion has been questioned; see Gal (2006).

discovered by the crass methods of the sciences. But when some (apparent) positive evidence of this crass kind comes along, it is greeted by many with uncritical enthusiasm. A 2013 study by Emanuele Castano and David Comer Kidd, purporting to show improvements in empathy skills brought about by specifically literary fictions caused a stir in the media, with one novelist whose work was used in the study commenting, 'This is why I love science ... [The researchers] found a way to prove true the intangible benefits of literary fiction.'[12] No clear replication of the results has been achieved.[13] I don't say that the advocates of the positive case invariably conform to this model; it is possible to gather interesting arguments from their writings, along with a supply of useful examples.[14] But a good deal of work in this genre does conform, and even the best work rarely avoids its temptations altogether.

My project is no righteous crusade. An enthusiastic and somewhat poorly evidenced commitment to the positive value of literature is not so very wrong: its drawbacks are modest by comparison with many evils abroad; it may, all things considered, be the right attitude to take. Perhaps a somewhat dogmatic and emotionally driven belief in the positive effects of literature goes with a generally optimistic, life-enhancing outlook; reading literature is certainly enjoyable, and it is hard to believe that anyone will be seriously harmed by reading Proust or Henry James, even if they do so in the expectation of cognitive gains that turn out to be illusory. I do not pretend that this book is a defence against a civilization-threatening ideology. All I suggest is that serious academic scholarship on the subject should not be blind to the evidence and arguments I shall highlight.

Isn't setting up literature to be judged by the standards of science setting it up to fail? Writers through the twentieth century have thought so: T. S. Eliot, John Crow Ransom, I. A. Richards, Cleanth Brooks along with Nietzsche, Wittgenstein, Rorty, Scruton.[15] Writers in the tradition of post-structuralism and deconstructionalism have not generally been moved to offer defences of a rigorously empirical and scientific approach. The very disparate outlooks represented by these thinkers cannot be reviewed here. I make just a few simple points. The first is that

---

[12] *New York Times*, 3 October 2013. See http://well.blogs.nytimes.com/2013/10/03/i know how youre-feeling-i-read-chekhov/?_php=trueand_type=blogsand_r=0. The study in question is Kidd and Castano (2013). According to Vera Nünning (2015) 'There is even one pioneer study, recently published in the journal *Science* (2013), demonstrating that reading literary fiction improves social cognition, while reading popular fiction did not have such an effect (Kidd and Castano)'; see also Young (2017): 'The results of Kidd and Castano (2013) could be taken as the basis for a reliabilist defence of literary fiction as a source of true belief' (p. 88). See also Buckwalter and Tullmann (2017: 206). For doubts about the soundness of the Kidd and Castano study's methods, see https://slate.com/human_interest/2013/10/empathy_gap_dont_believe_that_widely_reported_study_in_science_about_literary_fiction_and_social_intelligence.html.

[13] For failure to replicate see Panero et al. (2016). Kidd and Castano have replied, claiming that the conditions of the replication were unsatisfactory (Kidd and Castano 2017). Their own (2018) attempt to replicate some of their earlier results has had mixed success.

[14] Particularly thoughtful and developed versions are Carroll (2002) and Engel (2016).

[15] See Novitz (1987: Chapter 1) for discussion of these views.

it is one thing (and a wrong thing, perhaps) to suppose that literature gives us knowledge of the same kind and in the same way that science does. It is another thing (and I claim a correct thing) to insist that the claims of literature to give us knowledge of whatever kind be judged by the very standards that are used in assessing the claim of science to do the same. Whose standard do we use? Those of science, I say. But isn't that just what's at issue here?

No. The standard of science is empirical evidence and that is, or should be, everyone's standard—at least in factual matters.[16] It is not only science that requires empirical support for the claims it makes: in the courts, in folk psychology, in controversy over spiritualism, in finance and business. In all these areas and more we regularly expect claims to be supported by evidence taking the form, roughly speaking, of observable events which the claims, if true, would lead us to expect to occur. There are areas of inquiry where some people are prepared to depend on other things to validate their opinions. In religion many take the fact that it says something in a book as definitive proof of some proposition; it seems to me unlikely that anyone will seriously claim that arguments about the epistemic efficacy of fiction ought to be supported in this way; at the least, no one I know of has claimed that, and without any such argument on the table I won't consider that view further.

There are distinctively scientific ways of arriving at the sort of evidence I'm talking about here; witness the psychological work reported in some of these chapters, which involves large numbers of subjects, controlled experimental situations, and statistical analysis of the results. This is not what we find in ordinary debates between critics or book-lovers. But all these things are simply *refinements* of the common-sense notion of empirical evidence, devices for finding empirical evidence that would not be visible in less structured situations or without large numbers of people to study or without finely grained techniques to assess the difference between outcomes. It is not controversial that we sometimes need to intervene in situations in order to see whether a certain claim is true—simply staring at the world is not always good enough. It is not controversial that some effects are only related to their causes in quite complex ways, that to see how they are related we need to shield our results from other and confounding factors, that the contribution of different factors to an outcome vary a lot, and how much each factor contributes is not always easy to see. Experimental methods simply provide us with ways of getting around these difficulties.

My enthusiasm for an empirical approach to learning from fiction goes, however, with a cautious approach to the empirical data currently available.

---

[16] Quine said '[t]he scientist is indistinguishable from the common man in his sense of evidence, except that the scientist is more careful. This increased care is not a revision of evidential standards, but only the more patient and systematic collection and use of what anyone would deem to be evidence' (1976: 233).

Empirical results never provide an absolutely firm foundation for inquiry and those in psychology are high on the contestability scale. The empirical study of fiction is of recent invention and, as noted earlier, results of any kind are few. The replication crisis is as likely to be of concern here as anywhere.[17] At this stage philosophical argument is a great stabilizing force and I will use it a good deal. In the places where I draw most extensively on empirical results (Sections 10.2 and 11.7 are particularly burdened with references to the evidence) the work concerned is often of indirect relevance to learning from fiction: it concerns such issues as illusions of expertise, self-licensing, and the psychology of creativity. The literature I have struggled with most, though, is philosophical. In recent years there has been a great outpouring of work on learning from fiction, and giving serious consideration to much of it would have broken up the argument in a way I thought undesirable. The compromise was to comment briefly—sometimes in the text, sometimes in longer notes—on contributions that had relevance to just that stage of the argument. This meant simply ignoring a lot of good work.

In drawing on empirical research I have also been selective. Have I made a mistake Murray Smith (2017: 3) calls attention to: cherry-picking the results that suit me? It's unlikely I am free from confirmation bias, but I also do not see it as my task here to produce an even-handed survey of what the evidence tells us about the idea of learning from fiction. My aim here is to argue that this idea faces a harder struggle for rational acceptance than is generally recognized. We hear a lot about fiction's role in promoting knowledge and understanding, enlarging the imagination and expanding our capacity for empathy. Evidence for some of these claims is available and more can surely be found. But the relation between fiction and learning is massively complicated; we should not let our humanistic values drive us to a defensive posture every time it is suggested that knowledge from fiction might not be so easy to get, that we might sometimes end up with ignorance and error, that it's sometimes easier to have an illusion of knowing than it is to know, that the contours of the fiction/knowledge landscape can't be mapped from the philosopher's armchair. For all that I have, I believe, been fair to those who are generally positive towards the idea of learning from fiction. The book considers as many of the plausible pathways to such learning as could reasonably be included, as well as various kinds of learning those pathways could deliver. In criticizing arguments, I have granted controversial assumptions where I can and sometimes considered at least the first line of response that their defenders might give. But my primary aim is to display a side of the argument not

---

[17] The replication crisis has emerged over the last decade and has undermined confidence in experimental results in social psychology and other areas of empirical research. When experiments with apparently significant outcomes are repeated it often turns out that the previously reported result is not found. See e.g. Pashler and Wagenmakers (2012). In earlier work I cited Williams and Bargh's (2008) study purporting to show that holding a cup of hot coffee affects people's judgements of personal warmth; attempts to replicate this result have failed (Chabris et al. 2019).

often heard. For an attempt to make out the best case for learning from fiction the reader will have to look elsewhere.

*

Finally in this introduction I acknowledge some restrictions I have accepted, or perhaps imposed on myself, regarding the kinds of positions and arguments to be considered. The long tradition of valuing fictions for their insights into human nature and conduct has been focused mostly on drama (largely Greek and Elizabethan) and the novel (largely through the last two and a half centuries). Very recently film has come in for special attention. The kinds of arguments I am considering are intended to have very general application and I have avoided extended discussion of particular works, periods, or genres; nor have I given separate consideration to distinct media. So while, for example, I have responded occasionally to some claims that are made about the epistemic value of film I have considered them within the context of more general discussions. I have not therefore given serious consideration to a position which has come lately into focus according to which film has a special, perhaps unique, role in the creation of philosophical knowledge. I agree with Paisley Livingston and others that film is well able to illustrate philosophical ideas in distinctly cinematic ways (analogous claims being allowed concerning drama and the novel).[18] But I offer no view as to whether cinema, as a distinctive vehicle of fictional narration, can contribute through illustration or in other ways to the uncovering of truths important to philosophy. Resolving this question seems to me to depend on what we say about the role of images in argumentation, on the proper understanding of the relation between imagination and perception, and indeed on how we see the relation between philosophy and the discovery of truth. It may be a failing that I have not tackled these difficult issues here, but it is not a fatal one. Gödel would be much less revered if he had said, 'I have shown that it's impossible to prove the consistency of first-order arithmetic by finite means, except perhaps in one or two ways I have not examined.' Since I am far from offering an impossibility proof for learning from fiction I am not open to criticism of that sort.[19]

Finally, a note on terminology. I have said that in this debate attention is often on works in the novelistic and dramatic tradition regarded as canonical, most often Shakespearean drama, the English, Russian, and French realist novels of the nineteenth century and their modernist descendants. 'Literature' is for my

---

[18] See Mulhall (2001), also Livingston (2006), Wartenberg (2006), and Smith (2006), all in the *Journal of Aesthetics and Art Criticism*'s issue on film and philosophy, 64 (2006). More recent contributions to the debate include Smuts (2009) and the response in Chapter 1 of Livingston (2009). Wartenberg (2007) develops the idea of film as thought experiment through a number of detailed case studies; for criticism of the general idea of seeing fictions as informative thought experiments see below, Section 8.4.

[19] That philosophical understanding can contribute materially to the interpretation of films is illustrated by a fine essay from Levine (2009).

purposes in many ways a misleading term: I'm interested in the epistemic claims of film, I see a case for genre fictions of various kinds, and I have no commitment (for present purposes) to the traditional canon. But occasionally referring to literature and the literary reminds us that it is a perfectly acceptable move in the argument to insist that it is only fictions of a certain quality that are likely to be epistemically valuable; it is a too easy victory for scepticism to point to the many agreed examples of worthless fictions.

PART I

IMAGINATION'S EMPIRE

It is easy to exaggerate the power of the imagination; as Bolingbroke noted, we cannot cloy the hungry edge of appetite by bare imagination of a feast. But imagination is a powerful tool for planning, invention, connection with others, and entertainment. It makes available to us the practice of fiction in which vast amounts of human energy and interest are now invested. Though too much is asked of it sometimes its extensive domains are very real.

The first two chapters in Part I respond to a variety of objections that have been put to the idea of a close (very close) connection between fiction and the imagination, and to some more general claims that the imagination is not so important in our lives as some have thought. Having, I hope, put these concerns to rest and stabilized the situation, I get more expansive in the following two chapters; each identifies aspects of cognitive functioning that deserve to be seen as varieties of imaginative activity. They concern desire and emotion respectively.

Imagining and Knowing: The Shape of Fiction. Gregory Currie, Oxford University Press (2020). © Gregory Currie.
DOI: 10.1093/oso/9780199656615.001.0001

1

An essential connection

1.1 First thoughts on fiction, imagination, and learning

Fictions come in many varieties. Some stay close to the historical facts, their authors taking care to tell us only of the thoughts and actions of real people, though typically those thoughts and actions are not claimed to be, in all detail, the ones those real people had and did. I assume that to be worth the name, a fiction must contain *some* content which is not presented as true; even those who dispute this will agree that fictions presented as entirely true are rare.[1] And those who think we can learn from fiction don't focus their hopes on these rare cases; they don't claim that nearness to truth is even a rough surrogate for learning potential.[2] People who prize learning from fiction don't rate Henry James and George Eliot low in epistemic potential because their characters and situations are largely invented; on the contrary, they place high value on the insights of these authors and their fellow canonicals in the novelistic tradition. It's a natural thought that the imaginative freedom of authors like these contributes strongly to their ability to generate and spread the kinds of learning we will later discuss. In these cases high levels of imaginative content are said to go with high learning potential.

We might say the same about the other side of the transaction: the reader's. Despite talk of the believability of fictional stories we hardly ever actually believe in the existence of Anna Karenina or Mr. Lydgate, and things have gone badly wrong if we do.[3] We imagine them existing and doing the things the story says they do. And it is only when the reader's imagination is fully engaged with the characters' motives that we may learn something important about the complexities of decision and action. But how can *knowledge* arise from that sort of enterprise? How can we learn from an engagement with something that depends so crucially on what can seem like the antithesis of knowing—imagining?[4]

---

[1] For more on this issue see below, this chapter, Section 1.3.

[2] Attempts to explicate the notion of nearness to truth or verisimilitude have failed (see Oddie 2014).

[3] While this is close to a consensus view in philosophy at present there are deniers, e.g. Buckwalter and Tullmann (2017), who argue that we can explain our engagement with fictions in terms of 'genuine attitudes' such as beliefs.

[4] Allan Hazlett argues that cases of imagining prompted by fictions can be cases of knowledge, thus denying that a person's propositional knowledge is a proper subclass of what they believe (Hazlett 2017). I am not persuaded by the arguments given. But while I here treat knowledge as belief, that is largely for purposes of exposition; the arguments I will give could be reformulated to accommodate propositional knowing which is not believing.

Imagining and Knowing: The Shape of Fiction. Gregory Currie, Oxford University Press (2020). © Gregory Currie.
DOI: 10.1093/oso/9780199656615.001.0001

We should avoid answering the question with a trivializing account of the relation between learning and imagination. Given a broad enough conception of the imagination, it will turn out that imagination is involved in any process of learning we can find, because imagination is involved in all mental activity. McGinn (2004:148) argues that grasp of meaning requires the exercise of the cognitive imagination—something he distinguishes from the use of mental imagery. That implies that learning anything that involves meaning (and what doesn't?) involves the imagination. Think also of Hume's idea that we use imagination when we assume the continuity of objects between episodes of visibility; in that case the imagination is a pervasive feature of even low-level cognition.

To make the question more interesting I propose to focus on imaginative activities which are a bit more sophisticated, and are, or can be, under some degree of conscious control: things like coming up with novel explanations, thinking through a supposition, putting yourself in an imagined situation. These are things most of us do a great deal of the time, and they can be done well or badly. Done well, they mark the doer as 'imaginative'. But I am not focusing on flights of imaginative genius or even notable talent here. My focus is on the middle range where the sensitive, diligent, but otherwise unremarkable reader can be expected to think imaginatively about what the maker of fiction puts before them.

From here we can proceed in either of two ways. The first is to argue that there are, after all, ways to learn from what people invite us to imagine, and ways to learn partly from the imaginative acts we perform in response. Part II begins an interrogation of that kind of argument. The other response is to say that, whatever the problem is, it is not specially to do with imagination because there is not, after all, the kind of close connection between fiction and imagination that my state- ment of the problem suggests. The following claims have recently been made:

1.   We cannot define fiction in terms of imagination;

2.   Appeals to the imagination are not helpful for explaining how an audience engages with fiction.

Additionally, there is a more general thesis around, available in several versions. Here is the most general formulation I can think of:

3.   The imagination plays a less significant role in explaining human cognitive capacities and behaviour than we have supposed.

I consider these three views in turn. It's obvious why we need to consider 1 and 2. Why consider 3? After all, 3 is consistent with the idea that imagination is important for fiction; it might be that it is not important for much else, and that fiction is not very important. Yes, one may hold that combination of views. But if we get a sense that the imagination is in retreat, that it has generally been oversold in recent theorizing about the mind, we may start to suspect that its role in our engagement with fiction has been exaggerated as well. I don't believe there are any grounds for that suspicion.

In the course of arguing for this I will address a related issue. As advertised, I will be arguing for a close connection between fiction and imagination. There is some tendency among historians of literature to scepticism about claims of this kind when they are not carefully relativized to particular places and time; some of these scholars are also apt to say that the idea of fiction is of relatively recent invention. I believe they are wrong on both counts.

First, I need to say something brief about the kinds of imagining that operate in fiction.

1.2 Kinds of imagining

What counts as imagination for our purposes? There is, first, imagining that such-and-such, called propositional imagining: the kind of imagining that compares instructively with belief. We may believe that we are being followed on a dark street, and we may imagine that we are. There are differences and similarities between the two: the believer is more likely to take evasive action, though even imagining danger can make you look nervously behind you; note that both kinds of states are likely to generate mental images, on which more later. And when the episode is over the believer may make inquiries about who might have been following them; the imaginer probably won't. But there are many ways to complicate the picture. Imagining can kindle belief; you start by imagining someone following you and end up suspecting that someone is following you; your attention to the issue has caused you to discover some real or supposed evidence for that proposition. We can be mistaken about whether we believe something or imagine it; imagining something happening can make it more likely that you will claim to recall later on that it happened, and it has been argued that some delusional states and some religious or superstitious ideas are imaginings taken by their possessors as beliefs.[5]

Another way to complicate the picture is to suppose that when we imagine a situation and become progressively more 'immersed' in it, we start to move from a state that is one of pure imagination to one that is or approaches the condition of belief. Susanna Schellenberg says:

---

[5] On mistaking imagining for remembering, see e.g. Garry et al. (1996); on delusions see Currie (2000); on religion see van Leeuwen (2014).

> Arguably, one thing that marks a good actor is the ability to swiftly move up and down the continuum between imaginings and beliefs, that is, to swiftly slip in and out of character. When a good actor plays a villain, she does not simply imagine that she is a villain. She immerses herself in her role. In doing so, she arguably adopts mental representations that are to some extent imagination-like and to some extent belief-like.   (2013: 510)

I agree that there are states intermediate between imagination and belief as classically understood.[6] Such intermediate states may be described as 'quasi-' or 'near-' beliefs: states which are apt to be endorsed very firmly by their owners but with a tendency to guide action only rather selectively, to be sensitive to evidence of a very restricted (usually positive) kind, to be brought to activity by emotionally gripping stories but to fade somewhat in other contexts. Some forms of religious cognition may fit well into such an intermediate category while not being comfortably described as either imaginings or beliefs. But immersion is not, I claim, a matter of moving through a continuum of states that are progressively more belief-like. I might be very immersed in a fantasy of winning the newly established Nobel Prize for philosophy without having any suspicion that I have won it. As Liao and Doggett (2014) note, the immersed actor on set speaks the lines she has been given and follows the camera with utter precision; she shows no sign of losing her grip on the fact that this is all pretence or of moving towards the belief that she really is the character, who is not on a set and has no lines. A progressive state of immersion may occur without any move towards belief.

While some kinds of imaginings are suitably compared with beliefs, suppositions, suspicions, and guesses, others are more comfortably placed in the company of perceptual states: seeings, hearings, touchings, and awarenesses of the disposition and movement of our bodies.[7] States of visualizing or visual imagery are the most obvious and the most studied, but we have images in all sensory modalities as well as motor images: images as of moving our bodies. I don't assume that imagery in any modality is essential for an episode of mental activity to count as imagining, though the two forms often go together and it is likely that mental imagery is responsible for much of the affect that is generated in imagination.[8] Any sustained imaginative enterprise will likely involve several forms of imagining along with other parts of our mental economy. If I imagine reading an important

---

[6] See Currie and Jureidini (2004).

[7] For more on this see Currie and Ravenscroft (2002: Chapter 1). Roger Scruton once said that 'imagination, if "asserted", amounts to genuine belief' (1974: 120), suggesting that imagination and seeing-as are of a kind, the latter being a kind of 'unasserted' perception.

[8] For an argument that imagery is essential to acts of imagining see Kind (2001). Kind suggests that imagery is the 'paint' that enables imagination to be about particular things. But it is unclear why such paint is necessary. Our beliefs may be about particular things without there being an imagistic or otherwise sensory accompaniment to go with them—an obvious truth in the case of dispositional beliefs. If content can be secured non imagistically for belief, why not for imaginings also?

message this will typically involve visual imagery of the words on the page; it may also involve imagined motor events as I imagine turning the page or scanning across; it will recruit other mental capacities and processes, such as semantic and pragmatic competencies as I gain a sense of the intended meaning of what I imagine reading; it will involve propositionally imagining what I take to be meant; it will involve awareness that my desires are more or less likely to be fulfilled by what the message suggests about the future; it will involve emotional responses to what I propositionally imagine.[9] Later chapters in Part I will ask whether these references to desire and to emotion are references that lie within the domain of imagination itself. I will argue that they do.

1.3 The idea of fiction

Roughly speaking, the project of explaining fiction in terms of imagination has been based on the simple thought that when we read in a story, 'Holmes lived in Baker Street' we understand that this is not being put forward as something which the speaker wants us to believe, or that the speaker is committed to, but as something we are being offered as part of an imaginative project. Putting it this way makes it clear how important the idea of intention is to the project: I follow Grice and others in regarding assertions as distinguished by the distinctive intentions of assertion makers; I extend that idea by marking out fiction-making as a distinctive kind of communicative act, characterized in terms of the intention that what is communicated be imagined (Currie 1990). One might quarrel with this on (at least) two grounds. First, that such communicative acts as assertions and acts of fiction making should not be assumed to have a psychological nature. Secondly, that the association of fiction-making (and fiction) with the imagination will not serve to distinguish works of fiction from works of non-fiction. The second worry will turn out to be more troubling. I start therefore with brief remarks about the first and will say rather more about the second.

Tim Williamson and others have argued that what is distinctive of assertion is not something psychological but something normative: that one is entitled to assert P only if one knows P (Williamson 2000). Adopting an analogous approach, Manuel García-Carpintero suggests the following as a comparably normative account of fiction-making:

> For one to fiction-make p is correct if and only if p is worth imagining for one's audience, on the assumption that they have the relevant desires and dispositions.
>
> (García-Carpintero 2013: 351)

---

[9] See below, Section 8.2 for a case of this kind.

García-Carpintero's proposal is a challenge to the kind of intention-based account of fiction I continue to support.[10] I do have doubts about the proposal and in particular wonder whether the reference to 'relevant desires and dispositions' can be spelled out in a way which avoids trivializing the idea; for any product of fiction-making, however tedious, lacking in narrative invention or literary merit, there will always be some combination of desires and dispositions that makes engagement with that product seem worthwhile (you want to read a really boring story). I don't rule out the avoidance of this and like difficulties and García-Carpintero is right to point out that normative accounts of acts of communication have, in general, some advantages not obviously enjoyed by their psychological, Gricean rivals. But if García-Carpintero's proposal, or something like it, is right it is not a challenge to the idea I am defending here and now, which is that there is a very close connection between a work's being fiction and the imaginative response to that work of its audience. Indeed, it is a strong endorsement of that idea, since the norm García-Carpintero offers is specified in terms of what it is worthwhile imagining. This is not to say that García-Carpintero and I attribute to the imagination the same role in accounting for what is and what is not fiction. García-Carpintero is offering us an imagination-based account of what it is for a *work* to be fictional and, as we will see immediately, I do not claim to define the concept of a fictional work. But this does nothing to show that García-Carpintero is less dependent for the success of his aims on there being a vital connection between fiction and imagination than I am for mine; as he says: 'that fictions contain utterances whose contents we are to imagine is . . . an essential property of them' (p. 355). For present purposes García-Carpintero and I have no quarrel.

I come now to the idea that appeals to the imagination won't enable us to distinguish works of fiction from those of non-fiction. Victor Hugo includes in *Notre Dame de Paris* a great deal of information about mediaeval architecture, life, and customs, including such things as the complex rules of sanctuary: precisely where, when, and under what circumstances sanctuary could be claimed in Church property. As a result, extended passages of text read much like history, which is in part what they are (or so I grant).[11] It has been suggested that cases like this make difficulties for imagination-based theories of fiction: theories which claim a conceptual connection between fiction and imagination and which say that fiction is utterance intended to be imagined, rather than, say, believed. Stacie Friend offers another example:

---

[10] It will turn out (Section 3.3) that we can give a partial characterization of imagining in terms of what makes states of imagining appropriate. But it is only partial.

[11] George Wilson discusses the intermingling of fictive and assertive utterance in *Notre Dame*, but his concern is with the identification of an internal narrator responsible for both types of utterance (Wilson 2011: 135); see also the discussion of Dan Brown's work in Worth (2017: Chapter 3).

Elizabeth Gaskell's *Mary Barton* opens with this sentence: 'There are some fields near Manchester, well known to the inhabitants as Green Heys Fields, through which runs a public footpath to a little village about two miles distant.' This statement is not only true, it was intended to be true and any informed reader of Gaskell will believe it. It meets all the standard requirements on sincere assertion.

(Friend 2012: 184)[12]

The same could be said about extended passages from Victor Hugo. The standard response at this point is to remind everyone that stories are a mixture of fiction and non-fiction and that such passages merely constitute non-fictional elements within a hybrid text. But this raises questions, notably, What makes *one whole work* to be fiction rather than non-fiction?

I have earlier (1990) expressed a lack of interest in this question, regarding it somewhat as we might regard the question 'Is this quantity of liquid water?' To such questions we tend to get unsystematic answers that do not line up well with such true principles as 'water is H_2O'.[13] As Paul Bloom points out, there is often more water (that is, more H_2O) in *Sprite* than in pond water but we call only one of them water, perhaps because the non-water in *Sprite* is put there deliberately (Bloom 2007). But Stacie Friend thinks that there is something more general and more systematic that we can say, and we say it by thinking of fiction as a *genre*, a notion which she regards as best explained by appeal to Kendall Walton's (1970) idea of a category. It is the idea of a category that I will focus on here, and on the ideas of standard and non-standard features, which help to explain the idea of a category.

Friend's idea is not that imagination is irrelevant to fiction, but rather that it is not an essential property of a fiction. It is, in Kendall Walton's phrase, a *standard property*. Walton says:

A feature of a work of art is *standard* with respect to a ... category just in case it is among those in virtue of which works in that category belong to that category— that is, just in case the lack of that feature *would disqualify, or tend to disqualify,* a work from that category ... a *contra-standard feature* with respect to a category is

---

[12] A view much closer to mine is that of Stock (2017), though there are significant differences between us. Stock defines a fictional utterance as one which is (Gricean) intended to cause imagining. In this her view is somewhat like the proposal I gave in Currie (1990), though I there argued for the importance of another condition (non-accidental truth) which Stock thinks may be dispensed with. A fiction, for Stock, is 'one or more fictive utterances' (149). On Stock's account fictional works are not (generally) fictions; I, to the contrary, have no concept of fiction in addition to fictional utterance and fictional work. And Stock argues, as I do not, that 'the fictional content of a particular text is equivalent to exactly what the author of the text intended the reader to imagine' (1).

[13] Is water really identical with H_2O? There are arguments for thinking that the essentialist account of water will have to be a bit more complicated, but they are not arguments against the truth of some such essentialist identification (see Hoefer and Martí 2019).

the absence of a standard feature with respect to that category—that is, a feature whose presence tends to *disqualify* works as members of the category.

(Walton 1970: 339, some emphasis mine)

Friend echoes the normativity in this characterization: 'A feature is contra-standard if possession of that feature *excludes or tends to exclude* the work from a category' (2012: 188, my emphasis). So the presence of standard/contra-standard features gives us *reasons* for thinking that a work does/does not belong to a given category, though the reasons will not always be conclusive. In particular, contra-standard features indicate that a work is a doubtful, marginal, peripheral, or at least non-central case; a work with a contra-standard feature might thus be a member (perhaps partial member) of the category, but there would be a legitimate doubt about that, resolvable perhaps in favour of membership, but one would not put the example forward as a paradigm of membership in the category. And this normative conception is not reducible to the descriptive idea of 'what we as a matter of fact expect of works of this kind'. There was a time when people expected movies not to contain explicitly sexual material but there is little doubt that viewers shocked by more recent practices would have no uncertainty that what they were watching was a movie. There was also a time, I am told, when it was expected that fictions would contain 'impossible' events; the rise of realistic fiction in the eighteenth century then caused confusion in readers who took those realistic works not to be fiction. This might well be true (though I have also heard it denied). Indeed, readers at any given time will have expectations about what fictions are like, where the features in question correlate less than exactly with the actual fiction/non-fiction divide; they may sometimes therefore be mistaken in their judgements about what is and is not fiction, just as people unfamiliar with ice will not immediately see that what they have in front of them is water. I will return to the issue of misidentification in Section 1.4.

Given this normative understanding of the ideas of standard and contra-standard features, we can see that they do not do the explanatory work Friend requires of them. She says:

> It is currently standard for a work of fiction (and contra-standard for a work of non-fiction) to contain many statements that are not intended to be believed. It is also currently standard for a work of fiction (and contra-standard for a work of non-fiction) to be constructed with objectives other than truth-telling in mind, or to contain parts constructed with such objectives in mind.   (2012: 190)

So it is contra-standard for a work of non-fiction to contain many statements that are not intended to be believed. Such a work would therefore be doubtfully, or partially, or marginally a work of non-fiction at best. But this is not in line with my (or indeed Friend's) judgements. She cites the passage below from an opinion piece in the *New York Times*, which invites us to imagine a scenario for future conflict in Sudan:

> JAN. 18 The South declares that 91 percent of voters have chosen secession. The North denounces the vote, saying it was illegal, tainted by violence and fraud, and invalid because the turnout fell below the 60 percent threshold required.
>
> JAN. 20 The South issues a unilateral declaration of independence.
>
> JAN. 25 Tribal militias from the North sweep through South Sudan villages, killing and raping inhabitants and driving them south. The governor of a border state in the North, Ahmad Haroun, who is wanted by the International Criminal Court for war crimes and organizing the Janjaweed militia in Darfur, denies that he is now doing the same thing in the South.   (Friend 2011: 172)

Friend says, 'The article is comprised mostly of utterances we are not supposed to believe, but it is a clear case of non-fiction' (Friend 2011: 173). I agree that it is as clear a case of non-fiction as one could wish for. But that cannot be because our judgements of a work's status as non-fiction are guided by sensitivity to what is contra-standard for that category; if they were we would regard the article as marginal, contestable, or at least an *un*clear case of non-fiction.[14]

Why then is this a clear case of non-fiction? A plausible answer is easy to generate. The fictive material—the South declares independence, the North claims the vote was illegal, and so on, as given in the passage above—is there not because it is of independent interest *as* fiction but because it serves to make vivid what the writers regards as a likely outcome in the real world, namely an attack by the North with consequent atrocities. Similarly, an academic article on the literary style of Virginia Woolf might have more words in it from her fiction than it has words soberly analysing her style, and it might be important, in order to appreciate the stylistic points made, that the reader engage with those fictional passages in fully imaginative mode. Again, the article is easily classifiable as (a very clear example of) non-fiction, with a good deal of fiction embedded in it. The intention to engage the imagination with the fictional parts is subservient to having the reader understand the literary devices they employ.[15]

I am not claiming these judgements derive from my theory alone. I am drawing also on what strike me as commonsensical assumptions we use to judge people's intentions, motives, and purposes and which enable us to identify hierarchies of intentions, as we so often do. We say that his primary motive was malice and that providing a warning was only secondary, that her dominant intention was to signal virtue and only secondarily to contribute to a cause. Without recourse to

---

[14] For a related point about normativity see Stock (2017:166).

[15] The idea that in cases cited by Friend as problems for imagination-based views of fiction what we have is fiction embedded within non-fiction is used to good effect by Stock (2017), e.g. 149, 160.

this commonsensical background my theory would do no explaining when it comes to the judgements that we make about whether this work is, as a whole, fiction and that one non-fiction. Friend's objection to my theory is that it places me in exactly this position, unable to derive work-level judgements from my theory alone. My response is then to say two things: (i) Friend's theory is in no better state, for the reasons given two paragraphs back, and (ii) my theory, while it is not the only thing I appeal to, plays a non-redundant role in the explanation. For example, I gave an account just now of why it would be reasonable to regard the *New York Times* op-ed as non-fiction, and the explanation made use of the idea that while parts of the work are clearly the products of a fictive utterance— namely the narrative of imagined conflict quoted above—those parts were clearly subservient to the overarching aim of shaping belief. The explanation thus draws heavily on the contrasting kinds of utterer's intentions given centre-stage in my theory.

The same thing happens when we look, not at people's all-up judgements about whether this or that is fiction, but at what evidence people would bring forward to support the claim that a given work is fiction or non-fiction. For example, I am confident that people, asked to illustrate the concept of fiction, will gravitate towards bits of discourse which seem most obviously intended to play a significant role in the reader's imaginative engagement and which also seem not to be intended to be believed, or seriously considered as candidates for belief. If asked to illustrate the idea of fiction by reference to passages from *Notre-Dame de Paris* people would be much more likely to offer the part where Quasimodo rescues Esmeralda from the gallows, than they would be to offer the descriptions of sanctuary practices in fifteenth-century Paris. And if there was an argument about whether *Notre Dame* is to count as fiction rather than non-fiction, they would support the idea that it is fiction by pointing to the rescue section rather than the sanctuary material. So we can say at least this: while the fictive-utterance theory does not by itself explain judgements about the fictional status of works, there is strong evidence that rationally defensible judgements of this kind are made with a sensitivity to the theory's distinction between assertive and fictive utterances.

I won't try to rebut all the objections to fictive-utterance theories that there are or might be; we would not then get on to other matters. I'll consider just one more. It is said that Victor Hugo was keen to make his readers better informed about the history of Paris. Suppose this was his primary aim, and that writing the story of Quasimodo, Esmeralda, and the rest was considered by him as simply a means to that informative end. Would we then have to count *Notre-Dame* as non-fiction? That seems an undesirable conclusion. But is it one I am driven to by my commitment to the explanation, given above, of why the op-ed and the academic article are to be counted non-fiction? I believe not. Like others, I emphasize that the intentions it is relevant to consider are those that are manifested in the work itself, not those which are merely the undisclosed wishes of the author. An attentive reader of the work itself would not, I think, conclude that the story of Quasimodo and the others was intended merely as a way of fixing the facts about mediaeval Paris in one's mind; the fictional construction is too elaborate for that to be plausible (though of course the implausible is sometimes true). But in the case of the op-ed piece from the *New York Times* one does get the impression of a dominant intention to affect the reader's beliefs. At this point Friend may cite another case: Solzhenitsyn's *One Day in the Life of Ivan Denisovich*, wherein 'the fictionalized presentation serves mainly to promote certain beliefs' (2008: 8). This, she claims is a work of fiction. How does that case differ from the op-ed? I agree that *Denisovich* is conventionally categorized as fiction and have no desire to quarrel with that judgement. Again, it is not difficult to see how such a judgement gets arrived at and becomes stable. When what we have is a long, engaging stretch of discourse the explicit content of which (the details of characters and occasions) is clearly not presented as factually correct, which is not prefaced by or interspersed with substantial argumentative commentary, which does not conclude with a comparably extended distillation of ideas, we have something very different from the op-ed case and something where the fictive content is much more salient and vivid. Is it really right, though, to claim a categorical distinction between this case and the op-ed case? No. I don't think we should give a great deal of weight to these acts of labelling beyond the convenience of booksellers. What matters from the point of view of understanding *Notre-Dame*, the op-ed, and *Denisovich* is that we identify the material that is fictive, the material that isn't, and the relations between them; doing that gives us the right account of how these three cases are similar and also different. The fictive utterance theory makes a distinctive contribution to our doing that.

I don't claim that our overall judgements of the fictional/non-fictional status of works always conform to a consistent pattern explicable in such clear, argumentative terms as I provided in discussing previous examples. By and large we depend on the prior categorizations of publishers and other institutions to provide the judgements for us, and these can be driven by commercial motive, while many cases seem to be of indeterminate status or simply baffling. Hesitation and confusion on this issue among people who have not been called on to think deeply about the nature of fiction surely abounds. But the idea that some things are communicated to us with the intention that they be imagined rather than believed is surely a significant driver of people's personal judgements about the fiction/non-fiction distinction. We can see this by looking both at people's all-up judgements about whether this or that is fiction, and at what evidence people would bring forward to support the claim that a given work is fiction or non-fiction.

1.4 Fiction and its history

It should be clear by now that in defending the centrality of imagination to our understanding of fiction I am not making a local, historically restricted claim. I am not saying merely that this close connection holds now in some community of which I regard myself a member and that with other communities it might be different. I say that the idea of fiction, understood as crucially dependent on a grasp of to-be-imagined discourse is vital for anyone, at any time, who is negotiating the human social world. Historical scholars of literature are often resistant to this presumption of long-term conceptual stability when it comes to such notions as fiction. Two views, not always distinguished, are often heard: that fiction has radically changed its nature over time, and that fiction is the invention of some comparatively recent period (cynics comment that this period usually coincides with the period specialized in by the scholar concerned). Let's consider examples of both views, the second view first.

William Egginton is surely wrong to describe Cervantes as 'the man who invented fiction' (2016: 1). If anyone did invent it, that was long before Cervantes. There is fiction in Greek drama and comedy, in mediaeval romance and, I would say, in just about every time and place of recorded culture. We even have some slender evidence for fiction in the European Paleolithic from chimerical figures which may have featured in stories told. Most likely, nobody invented fiction, and it emerged in something like the way that cooking probably did, by increments of control over naturally occurring flames and embers. Egginton seems to grant all this, since he allows that fiction is 'an untrue story we read for entertainment, in full knowledge that it's not true' (5) though by saying 'this much is accurate' he seems to suggest that there is, all the same, something inadequate about it. He does not tell us what that is.

Similarly, Catherine Gallagher says in an influential essay that the novel 'discovered' fiction. I think, however, that her view better illustrates the fiction-has-changed-its-nature view. For she goes on:

> It used to be assumed that fictions form a part of every culture's life, and if evidence for the assumption were needed, one could point to the seemingly universal existence of stories that apparently do not make referential truth claims, such as fables and fairy tales. It seemed to follow that something resembling the modern acceptance of the word *fiction* must be universally comprehended and the phenomenon at least tacitly sanctioned. A general human capacity to recognize discourses that, in Sir Philip Sidney's words, 'nothing affirmeth, and therefore never lieth'... made the term appear unproblematically applicable to narratives from all times and places. Recent scholarship has shown, though, that this modern *concept* of narrative fiction developed slowly

in early-modern Europe, a development reflected in the changing uses of the word in English.   (Gallagher 2006: 337–8, emphasis in the original)

Gallagher's 'though' in the last sentence quoted suggests that the universalism she has just described is a complacent view tenable only as long as one fails to attend to the history of the 'changing uses of the word [fiction]'. Here is the argument she gives to support that:

> From its common use to denote, 'that which is fashioned or framed; a device, a fabric,... whether for the purpose of deception or otherwise' (*Oxford English Dictionary*, 2nd ed., s.v. 'fiction') or 'something that is imaginatively invented', a new usage came into existence at the turn of the seventeenth century: 'The species of literature which is concerned with the narration of imaginary events and the portraiture of imaginary characters; fictitious composition.' As this sense of the word gained greater currency, mainly in the eighteenth century, an earlier frequent meaning of 'deceit, dissimulation, pretense' became obsolete. Although consistently contrasted with the veridical, fictional narration ceased to be a subcategory of dissimulation as it became a literary phenomenon. If the etymology of the word tells us anything, fiction seems to have been discovered as a discursive mode in its own right as readers developed the ability to tell it apart from both fact and (this is the key) deception.   (2006: 338)

Readers should know that I am the last person to ask for a view on the history of words in English—or any language. But I do not need to take a view about those issues in order to show that Gallagher's argument is flawed. Gallagher's argument about the emergence of the concept of fiction relies on a claim about changes in the meaning of the word 'fiction'. 'Fiction' we are told, originally meant something fabricated for any reason, and then came to be used for that which is nondeceptively fabricated for imaginative purposes. Let's assume that is true. This does not show that, prior to the change, people lacked the concept *that which is nondeceptively fabricated for imaginative purposes*; it does not show that, prior to the change, people lacked the concept of fiction in roughly what Gallagher herself takes to be the modern sense. There can be changes in word meaning without changes in concepts possessed. And the assumption that, before some relatively recent point in history, people lacked the concept *that which is nondeceptively fabricated for imaginative purposes* is not credible, as we shall quickly see.

What possession of a concept amounts to is a deeply contested philosophical question. But it is enough for present purposes to say that people possess the concept of fiction in roughly the modern sense if they display a reasoned sensitivity to the distinction between things fabricated for deceptive purposes and things fabricated to provide a nondeceptive narration of imaginary events and characters. Given the importance of identifying deceptive invention in human social life it is all but impossible that people prior to the seventeenth or eighteenth or any other centuries would have been unable to distinguish deceptive 'imaginary invention' from its nondeceptive relative; that they put the comedies of Menander and the tragedies of Shakespeare in the same category, so far as narrative invention goes, as the lies of a neighbour or the doubtful rhetoric of a political opponent. I am sure they did not.[16]

There is, of course, an important subject to be investigated: the history of fiction. Its practitioners track and account for changes, sometimes radical, in the production and reception of imaginative literature. They may identify occasions on which some of these changes confused audiences to the extent that they identified this or that item as non-fiction when it was actually fiction or vice versa. Episodes like these need not indicate conceptual change. It is crucial in this endeavour to distinguish between the possession of an ability and the *refinement* of an ability. I possess the ability to ride a bicycle. Unfortunately this does not mean that I ride one very well, that I would be able to weave my way expertly through busy London traffic, that I could win the Tour de France, or that I could perform juggling and acrobatic feats while riding. My ability, like most abilities, is less than perfect (if there is such a thing as perfect riding of bicycles); the same is true of our ability, individually and collectively, to distinguish fiction from non-fiction. The fact that one may not be able always and infallibly to distinguish fiction from non-fiction does not show that one lacks the ability to distinguish them.

This is important because fiction can, as Gallagher emphasizes, be hard to distinguish from non-fiction, particularly when one lacks the institutional structures—libraries, book reviews, helpful bookshop classifications—that now-adays support the distinction. That the language of fiction is simply our ordinary language of assertion makes it especially possible for fiction to be mistaken for non-fiction, and vice versa. The author can say 'I really believe the following...' but that may be understood as the speech of an unreliable fictional narrator or, if we prefer the author's own voice, an ironic utterance. There are no words shielded from fictional use: 'really', 'truly', and 'in fact' can be used as much within fiction as outside it. If it was unclear whether you were making an assertion when you said 'It's raining outside', saying 'I'm asserting that it's raining outside' won't automatically settle the matter. It is possible, of course, for a story to begin with an announcement of its own fictionality, as with 'Once upon a time'. But even this positive test for fictionality is not decisive: an historian, frightened of the regime,

---

[16] In fact it seems from what Gallagher herself says that people immemorially possessed the concept, for she recognizes a 'general human capacity to recognize discourses that, in Sir Philip Sidney's words, "nothing affirmeth, and therefore never lieth"', which is not far off the contrast I have outlined between assertion and paradigmatic fictional utterances like 'Holmes lives in Baker Street' (2006: 337–8).

may preface his account of the decades of tyranny with those same words, hoping to confuse the not very intelligent censor but knowing that the intended audience will see through it. One must always trust to uncertain indicators when it comes to judging whether this or that is fiction, and there are times when we rely on the implausibility of the plot, or the presence of a narrator who knows more than any real narrator could know to make our judgement.

In situations where readers are used to fictions that declare their fictionality through the fantastical nature of their plots, a story with a naturalistic approach can easily be mistaken for non-fiction—as may perhaps have been the case with some readers of *Robinson Crusoe*. Such readers cannot be automatically convicted of lacking the concept ('our concept') of fiction; people who grasp the concept *duck* are sometimes confused by decoy ducks and when decoy ducks first came into use people were probably more easily confused than they would be now that they know that there are such things around. None of that shows that the concept *duck* has changed since decoy ducks came into use. And given the ever-present possibility of mistakes about what is and what is not fiction, it is not surprising that communities make finer distinctions than the simple fiction/non-fiction distinction I am proposing here. Dennis Green, in his excellent study of literature in the twelfth century, describes a tripartite distinction between *historia, argumentum* and *fabula*.[17] *Historia* is reported truth, though generally understood to be a reporting of events at some time before the reach of present memory. *Fabula* consists of that which is manifestly untrue, describing events which are 'against nature', as with much in Ovid. *Argumentum*, on the other hand, is fiction which is plausible, making reference only to kinds of things that could happen. Green suggests a strong but not universal tendency at this time to condemn the two fictive categories, either on grounds that anything other than a strict regard for truth is to be deplored, or as a tactic adopted by story-tellers to discredit the activities of their rivals. At the same time there was a recognition, at least in scholarly commentary, that it was possible to achieve an acceptable harmony with one's audience, as Virgil was assumed to have done in flouting the limits of commonly known historical truth in the episode of Dido and Aeneas. Green finds similar cases in the *Tristan and Isolde* of Thomas of Britain, and the Latin epic *Ruodlieb*. We would certainly go wrong if we thought that writers of this period worked only with the fiction/non-fiction divide, but Green's discussion, for all the complexity it reveals, strikes me as consistent with the belief that this divide was understood; understanding a distinction is not the same as approving activity on both sides of it.

---

[17] Green (2002: 4) acknowledges the close connection between fiction and imagination or make-believe: 'Fiction is a category of literary text which, although it may also include events that were held to have actually taken place, gives an account of events that could not conceivably have taken place, and/or of events that, although possible, did not take place and which, in doing so, invites the intended audience to be willing to make-believe what would otherwise be regarded as untrue.'

Of course, if imagination is the key to what is distinctive about fiction—as I believe it to be—there is much more to be said about the history of the practice of fiction, from a maker's point of view and from the point of view of reception. We owe a debt to scholars like Ian Watt and Gallagher herself from whom we have learned about the institutions of fiction, the presumptions of readers, the various means by which author's signalled their fictive intention and the difficulties sometimes encountered by authors who wished to express their fictive intent when developing new genres of fiction. An especially interesting topic is the options open to an author who wishes to create uncertainty about whether their intent was fictive or not, or to speak to two audiences, one of which can be expected to recognize the fictive intent while the other is for some reason insensitive to it. But none of this suggests that fiction itself is an invention of the comparatively recent historical past. The fact that what is fiction can be mistaken for something else need not undermine our confidence that fiction existed at the time of the mistake—witness all the trouble caused by Orson Welles' too-realistic radio version of *War of the Worlds*.

1.5 Conclusions

In this chapter I have argued for a bottom-up approach to understanding fiction. The bottom in this case is the single utterance (of very variable length) intended to convey the intention that the audience imagine what the utterance expresses; I call this a fictive utterance. I have no ambition to move up from there to a definition of what it takes for something to be a work of fiction, claiming that the conditions under which it is reasonable to call something a 'work of fiction' are too variable and context-dependent to allow of any such generalization. What is possible in at least many cases is to see that the definition of fictive utterance, in conjunction with other plausible principles concerning such things as the overall aim of the work and the context of its presentation, explains why a certain judgement ('this is a work of fiction/non-fiction') seems intuitively right. I've also argued that when fiction is understood in this way we have no reason to endorse claims about the historical variability of the notion: the core-concept of a fictive utterance is one that is visible in ancient as well as modern writing and thinking. Claims that what constitutes fiction has changed substantially, or that *fiction* is a concept of recent invention draw on historical evidence that does not support these notions: evidence for variation over time in (i) the use of the word 'fiction' and (ii) the kinds of fictions produced, which often brings with it increased temporary like-lihood of mistakes in the identification of instances of fiction for subjects who rely on stereotypical features, which certainly do change over time.

In Chapter 2 I confront some radical challenges to things I believe: that the fiction/nonfiction divide is psychologically significant; that imagination deserves the attention it has enjoyed in recent discussions of our cognitive lives; that imagination is a basic category, not explainable in other terms.

2

How fiction works

This chapter continues my defence of the importance of imagination for under-standing fiction. Here I focus particularly on the issue of how fiction works. The questions to be addressed are continuous with those of Chapter 1 but we will gradually embed the discussion of fiction in a larger context that includes the nature of mental representations in general, and the role of propositional attitudes in the explanation of behaviour.

2.1 Explaining engagement

Here is a broad principle Stacie Friend and I agree on: there is a close connection between fiction and imagination. As I indicated in Chapter 1, others deny this, saying that:

2.   Appeals to the imagination are not helpful for explaining how an audience engages with fiction.

Derek Matravers is a denier.[1] According to Matravers, it is wrong to think that there is an important psychological difference between our engagement with fiction and with non-fiction; rather, the distinction to focus on is the one between situations where we confront some circumstance directly, as in a direct perceptual confrontation, and situations where we engage with a representation of circum-stance. Our engagements with narratives, fictional and non-fictional, fall into the latter category, and so belong together from the point of view of psychological explanation. Matravers says this about the distinction:

> [I]n confrontation relations our mental states are caused by perceptual inputs
> from the objects of those states, and which cause actions towards objects in our
> egocentric space. In representation relations our mental states are not caused by

---

[1] Matravers (2014). He summarizes his claim this way: 'the most perspicuous account of our engaging with narratives available finds no role for the imagination. Furthermore, this account covers all narratives—whether non-fiction or fiction' (3). There is a great deal in Matravers' book that I won't discuss here; I confine myself to what I take to be his central claim. For other criticism of Matravers on this topic see Stock (2017: 167–9).

Imagining and Knowing: The Shape of Fiction. Gregory Currie, Oxford University Press (2020). © Gregory Currie.
DOI: 10.1093/oso/9780199656615.001.0001

perceptions of the objects of those states, and do not result in actions towards objects in our egocentric space.... (2014: 50)

I will argue later that understanding the relation of imagination to fiction depends crucially on a distinction between what is true, and what is represented as being true; to that extent I am with Matravers here. But the claim in his final sentence above is false. We do constantly use representations as guides to action, and representations do constantly result in actions towards objects in our egocentric space. Among examples of this are road signs, maps, thermometers, and the testimony of others. If I am in a protesting crowd and someone shouts 'they are firing', I may respond immediately and, with luck, effectively to the threat, better perhaps than if I was looking out for weapons in the hands of our opponents which, from my position, I could not easily see. It is not a feature of representations in general that they fail to lead to action on objects in egocentric space. Why is it important to Matravers to deny this?

Let's start with something he and I agree on. Those who think that it is characteristic of audiences to engage in imaginings when confronting fictions sometimes make the following point. People watching a fictional performance won't step in to save the heroine, which is what they would do in a non-fictional situation; that difference in behaviour is a reflection of the difference between the mental states of the people concerned: imagination in the first case and belief in the second. Matravers points out (i) that we should not be contrasting what people do when they confront fiction with what they do when they confront reality; we should be contrasting fictions with other, this time non-fictional, *representations*. And he goes on to claim that, when we get the contrast right we don't find a difference between fictional and non-fictional cases; non-fictions are representations, and (ii) all representations fail to enable responses to objects in egocentric space. So the motive for saying that fictions drive imaginings and non-fictions drive beliefs disappears.

(i) is surely true. But we have seen that (ii) is false. So Matravers can't conclude, as he wishes to do, that fictions and non-fictions are alike in action-guiding potential (because they are null in this regard). Now the fact that your opponent cannot prove P does not mean you can prove not-P. Can we, at this point, argue positively that fictions and non-fictions are *distinct* in action-guiding potential? Yes. We do this by constructing a pair of hypothetical cases about which we will, I hope, agree that they have different behavioural outcomes, and agree, I hope, that the only difference between them capable of explaining this behavioural difference is that one is fiction and presents its material to be imagined, while the other is non-fiction and presents its material to be believed.

Suppose the *Huffington Post*, in a bid to widen its audience, starts to provide up-to-the minute information about what is happening in people's local areas, which it emails to subscribers. The latest report I get is one warning of a group of marauding vampires in my village. I am likely to do something in response, though what will depend on my prior beliefs; it could be putting out garlic and sharpening stakes, or calling the health authorities to report the editor's worrying detachment from reality. Now vary the example. Suppose that I am a subscriber to the new *Huffington Ghost*, an online 'non-newspaper' which specializes in providing customized fictional stories; subscribers receive daily accounts of avowedly fictional supernatural events in their vicinity; an engaging item from yesterday's issue was headed 'Frankenstein's monster and the Wolfman meet to settle their differences at Epperstone Village Hall'. Suppose that today's story crafted for me is word-for-word identical with the emailed warning about vampires of the earlier example from the *Huffington Post*. The two stories are exactly the same in terms of what I take to be their contents. In both cases I think of their locations as related to me in the same way; with both I can think 'The vampires are about two hundred yards away at this point'. (It's one of the selling points of this sort of fiction that it has this kind of exciting egocentric dimension to it.) I construct, if you like, the same mental model of both situations.[2] Yet there is a very noticeable behavioural difference in these two situations: in one I am frantically calling the police (or the health authorities); in the other I am quietly reading the story. The difference is not due to the fact that one situation is representational and the other confrontational. They are both cases of representation. The difference between them is that I understand one to be an attempt to convey to me a representation of how things actually are in my vicinity, while the other is an attempt to engage me in an imaginative project which involves me in thinking of certain things as occurring in my vicinity when in fact they are not. I cannot see what is wrong or even controversial in saying that with the non-fictional *Huffington Post* I understand that an invitation is offered to me to believe something, while in the case of the fictional *Huffington Ghost* something is put forward for to me to imagine, and that this explains the difference between my behaviours, and my behavioural motivations, across the two cases.

Friends of Matravers may say that the counterexample to his thesis that I am offering here is entirely atypical. If all I am showing is that his thesis does not apply to narratives with egocentric content, what we have is a very untroubling restriction on the domain of its applicability; the thesis would still apply to just about everything that is recognized as a conventional fiction from Homer onwards. If we had considered as our toy example a case where the two narratives have exactly the text of *A Study in Scarlet*, with one of them fiction and the other understood to be sober reporting, we would not expect to see the kind of behavioural differences visible in the *Huffington Post/Ghost* case. I respond as follows. In fact there are plenty of behavioural differences that might emerge in the

---

[2] Such models are part of Matravers' own story about how we process narrative See his 2014, Chapter 5.

Study in Scarlet case: someone who took it for non-fiction might well make subsequent inquiries about the details of the case; inquiries they would not make if they thought it fiction. Of course there will not always be such differences: human responses to stimuli are very plastic and oftentimes one reads a piece of journalism with the same passivity one might apply to fiction. But no one, I hope, thinks that situations where there is no behavioural difference are always situations where there is no difference in cognitive attitudes. Matravers' thesis would be a very odd one if it came to saying that there is no psychological difference between our engagement with fictions and with non-fictions except where those differences do actually show up in behaviour. Anyone willing to say that will have to show why the same reasoning does not lead them to conclude that, where there is no behavioural manifestation of a mental state there is no mental state—an obviously unacceptable conclusion.

*

I come now to the third challenge described in Chapter 1:

3. The imagination plays a less significant role in explaining human cognitive capacities than we have supposed.

I'll consider two versions of this view; they have in common the idea that important work we have assumed to be done by the imagination is in fact done in other ways. The two versions are quite different. The first, due to Tamar Gendler, is thoroughly committed to the idea of mental representation; it is the claim that some of our representing of the world is not done by way of propositional attitudes such as beliefs, desires, and imaginings, but by way of a kind of non-propositional state which she calls *alief*. The second, the subject of Section 2.3, is inspired by ideas from phenomenology that have also made their way into cognitive science. It avoids mental representation and argues that our understanding of and dealings with other people are not guided by beliefs concerning what those people think and want but by more directly perceptual (or perhaps quasi-perceptual) encounters with them.

Both of these views are presented as general theories about the nature of human cognition. Both represent challenges to the kinds of philosophical theories of human motivation which developed and solidified in the final decades of the twentieth century: theories which give explanatory primacy to propositional attitudes such as belief and desire. Neither is aimed especially at our engagement with fiction. But if true, they would require us to rethink aspects of the nature of that engagement. When done with those two views I will consider a third: that while imagination is important for understanding other people it is not important for understanding fictional characters which are not—and are not like—real people. This objection is less of a problem for our proposition (3) than it is for:

2.   Appeals to the imagination are not helpful for explaining how an audience engages with fiction.

But I will consider the objection at that point because it is best dealt with directly after a discussion of how it is we understand real people.

2.2 Alief

We often explain people's actions in terms of what they believe and what they want.[3] When we do so we cite the cause of their behaviour and provide a way of understanding it as rational: wearing that clown suit to the party was the sensible thing to do given that I thought it was a fancy dress party and wanted to appear concordant with its theme. As it happens I was wrong—the party was black tie—but in light of my belief the behaviour made sense. That at least is one widely accepted view of action and its explanation. But some behaviours are hard to explain in this way. Tamar Gendler (2010) gives a number of examples. One, variants of which have long been noted in the philosophical literature, concerns the behaviour of someone invited to walk on the clear glass floor currently suspended over the Grand Canyon ('Skywalk'). People often hesitate, and some are unable to step on it at all, even though they have paid good money for the opportunity to do so. Is that because they believe that the Skywalk is dangerous? That seems unlikely; they know that the glass floor is solid and subject to very high safety requirements; besides, they let their children step on it, which they would not do if they had even a vague suspicion that it was unsafe.

Anyone in sympathy with philosophy's recent turn towards the imagination will at this point be thinking something like 'Yes, subjects don't believe that it is dangerous, but it would be difficult, in the circumstances, not to imagine it being dangerous, and such imaginings tend to bring on unpleasant sensations, making it difficult to step on the clear glass'. They will have similar reactions to cases where people avoid drinking water from a bottle marked 'poison' even when they know that the liquid in it is safe ('Poison'), or refuse to throw a dart at a picture of a loved one ('Dart'), knowing all the while that no harm would come to that person thereby. They will be especially prone to invoke the imagination in this well-known example ('Slime') which Gendler takes from Walton:

> Charles is watching a horror movie about a terrible green slime. He cringes in his seat as the slime oozes slowly but relentlessly over the earth destroying everything in its path. Soon a greasy head emerges from the undulating mass, and two beady

---

[3] Parts of this section are taken, with minor changes, from Currie and Ichino (2010).

eyes roll around, finally fixing on the camera. The slime, picking up speed, oozes on a new course straight towards the viewers. Charles emits a shriek and clutches desperately at his chair.   (Walton 1978: 5)

Gendler says this about Walton's example:

> How should we describe Charles' cognitive state? Surely he does not *believe* that he is in physical peril; as Walton notes, 'Charles knows perfectly well that the slime is not real and that he is in no danger' (Walton 1978: 6). But alongside that belief there is something else going on. Although Charles *believes* that he is sitting safely in a chair in a theater in front of a movie screen, he also *alieves* something very different. The alief has roughly the following content: 'Dangerous two-eyed creature heading towards me! H-e-l-p...! Activate fight or flight adrenaline now!'[4]

Why does Gendler say that Charles 'alieves' that he is in danger, when it seems so natural to say that he imagines this? The shift is certainly not just terminological; Gendler offers an explanation of the distinctness of alief and imagination as part of her account of alief, which I summarize below.

An alief is a mental state with three associatively linked components: a representational component R ('the representation of some object or concept or situation or circumstance, perhaps propositionally, perhaps non-propositionally, perhaps conceptually, perhaps nonconceptually'), an affective component A ('the experience of some affective or emotional state'), and a behavioural component B ('the readying of some motor routine') (263–4). The link between these three consists in the fact that they are co-activated by some feature of the subject's environment, and this co-activation is difficult to break. While traditional objectual or propositional attitudes are two-place relations between a subject and a simple representational content (naturally expressed, in the propositional case, as 'S believes that R'), alief is a four-place relation between a subject and a threefold associatively linked content of the kind just described ('S alieves R-A-B'). The difference between alief and traditional cognitive attitudes such as belief and imagination is a radical one: alief is 'developmentally and conceptually antecedent' to such attitudes, and it is not definable in terms of them (262; 288). Unlike beliefs, aliefs are, beyond narrow limits, insensitive to evidence; my alief that the skywalk is dangerous is not affected by the evident fact that people are walking safely on it,

---

[4] Gendler (2010: 258). Page references in the text and notes are to this work. The case of Charles might be complicated. It might be that he really is just pretending to be afraid, deliberately engaging in the sorts of behaviours associated with fear. Or is might be that the case is mixed: Charles' initial shock is the result of an involuntary response to the film image, but, delighted or intrigued by his reaction, he deliberately exaggerates it. But we can agree that it is possible—and does happen—that people show entirely involuntary signs of fearfulness as a result of exposure to fictions.

there have been no reports of casualties, etc. It also fails to connect inferentially with my belief that a highly salient and for other reasons controversial structure like this would be checked very carefully for safety. And alief's three components don't constitute a mere cluster of different mental states; rather they form a unified representational-affective-behavioural state, that 'there is no natural way of articulating' (289). Nor is the representational component of an alief a belief, or an imagining, or some other recognized state.

Gendler is surely right that there are behaviours not plausibly explained by appeal to beliefs and desires; she may also be right that some of these behaviours get no explanatory help from the imagination. She may even be right that we need something like alief to explain the residual cases, though there are questions to be asked about how aliefs should be characterized.[5] The important point to make here is that there are plenty of cases where imagination does respectable explanatory work, including cases which Gendler wants to mark off as in the explanatory domain of alief. I have already suggested that Skywalk, Poison, and Dart are cases where reluctance to act in a certain way is caused by imagination-induced feelings that are controllable only by avoiding the action in question.[6] In only one of these cases does Gendler offer a reason for rejecting the appeal to imagination. Gendler argues that in Poison, appeals to imagining are implausible because, as it turns out, people are also unwilling (to a degree) to drink from bottles labelled 'Not poison'. Faced with the choice of drinking from bottles labelled 'Not poison' or from ones filled with very same liquid but labelled 'Safe to consume', most subjects opt for the latter. In Gendler's view, it is not likely that seeing a 'Not poison' label induces one to imagine that one actually is drinking poison:

Is the reason for [the subject's] hesitancy supposed to be that *she had been imagining* that the bottle contained cyanide, though now she is not—and that what she imagined *in the past* (though fails to imagine now) somehow explains her action *at present*? Or that her current imagining that the bottle does not contain cyanide somehow contains within it (in not-fully-*aufgehoben* form) the antithetical imagining that the bottle does contain cyanide? And that somehow

---

[5] Gendler denies that aliefs are attitudes at p. 263; but one section heading (267) reads 'Alief and other attitudes'. Gendler grants that aliefs may not always have the tripartite structure of her formal characterization (264–7; 290); perhaps in some cases the tripartite structure shrinks to just a behavioural disposition, with no representational or affective component (or perhaps that structure is retained with the representational and affective parameters set at zero). Having introduced aliefs as the tripartite entities we have described in the text above, Gendler says later that they are 'propensit[ies] to respond to an apparent stimulus' (282; 288), thereby suggesting that only the third, behavioural component is in question.

[6] Actually in at least some of these cases more conventional belief/desire explanations may be available. One might refrain from throwing the dart because one believes that throwing it would be wrong and desires not to do wrong—at the same time perhaps as not being able to say what is wrong about it.

this negated semi-imagined content—content that she has, throughout the entire process, been fully consciously aware of explicitly disbelieving—sneaks into the control center for her motor routines and causes her to hesitate in front of the Kool-Aid? (269–70, emphasis in the original)

There is nothing mysterious in the idea that 'not Poison' induces imaginings of poison. In many situations it is entirely plausible that seeing a message of the form 'Not-P' provokes one to imagine P. When Donne says that no man is an island, a spontaneous, appropriate, and perhaps intended response is that we should imagine men (persons) as islands, though we go on to do other things with the metaphor. If a threatening Mafioso puts a label 'Not dead' on your loved one, that may very well be because it so easily prompts the contrary imagining. Notably, in the 'Not Poison' case, the label also bore a skull and crossbones image preceded by the word 'Not'. An erotically charged image preceded by the word 'Not' is unlikely to provoke images of celibacy.

We are now entitled to move back to a more orthodox account of what is happening in the case of Charles and the slime. Charles imagines the slime coming towards him—a state he gets into more or less automatically given the visual input he faces and the fact that he is thoroughly imaginatively engaged with the film by this time. The imaginative project he is caught up in involves a suite of bodily responses such as sweating, raised heart rate, gasping, and cowering, all manifest- ations of the bodily dispositions we associate with fear. This being a case of imagining though, the causal chain extends no further: Charles is not wondering what number to call the police on or whether he can outrun the slime; once reasons start to operate, the effects of imagining on non-pretend behaviour dissipate quickly.

Charles' reaction to the slime—more precisely, to the on-screen representation of slime—is towards one end of a spectrum of reactions we have to fictions. Charles' response is a visceral one provoked by a highly salient visual input as of something threatening coming towards him. This is quite different from our response, including our emotional response, to the actions and sufferings of a fictional character in a complex and sustained fictional narrative. One might respond to the fate of Anna Karenina, as it unfolds over a thousand pages, with a shifting mixture of admiration, sympathy, pity, and irritation, bringing to bear in your reflections all you understand about her situation and all you believe about human motivation, weakness of will, the place of women in Russian society, and a great many other things. A state of the alief kind could hardly account for such inferentially active and reflective processes. In these kinds of cases it is over- whelmingly plausible to say that we imagine all sorts of things concerning Anna, being guided all the while by what is said and implied in Tolstoy's text, bringing to bear in our imaginative project lots of things we actually believe about human society and psychology.

2.3 Understanding real people and fictional people

Fictions are usually about people, and most often about fictional ones, though real people sometimes make an appearance. From a reader's point of view, trying to understand a character's motivation, there is not much difference. Readers of *War and Peace* don't use one strategy to understand the motives of Pierre Bezukhov and another to understand Napoleon's, as they are represented in the novel. What is that strategy? A contest between two views of interpersonal understanding has developed over the last thirty years though recently there have been attempts to divide the territory between them.[7] The *theory-theory* says that we possess a theory of human motivation and feed information into it in order to get out conclusions about what people believe and want, much as we do when making predictions in physical science. The *imagination* (or sometimes 'simulation') *theory* says that we get the same sorts of conclusions by placing ourselves imaginatively in the position of the target person. Like others I think that both strategies play their part, though I put a lot of emphasis on the role of imagination and regard that as essential for fluent and sophisticated mind-reading. But the thing to keep in mind for now is the claim the two theories share: people have and are motivated by propositional attitudes, and an important part of understanding them is knowing what those attitudes are.

According to Shaun Gallagher and Dan Hutto (2008), both theory-theory and the imagination theory offer a too intellectual account of interpersonal understanding. Their aim is to give an 'adequate account of our everyday intersubjective abilities for understanding the intentions and the behaviors of other persons' (18).[8] On the account they offer intersubjective understanding is given to us directly (non-inferentially) in our interactive, properly contextualized face-to-face encounters with other people. These experiences, they say, are 'sufficient to deliver the nuanced adult capacity for understanding (as well as for misunderstanding) others' (17). My mistake (and that of others unable to escape from the theory-imagination dichotomy) is, apparently, to think that intersubjective understanding is a matter of trying to discover another's propositional thinking and inferring. In fact 'In seeing the actions and expressive movements of the other person one already sees their meaning; no inference to a hidden set of mental states (beliefs, desires, etc.) is necessary' (20). For Gendler much of the heavy lifting some thought was done by imagination is actually done by alief; for Gallagher and Hutto it is done by fast, automatic, and perceptual or perception-like mechanisms.[9] While this claim, if correct, annihilates both the theory-theory

---

[7] See e.g. Mitchell et al. (2009).   [8] See also Hutto (2008), especially Chapter 1.
[9] Might Gallagher and Hutto decide that aliefs are exactly the mechanisms (or parts thereof) they are looking for? I take it that the representational nature of aliefs would make that option unappealing to them.

and the imagination theory my present interest is from the point of view of the latter: it would show that one apparently important role for the propositional imagination in our lives is an illusion. For the imagination theory says that I put myself in your shoes by imagining something that matches in content what you believe, and that helps me to understand how you understand, and respond to, the world.

As with some other views I discuss in Part I, opinions that look deeply opposed to my claims turn out on closer inspection to be less threatening. Other things that Gallagher and Hutto say suggest a more peaceable opinion, allowing a legitimate region of interpretive phenomena to which the propositional attitudes may well apply:

> Thus, *before* we are in a position to theorize, simulate, explain, or predict mental states in others, we are already in a position to interact with and to understand others in terms of their expressions, gestures, intentions, and emotions, and how they act toward ourselves and others … [This] underpins those developmentally *later, and occasional*, practices that may involve explaining or predicting mental states in others.   (Gallagher and Hutto 2008: 17, my emphasis)

This concessive formulation is misleading in its suggestion that propositional attitude (PA) theorists have claimed that their favoured devices are the first to emerge in ontogeny. We all agree that interacting with others is a capacity which manifests itself from birth and which seems to be developmentally canalized. It has stages appropriate to the developing needs of the infant/child. Before young children acquire facility with belief-desire psychology there is much going on which underpins their interaction with other people, and some have speculated on what these precursor states might be. Believing in PAs does not commit anyone to a view about exactly what these precursor states are. So a PA theorist can agree that 'before we are in a position to theorize, simulate, explain, or predict mental states in others, we are already in a position to interact with … others', though how sophisticated that interaction is, and how informed by understanding is a complex empirical question.[10]

Note, however, that Gallagher and Hutto say that inferential methods are not merely later developments but 'occasional' practices. While PA theorists have treated intersubjective understanding as centrally a matter of inference to beliefs and desires, this sort of intersubjective understanding is, according to Gallagher and Hutto, unusual and peripheral to the normal range of human interactions,

---

[10] In more recent work Shaun Gallagher (2015) has acknowledged the possibility of 'pluralistic' models which combine elements of PA theories and direct perception approaches. For a clarifying intervention that aims to reconcile propositional attitude theories of mindreading and (one version of) the idea of direct social perception see Spaulding (2015). See also Carruthers (2015).

which proceed, by and large, without such cerebral and reflective activities. This is hard to accept. We interact with people in all sorts of ways: we negotiate our way past them on the subway, we occasionally attend to their urgent needs, we converse, barter, compete, and cooperate with them. Our dealings with them may last a few seconds or a lifetime. For anything more than a momentary interaction, where a person's current intention is clear from his or her bodily disposition, we need to understand a great deal more about them; we can hardly argue that a person's long-term intentions, say, to attend college in a year's time, are readable from their expression and bodily posture.[11]

It is not merely that we need to predict or explain their behaviour, though that is certainly something which has been much emphasized, perhaps overemphasized, in the literature on mentalizing. As Adam Morton and Jane Heal have both argued, there are all sorts of reasons for knowing what people believe or desire which have nothing directly to do with making predictions about how they will behave on some specific occasion, or giving explanations for how they have behaved.[12] We want to annoy or please or placate people; generally, this is part of wanting to make a difference to their behaviour, though it is a difference we do not easily associate with specific actions or predictions. Doing these things requires us to have views about their beliefs and desires. In deceiving people we try to get them to have false beliefs; we could hardly do this if we had no ideas about what they already believed. And cooperating with people depends on having some sense of what they desire, as well as of what they believe. I cooperate with you confidently as long as I believe that you share my desire, and my belief about how to achieve it; I will become doubtful or suspicious when that belief weakens or disappears. These assumptions about beliefs and desires can provide us with the materials on which to base our interactions with other people over the middle, long, and sometimes the short terms.

It is said against PA theorists that our explanations of people's behaviour rarely appeal to propositional attitudes but focus instead on aspects of their situations. Matthew Ratcliffe (2007: 191–2) points out that we explain the driver's pulling away when the light changes to green without invoking any belief; the driver simply responds to the light. Even in such situations of fluent behaviour there are assumptions we make about attitudes, the absence of which would defeat our

[11] Gallagher writes as if those who believe in the importance of inferential processes of mental state attribution are unable to accommodate two important facts: (1) that we recognize emotions non-inferentially; (2) that we are generally participants in interactions with those we seek to understand rather than passive observers of them (2008: 164, 166–7). Neither claim is true. Classical inferentialism is a theory about belief-desire attribution, not about emotion attribution, though it does need to be recognized that in some cases we cannot attribute emotion without making assumptions, presumably based in inference, about beliefs and desires: is that envy or jealousy you are displaying? And the rich source of information about people we access when we interact with them is often crucial to finely tuned judgements about what they think and what they want.

[12] See Morton (1996); Heal (2003: Chapter 12). That prediction is central to the project of folk psychology is assumed by Ratcliffe and Hutto (2007: 2).

situational explanations: we would be surprised to learn that the driver had wanted *not* to start on the green (she was part of a complex plot to delay traffic). Habitual behaviour can bypass desire, but if it did in this case that would be an interesting addition to the narrative; without it we assume that the driver's behaviour was coherent with her desire. Other kinds of situational explanations do quite substantially impose presuppositions about propositional attitudes on those who accept them. Ratcliffe (2007: 194) considers some of the different explanations one might give of umbrella-carrying:

1.   As always, John switched off his alarm clock and got out of bed at 7:30. He dressed, ate breakfast, picked up his briefcase and umbrella, and set off to work at the usual time of 8:30.

2.   John opened the door and saw the unusually dark sky. He went back into the house and picked up his umbrella.

These are certainly different, but both create presuppositions about attitudes. Consider these variants:

1*.   As always, John switched off his alarm clock and got out of bed at 7:30. He dressed, ate breakfast, picked up his briefcase and umbrella, and set off to work at the usual time of 8:30, *despite not wanting to take his umbrella with him.*

2*.   John opened the door and saw the unusually dark sky. He went back into the house and picked up his umbrella; *John did not want to go out with his umbrella.*

These versions do not merely add new information; they undercut assumptions implicit in the previous versions. Story 1 now becomes a tale of habit subverting one's wishes, while 2 is hard to interpret at all: does this mean that John took the umbrella under some strange compulsion? However understood, the addition is surprising; without it, we assume that the relevant desire is in place. Someone might object that adding 'John wanted to go out with his umbrella' would also be a surprising addition to 2. Agreed, but not because we were, to that point, making no assumptions about Johns desires. It would be surprising because making it explicit in this way raises a number of questions not previously salient: was it unusual for John to want to go out with his umbrella when rain is likely? Why might he be generally averse to carrying an umbrella? Similarly, if I say 'It's raining' and add 'I believe it's raining' this has the effect of suggesting that I am, on reflection, not very confident that it is raining. Making explicit what I can count on you to assume anyway would be pointless unless I wanted thereby to add something to the common ground of the conversation, and I can certainly count on you to understand that my believing that it's raining is implicated simply by my saying that it is raining. Making explicit things which people can be taken to have assumed changes the landscape of conversation in potentially confusing ways.

For these reasons I am inclined to accept, for mature human beings, something which Gallagher has called *the supposition of universality* and which he rejects:

> Our reliance on theory (or our reliance on simulation or some combination of theory and simulation) is close to universal. That is, this folk-psychological way of understanding and interacting with others is pervasive in our everyday life.
>
> (Gallagher 2004: 200)

Holding this principle is consistent with thinking that, while the use of some method—imagination, or theory, or both—for finding out beliefs and desires is close to universal, it depends on the use of more primitive modes of intersubjective understanding. Julian Kiverstein says:

> Embodied practices come before mentalizing not only developmentally. They are also the conditions of the possibility of understanding other people through mentalizing. Without embodied practices, we would have no sense of there being other people, and we would have no sense of what are the normal ways of comporting ourselves in relation to others.   (Kiverstein 2011: 58)

Perhaps that is true; for present purposes I need not dispute it. You cannot show that something is unimportant because it depends on something else.

If we turn from our relations to real people to the imagined others of literature, the case for propositional attitudes is even stronger. Fictional characters are not beings with whom we interact or have sensory access to. Their thoughts and motives are sometimes unusually complex; inferential methods are going to be of great importance—which is not to deny that we also respond to the characters of literature in strongly emotional ways. We have also to account for our engagement with the text which serves to represent the characters and events of the story. This involves purely linguistic processing which may well be the responsibility of a Fodor-style module.[13] But understanding a text also involves understanding what the utterer intends to communicate, which invariably goes beyond the words on the page. Except in very unusual circumstances we have no bodily or perceptual interaction with the author and must work out what was meant from the textual evidence before us, though it would be wrong to assume that the inferences involved are generally slow, effortful, or involve inner speech.[14] Where fictions are formatted in other ways, as with film and theatre, perceptual modes of access play an important role, but those modes of fiction-making don't turn us into

---

[13] See Fodor (1983) especially 44–5.
[14] For more on pragmatic processing in fiction see Chapter 9.

participants in the action; they also require us to make assumptions about the intentions of a perceptually absent story-maker, as when we assume that editing cuts and other transitions preserve (or don't preserve) elements of story continuity in film. In general, the case for thinking that inferential ways of understanding other people are important is even more persuasive for fictional cases than for 'real life'. Indeed, the conclusion generalizes if we bear in mind Matravers' point that fictions and non-fictions are alike in being representations. The same add-itional reliance on inferential methods holds when we read biographies or see documentaries.

What is claimed by me and by other advocates of the role of imagination in engaging with fiction is this: we imagine the characters in the story are real people, and try to understand their beliefs, desires, and motivations within the scope of that imaginative project. And within the imaginative project, we use the same strategies for mind-reading that we use in the cases of the real people we engage with. This idea is quite general and not peculiar to psychological understanding. If, when reading a story, we hear that houses have been flooded we bring to bear on the story's content our real-world assumptions about the causal consequences of flooding: the houses won't be habitable for a while, there will be a lot of clearing up, inhabitants may have died.

Might psychology be an exception to the rule: For any F, apply the same knowledge, skills, and methods to understanding F-type events in fiction as you would apply to understanding F-type events in the real world? It's hard to see how. John Searle (1975) pointed out that words, as they occur in fiction, have just the same meanings they have in non-fictional discourse, for otherwise we would have to learn new meanings for these words when we read fiction. But we don't do that; we bring to fiction our ordinary semantical competence. Similarly we don't notice a point in cognitive development where children have to acquire a new kind of competence for understanding fictional mental states before they can say things like 'Pooh and Piglet thought they were following a Woozle but it was only their own tracks.'

But that's childhood for you. Should we, as mature audiences with identifiably literary interests, see fictional characters as candidates for ordinary psychological explanation? Peter Lamarque has claimed that it is a mistake to see characters in literature as subject to the same explanatory constraints as those that apply to real human beings:

> ... the role of fictional characters in literature does not closely mirror the role of real people living real lives. Nor do real-life narratives bear a close relation to literary narratives. It is not just that ordinary lives tend to be more humdrum, less dramatic, or less structured. To see literary characters as our friends, as ordinary people like ourselves, their lives as essentially like our lives, is to set aside nearly everything that makes great literature what it is. In effect it is to ignore all

essentially literary qualities and to reduce literature to character and plot at the same level of banality as in the stories we tell of ourselves.   (Lamarque 2014: 68)

This seems hostile to the approach I have been taking. It turns out, however, that Lamarque is not denying that we should apply psychological explanations to characters in literature; he is denying that this is the *only* thing we should do with them. What he insists on is that we should be sensitive to two distinct perspectives one may take on a literary work. Taking the internal perspective 'characters are imagined to be real humans, speaking, acting, and interacting just as ordinary people do' (95). But:

When viewed, externally, as artefacts in a work of art they become subject to radically different kinds of explanation. Why do they act as they do? Perhaps because they must act that way to meet aesthetic, structural, and genre-based demands for works of that kind. Perhaps their actions have a symbolic function or a function connected with the development of a theme or because they represent a 'polarity' with another character.   (Lamarque 2014: 7)

So Lamarque and I agree about the legitimacy of psychological explanation as applied to fictional, and indeed literary, characters. Is there anything left to disagree about? Here's what may be a disagreement, or just a difference of emphasis. Lamarque speaks of the two perspectives—the work as telescope into the lives of agents, the work as a literary artifice—as having different concerns, raising distinct questions, trafficking in different concepts. As I see it, the two perspectives are much more closely connected. Our interest in the work as constructed artifice is not separable from what we think about the psychological plausibility of the character's behaviour. It can be a failure of literary construction that a character behaves in a poorly motivated way; we sense that, externally considered, the plot needed to go in this way but that the author has failed in the task of maintaining coherent motivation. In all cases, judgements of psychological plausibility or its absence are poised to feed into our view of the work as literary artefact. Conversely, what we think about the work as constructed artefact helps to determine how we treat character motivation. Absence of naturalistic psychological motivation is expected in some genres and some works gain by having motivation be opaque, with much depending on our sense that lack of, or unclarity about, motivation was an intended effect rather than a failure of artistic ambition.[15] Lamarque, I think, sees the two perspectives as two sides of a coin; one may look at the one and then the other. They seem to me more like the two halves of a torn page: things that need to be conjoined if either is to be made sense of.

---

[15] See below, Section 9.8.

Perhaps my problems are not over. If reading the minds of characters is inseparable from thinking about their roles in a literary construction, surely that shows that engagement with fictional characters is very different from engagement with real people, who we don't think of as embedded in narrative. My answer is: not so very different. There is a difference, at least in normal cases, and the difference is the range of considerations that may have a bearing on our thoughts about the thoughts of others.[16] One important fact about mind reading is that it is, in Fodor's (1983: 105–7) terms, *isotropic*: everything you know is potentially relevant to a conclusion you might draw about someone's mental state. As Currie and Sterelny put it:

> If Max's confederate says he withdrew money from their London bank today there are all sorts of reasons why Max might suspect him: because it is a public holiday there; because there was a total blackout of the city; because the confederate was spotted in New York at lunchtime. Just where are the bits of information to which we are systematically blind in making our social judgements? The whole genre of the detective story depends on our interest and skill in bringing improbable bits of far-away information to bear on the question of someone's credibility.   (Currie and Sterelny 2000: 149)

We can go further. The confederate's religion may forbid him to draw money when there is a full moon or when it's a Thursday; You look happy, but I know the solution to the four-colour problem—something you have been working on unsuccessfully for years—has just been announced. These are unusual cases, but we have no difficulty understanding how the relevant information, once noticed, is brought to bear on the problem.[17] What is distinctive about literary cases is the way that bits of information get lumped together for inferential use. Is the fact that this character in this novel symbolizes hope relevant to working out the mental states of my friend? Certainly, if she is a literary critic working on exactly that question. Is it relevant to working out the mental states of the character himself? Again, yes, but the inference would be a different one; it goes via a rough and ready principle to the effect that characters who symbolize hope are more likely to possess this or that mental profile than characters who don't. Both cases exemplify a mentalistic conclusion influenced by a variety of beliefs, including one about symbolism in a literary work. That's why I say the two cases are not so very different.

---

[16] I say 'in normal cases' because I've argued elsewhere (Currie and Jureidini 2004) that certain pathologies of thought involve something we might call the 'fictionalization' of others and ourselves.

[17] People who claim there is a 'mind-reading module' don't, I think, deny this. Peter Carruthers thinks there is a mind-reading module, but his modules are not at all Fodorian. In particular they are not encapsulated: insulated from information stored beyond the module itself. See his (2006: 12).

2.4 Reductions of the imagination

I have been arguing that there are things that happen, and things we do, that need the imagination for their explanation. But these arguments might be vulnerable to a reductionist strategy. The reductionist does not deny that there is such a thing as the imagination, just as the materialist does not deny the existence of the mind. The materialist's opposition to dualism is opposition to the idea that the mind is non-material; the materialist thinks that mind is made of something we all believe in: matter. Might the imagination turn out to be something we already, and for independent reasons, admit to our ontology? Peter Langland-Hassan thinks so.[18] He thinks the imagination is a certain kind of belief. His argument is confined to the case of imagination in pretence; we best approach it through an example. In an influential study, Alan Leslie (1994) introduced children to a game in which it is pretended that two cups are filled with water. One of the two cups is inverted, meaning that, in the game, that cup is now empty. Young children are easily able to point to 'the empty cup'. It seems that they are imagining that one is empty and indeed that this imagining is not reducible to what they believe: they believe (correctly) that both are empty. Langland-Hassan points out that the child's behaviour might well be driven by belief and desire alone, if we include a wider class of beliefs. The child understands that a pretence has been started in which water is poured into two cups, one of which is turned upside down. Believing that upended cups discharge their water, she realizes that it is now pretence that this cup is empty. Wanting to behave in accordance with the state of the game, she points to the upended cup when asked 'Which cup is empty?'

Let's grant that the pretence behaviour in this case can be accounted for by appeal only to beliefs (including beliefs about pretence) and desires. What should we conclude? We can say, with Langland-Hassan, that it is pretence in which the imagining that guides the pretence consists of having hypothetical beliefs. But there is an alternative: to say that what Langland-Hassan has described is a case of pretence to which imagination makes no causal contribution; it is a case of pretence driven entirely by belief and desire. That is the answer I favour. How plausible is it? Two things speak in its favour. The first is that it is by no means a priori that pretence is always guided by imagination. One can engage in a calculated pretence by following a script or routine which one associates with the scenario one is pretending. And while some actors seem to be imaginatively immersed in their roles there are approaches to acting which dispense with such immersion. Indeed, there are theories of pretence available which explicitly make a space for pretence-without-imagining.[19] The second is that Langland-Hassan's

---

[18] Langland-Hassan (2012: 155); "propositional imagining just is a form of believing". See also his (2014).
[19] See my (2016). See also Velleman (2000).

reductionist program does not seem to work for other cases of imaginative activities, including those not tied to the notion of pretence.[20] Take the reader absorbed in a fictional work. The more or less standard view now is that the reader does not believe that there was any such detective as is described by Doyle, but imagines that there is one. I assume that Langland-Hassan is not going to say that the reader does, after all, believe this; if he did he would surely count as an error-theorist about imagination rather than a reductionist, for saying that imagining P is really just believing P is a way of dispensing with imagination in favour of something else. But there is no way for Langland-Hassan to tell a story about the fiction-reader that parallels the story he tells about the child pretending that a cup is empty. Langland-Hassan's strategy in that case was to show that a certain kind of behaviour—specifically a certain kind of pretending—could be motivated by beliefs and desires. But with the reader there is no behaviour (beyond the minimal behaviour associated with reading: eye movements, page turning) to be explained. Langland-Hassan could claim a partial reduction of the imagination, limited to cases of pretending. I am unwilling to grant him even that until he can show that his account of the pretending case is not simply a way of understanding it as a case of pretence-without-imagining.

2.5 Conclusions

I've examined a range of views which, taken collectively, suggest that imagination (understood as a *sui generis* attitude) is a much less important phenomenon than many of us have thought, both for understanding fiction and how we engage with it, and for understanding human cognition in general. I've given some reason for thinking that those views are either wrong or, where correct, provide no reason for denying the importance of imagination. In Chapter 1 I briefly mentioned some forms that the imagination takes but which are less often discussed in connection with fiction than the propositional imaginings which have been the focus of this chapter. The next two chapters (3 and 4) examine the workings of these imaginative forms. Chapter 3 presents a philosophical argument for believing in conative or 'desire-like' imaginings. Chapter 4 turns to the emotions. It has been said that our responses to fiction require us to recognize a category of 'quasi-emotions' that depend on imagination in the way that ordinary emotions depend on beliefs. That chapter examines this connection between emotion and imagination, as well as the complex ways that emotions can be said to be appropriate to a fictional context, depending on their connection to what is imagined.

---

[20] Langland-Hassan does not consider other cases; see 2012, n13.

3

Imaginings like desires

To this point I have focused largely on the form imagination takes when it mirrors certain characteristics of belief. There are other attitudes, notably desire. In this chapter I will argue that there is a kind of imagining which is like desire and is indeed easily mistaken for it. This kind of imagining is extremely important for understanding how we engage with fictional stories. Later we will consider the case for thinking we can learn from fiction; that case subsumes a great many arguments and accommodates several distinct forms of learning. But what is common to the variants I will consider is the assumption that learning from fiction happens through the kind of engagement that is appropriate to fiction, and not in some other way. So I treat claims about learning from fiction in the way we would ordinarily treat claims about learning from telescopes. One can learn from the examination of telescopes about the materials and construction of telescopes, but that was not what was up for debate when Galileo claimed, against certain Aristotelian objections, that telescopes could inform us about the superlunary realm. Rather, the claim was that using telescopes in the way they were designed to be used—to magnify the visible features of the things they are aimed at—enables us to learn about superlunary objects. Against this, the objection that the terrestrial success of telescopes is no guide to their usefulness in other regions, governed as they are by other principles, was one the Aristotelians were fully entitled to make—though it ultimately failed. I take it that the interesting arguments for learning from fiction parallel Galileo's stance: the claim is that ordinary processes of engagement with fiction (amplified perhaps by high levels of attention and accompanying reflection) are apt to lead to knowledge. If that is right it is important to know what sorts of imaginative resources we do regularly deploy in engaging with fiction.

Certainly, imaginative engagement with a fiction does not consists simply in our imagining that things happen in the way the story tells us they happened. Part of the more that is going on is no doubt a matter of sensory and bodily imagining. But importantly, our desires and our emotions are involved, and that is what concerns this chapter and Chapter 4. There is not much one will learn from watching *Othello* or from reading *Middlemarch* if one has no feelings towards the characters and their situations and no preferences as to how things should turn out. So I want now to bring those aspects of fictional engagement into the domain of discussion. And I will do that by asking whether there is something distinctive about the desires and emotions that fictions promote—something

Imagining and Knowing: The Shape of Fiction. Gregory Currie, Oxford University Press (2020). © Gregory Currie.
DOI: 10.1093/oso/9780199656615.001.0001

distinctive enough for some to say that we are talking about states which are desires and emotions only in an extended sense, or even that they are not desires and emotions at all.

3.1 Desire

I will say more about emotions in Chapter 4 but for now let's note that the emotions we have—positive or otherwise—are often dependent on the desires we have. *Othello* would not be for you the emotional experience it is for most people if you *wanted* Desdemona to be killed. And where emotion depends on desire, it also depends on belief. Why is Elspeth sad? Because she wanted to win and believes (perhaps knows) that she has lost. But when it comes to *Othello*, we have already seen reason to think that belief is not in question. I don't believe that Desdemona is in danger; I imagine she is. It sounds as if my emotion in this case depends on a desire and an imagining. Might there be a reason to go further? When we consider fiction cases we find the need, for many questions at least, to go from talking about belief to talking about imagining. Is there a need in those cases also to go from talk about desire to talk about—what?

We don't have a familiar word or even a phrase for what we want. It has been labelled 'imaginative desire', 'desire-in-imagination', 'desire-like imaginings', and (the one I'll use most often) 'i-desire'.[1] The common thought behind these philosophers' inventions is that we need a kind of imagining that stands together with desire, rather than making do with, as we more commonly think of it, one that stands together with belief. The argument for this will draw on the distinction between how things are and how they are represented in a fiction as being.

3.2 Truth and representation

The idea that there is an essential connection between belief and truth is widely accepted, though formulations of the idea vary. 'The aim of belief is truth' say some, and a critical literature has developed.[2] For present purposes, we need no more than this: in deciding whether a certain belief is the right belief to have, we should always ask how that belief stands to truth: Is it true? If not, how far from

---

[1] See Currie and Ravenscroft (2002: Section 1.4); Doggett and Egan (2007), Doggett and Egan (2012).

[2] 'Beliefs aim at truth, and are defective in a certain way if they are not true' (Burge 2003: 511). See also Williams (1973); Velleman (2000: Chapter 11). See also the essays in Chan (2013). I am influenced in this discussion by Walton's remark that 'Imagining aims at the fictional as belief aims at the true' (1990: 41).

the truth is it? It would not be in the same way relevant to assessing the rightness of the belief to ask how close it was to what was said in last night's news broadcast, today's sermon, *War and Peace*, or any other representation. Asking how the belief stood in relation to these or other representations would be legitimate only to the extent that one thought that those representations are themselves a guide to what is true.

That is not so for imagination. In many cases of imagining, there is nothing relevant to compare the imagining with; I idly imagine there being a frog in the next-door garden and the relation of this imagining to truth, and to pretty much anything else, is of no interest to me or anyone. But where one is imagining as part of engagement with a fiction, there is something—a representation—that is very relevant to it: the content of the fiction itself. In such cases I don't need my imaginings to be in line with the way the world is, but I do need them (some of them at least) to be in line with the way the fiction represents the world as being.

So, consider these two related notions: being true and being represented as true. It may be true that it is raining, and it may be represented as true that it is raining: represented in the TV weather report, in my statement to you, in a religious text, in a novel which tells us, at a certain point in the narrative, that it is raining. It may not be raining, but it may be raining *according to* one or other of these representations.[3] Many of these systems of representation are there because they aim at truth; as noted above, we try to align our beliefs with the weather forecast when we think the forecast is, or is likely to be, or is close to being, true. Fictions are somewhat different; on the contrary, they aim to deviate from truth; as we will later see, they never do that more than very partially.

We have the following idea. Both beliefs and imaginings can succeed (in one way) by matching something external to the mind of the believer or imaginer. In the case of belief, this is a state of the world; in the case of imagining, this is a state of some representation of the world. The state of the world can help us determine what it is right to believe, and the state of a representation of the world can help us determine what it is right to imagine. In particular, it is right to believe that The Prime Minister has resigned when she has resigned; it is right to imagine that Prime Minister has resigned when she has resigned according to the story with which you are imaginatively engaged.

All this has been in the service of distinguishing between belief and imagination. At the same time, we should remember that they have a lot in common. They are, for example, inferentially and emotionally similar. We infer from what we imagine much as we do from what we believe, and imagining yourself in danger can have affective consequences rather like those of believing you are. And there is this much in common between them as regards truth: both are

---

[3] See Currie (2010b: 8–9) for more discussion of this issue.

truth-directed (Velleman (2000: 250–1)) in that both believing and imagining something is believing (imagining) it as true. As Alex Byrne puts it: 'What "appears to be so", when one imagines a purple polar bear, is that purple polar bears exist, not (merely) that they could have existed.'[4]

3.3 Formulation problems

It is time to see that there are problems with the way I have put all this so far. First of all, I have contrasted the state of the world with the state of some representation of the world. But sometimes, when we have a belief, what makes that belief appropriate *is* the state of some representation of the world. Take my belief that last night's weather report predicted rain; what makes that a true belief is how the world is represented in the report. A state of some representation of the world is, after all, a state of the world. To get around this difficulty we need a more complicated formulation of our distinction between belief and imagination:

> When a state which is either a belief or an imagining has content *P*, the state is a belief if it is made appropriate by the fact that *P*; it is an imagining if it is made appropriate by the fact that *According to the fiction, P*.

The fact that *P* and the fact that, *according to F, P* are equally facts about the world, for any substitute for *P*. If the particular proposition that substitutes for *P* is 'According to the novel *Atonement*, Cecilia and Robbie are in love' our principle holds. Angelika has the thought 'According to the novel *Atonement*, Cecilia and Robbie are in love'. Is it a belief or an imagining? It depends on what would make it appropriate. If it is made appropriate by it being the case that

According to *Atonement*, Cecilia and Robbie are in love

it is a belief, a belief about the novel she is reading. But suppose Angelika is reading the metafictive sequel, *Atonement II*, in which the characters come up with a revisionary but convincing reading of *Atonement* according to which Cecilia and Robbie are not and never were in love. Angelika, it now transpires, has the wrong thought; she's like someone who reads *Pride and Prejudice* imagining that Elizabeth and Darcy are not in love. Her thought is an imagining.

The second difficulty is that what I have said provides a sufficient condition for something to be an imagining rather than a belief; it does not offer a necessary condition. I am not sure how to get to both necessary and sufficient conditions here. But we have done enough to show that there are clear cases where a belief

---

[4] Byrne (2007: 134). Byrne is discussing sensory imagining, but the point generalizes.

and an imagining can be distinguished by appropriateness conditions. So, where we have two states with the same content, P, where one is agreed to be a belief and one an imagining, and both have appropriateness conditions, the question which is the belief and which is the imagining can be settled by asking what their appropriateness conditions are. For present purposes that is all we need.

Finally, I said that it is appropriate that we imagine the things which are true according to that fiction. This needs some qualification. First, it cannot be expected that we imagine everything that is true according to the fiction, for there is a more or less unlimited stock of such fictional truths. Readers must choose their pathways through a fictional text, stopping to consider the implications of this or that event and then moving on, but rarely if ever investigating the full set of consequences that belong within the world of the fiction. It is also true that, on many theories of fictional truth, a lot of what is true according to the fiction is 'junk fictional truth'—rather like junk DNA, which has been thought to be redundant coding in our genes.[5] Thus some theories have it that it is true according to the stories of Sherlock Holmes that Venus is the second planet from the sun, that Edinburgh is east of Stirling, that whales are mammals. These are all things which might have been important for the stories—suppose for example that Holmes had to work out whether a suspect won his bet on the proposition that whales are mammals.[6] But none of them, I take it, are in fact important for the stories and it would be absurd to require of the diligent reader that she should imagine these things as part of her engagement with the fiction. So we should not say that the reader is required to imagine everything that is true according to the fiction. Nor should we say that the reader is required to confine her imaginings to what is true according to the fiction. There are many things which it is appropriate for the reader to imagine, which are not true according to the fiction. For example, there are many stories in which we are led to believe that something has occurred, but later we find that it did not. Readers of *Atonement* are led to think that certain things happened to Cecilia and Robbie, only to discover very late in the narrative that these events were imagined by the guilt-ridden Briony, and that Cecilia and Robbie died without being reunited. And without being misled ourselves, we are often able to deepen our engagement with the work by imagining its events from the mistaken perspective of one of the characters; Faulkner's *The Sound and the Fury* is an elaborate exercise in this.

So, it is wrong to say that an imagining undertaken as part of engagement with a fictional story is appropriate if and only if it is an imagining of some proposition true according to the story; the relation between appropriate imagining and truth

---

[5] Though it, or some of it, may have so far unidentified functions.

[6] Holmes once chided Watson for telling him that the moon goes around the earth on the grounds that it was taking up valuable memory space but would be no use to him. He could not have been sure of this. See above, the discussion of isotropy, Section 2.3.

in the story is weaker and much less orderly than that. Still, there are things it is appropriate to imagine *because* they are true according to the story, and one will not engage with the story unless one's imagining track the most central, most salient propositions of the story. And while it might be wrong for one reason to engage in imagining that Sherlock Holmes has two lungs (because it distracts one from important story content) it would be right compared to imagining that he had three lungs, given the plausible assumption that the story represents him (implicitly) as having two.

I grant, finally, that the distinction between belief and imagining is not well marked in our common talk. In particular, it is not always evident in talk provoked by fictions. Discussing the play as we watch (this is the first time we have seen it and we are somewhat confused by the unfamiliar language), I say 'I believe Desdemona is innocent'. But here we fall naturally into the pretence of being agents who are acquiring beliefs about real characters and events. Why not simply say 'Desdemona is innocent'? Because implicatures work within pretence as well as they do outside it. 'Believes' has a certain use to which Grice drew attention and which we have already noted: to indicate that we are less than sure that something is true.[7] Given that the speaker in the theatre is less than certain, at this point, of Desdemona's (represented) innocence, she uses 'believe' to indicate this; with more certainty she would just say 'Desdemona is innocent'. Substituting 'imagine' would not create the same implicature; to say that I imagine that Desdemona is innocent indicates, in ordinary speech, a very low level of confidence in the proposition, or at least a level lower than is indicated by 'believe'.[8]

3.4 Desires in imagination

For all the complexity that the debate over the aim of belief has produced, we can say this much: belief is related to truth in ways that imagination is not. And truth is so important to how we think about belief that it is right to think of imagination, which is not so related, as distinct from belief and not as a kind of belief—a less vivid, a less motivating belief, as has sometimes been suggested. I want to draw a parallel conclusion for desire: what we call 'desiring' that Othello see his error is no more a real desire than 'believing' Othello is about to murder Desdemona is a real belief. That last is a kind of imagining, and what is going on in the case we call a 'desire' is an imagining also; it is what has been called an i-desire.

Why think of i-desires as 'not really desires'? Here is an argument we should be wary of. It is said that, since we don't leap on stage to save Desdemona, we can't

---

[7] On conversational implicature see Grice (1989); on knowledge as the standard of assertion see Williamson (2000: Chapter 11).

[8] I made a similar point about the pragmatics of 'believes' at Section 2.3.

really desire her survival. But we learned from Matravers not to compare fiction with how we would respond in real life but to compare it with non-fiction—another form of representation.[9] Watching the re-enactment or filmed record of an actual murder, I do nothing to intervene, not because I lack a desire for the survival of the victim but because I don't believe there is anything I can usefully do at this stage: desires motivate only in conjunction with beliefs. It is said that 'desire' is the appropriate term only where action is a possible result; it may seem odd to say that I desire the survival of someone who I know is dead. Still, this is something towards which I have a pro-attitude; I can certainly wish that this person had not died. And there is a difference, I will argue, between wishing some real death had not occurred and wishing that Desdemona survive, for all the motivational inertness of both. As I use it, 'desire' will include these sorts of motivationally inert wishes as well as those pro-attitudes which are apt to motivate and which we more happily call desires.

Here's a better argument. Desires are as importantly related to how things are in the world as beliefs are. Our beliefs are true when they match how the world is, and our desires are *satisfied* when they match how the world is. Suppose I have a friend whose survival concerns me. What would make my belief that she has survived correct would be the non-occurrence of her death. That's also the thing that would satisfy my desire (wish) that she had not died. If it turned out, surprisingly, that she survived, my desire for her survival would have been satisfied all along and I need not have been concerned. If people on other planets turn out to have lived happy lives my desire that they do will be satisfied, though I will never know that they do. What satisfies my desires is the world turning out to be the way that corresponds to the content of my desire.

It isn't like that with 'desires' (so called) concerning fictional outcomes. Take my 'desire' that Desdemona survives. What would satisfy that? The survival of Desdemona? There are reasons to say that this is not even a possible state of affairs, for there is no such actual person as Desdemona and no even possible Desdemona: no person residing in a non-actual world who is Desdemona in that world.[10] Suppose, though, that this is wrong, and there is a possible person—a person in some non-actual world, who is Desdemona in that world. Suppose that she exists in many worlds, being murdered in some and surviving in others—even Desdemona isn't murdered *of necessity*. But the survival of this woman in some worlds is nothing to me, at least as far as my relations to the persons and events of the play is concerned. Her survival in some world does not satisfy my desire (so called) that Desdemona survive. What matters to me is what happens in the

---

[9] See above, Section 2.1.

[10] Kripke holds that, while what we take to be fictional characters like Sherlock Holmes (an easier example) might turn out to be real people really referred to by authors, as long as that is not so then there is no possible being who is that fictional character. See Kripke (2013, Lecture II); also Kripke (1980: 158).

actual world *on stage*. What happens on stage is a representation. My desire (we will go on calling it that for the moment) is satisfied if, according to that representation, Desdemona survives. As play-goers know, it does not work out that way.

To make this point more vivid, consider a fiction involving a real person. Suppose I want The Prime Minister to remain in office for the next five years; I also enjoy political theatre and attend a performance that tells of a possible future in which the government chaotically and amusingly progresses towards a collapse within days. Catching the satirical mood of the piece I find myself 'wanting' the collapse. What would satisfy my want? I glance at my phone during the performance and read that the government has fallen and the PM has resigned. That's not what I wanted! My want gets satisfied only if the play *represents* the government as falling.

The parallel with belief is clear: Beliefs are supposed to match the world; imaginings, where they are supposed to match anything, are supposed to match the world *as it is according to the fiction*. Beliefs and imaginings are, we agreed, not the same kinds of things. My desire that the PM stay in office is satisfied by her staying in office; what I've been calling my 'desire that the government collapse' is satisfied by the fiction representing the government as collapsing. This 'desire' stands to real desires as imaginings stand to beliefs. So we should think of them as members of a species of imagining—desires in imagination, or i-desires.[11]

It may be said of the case just considered that the object of my thought is not the real Prime Minister, but an unreal Prime Minister-of-the-play, so my desires about The Prime Minister are irrelevant; I really do want The Prime Minister-of-the-play to have to resign within the year.[12] As Stacie Friend (2003) has argued, there are heavy costs in assuming that fictions are never about real people; if they sometimes are, why isn't this play one of them? When I tell my daughter (fictional) stories about her adventures with her friend the lion their appeal for her depends on it being *she* herself who figures in them; they are invitations for her to have imaginings about herself. Why can't I just stipulate that it is she, that very person, who is the main character in the story? I might tell outlandish lies to

---

[11] Fiora Salis (2016) objects that this generalizes unwontedly: I want the lab experiment to succeed which requires the death of the rat, yet I don't want the rat to die; that seems to call, on my way of seeing things, for an intervention that ascribes to me another desire-like state (an 'x-desire' as she puts it) that is not really a desire. Salis was responding to an earlier formulation of my argument (2010c) which may be vulnerable on this issue but for the present I would say that the lab experiment case does not exemplify the contrast between what happens and what happens according to something. A death in a lab is a death, and not the representation of one, whereas a death in ('according to') a theatrical performance is merely a representation of one. As far as I can see, then, we can't generate a desire/x-desire contrast of the kind I am advocating for desires and i-desires. But there are important issues raised by Salis's discussion concerning the possibility that the desire/i-desire contrast might be helpful in some non-fictive cases. I am grateful to her work on this and hope to discuss this elsewhere.

[12] I am using 'The Prime Minister' in something like Donnellan's referential way. I am doing it that way to avoid proper names which will too quickly go out of date.

someone about my daughter having a friend who is a lion. They are lies because they are about my daughter, who incidentally does not have a friend who is a lion. Why can't it be the same with fiction-making? Lies and fiction telling are different in many respects, for example in respect of honesty: but if it is possible to say something deceptively untrue about a real person, why isn't it possible to say something undeceptively untrue about them? Of course, the fictions in question tell of things which may not happen to The Prime Minister and certainly didn't happen to my daughter; they are about The Prime Minister and my daughter *fictionalized*. The Prime Minister fictionalized is The Prime Minister and the same holds of my daughter.

Accepting this, an objector might insist that The Prime Minister example involves only genuine desires, though in this case desires of different kinds. I have, as stipulated, the desire that The Prime Minister not resign. That's a stable, background desire of mine. But I also, the argument notes, have the desire that she resign. That's a highly salient, *condition-dependent* desire, triggered by watching the drama. For the duration of the drama, the condition-dependent desire dominates my thinking, pushing into the background my other, contrary desire.

People do sometimes have condition-dependent desires which contradict their more stable desires. A person whose long-term background desire is to stay sober may, when confronted with temptation, acquire the desire to drink. This is a condition-dependent desire, and not a conditional desire; it is not the desire to drink if confronted by certain things, but the desire simply to drink: a desire the subject has just when so confronted. The condition in which one has that desire is a trigger; it is not part of the satisfaction condition of that desire; the satisfaction condition is merely that I drink. The subject has a desire of the one kind to drink, and a desire of the other kind not to.

All that is certainly possible. But that is not how it is with me as I watch the amusing political satire. My long-term, stable desire that The Prime Minister remain in office has a certain satisfaction condition; it is satisfied if she thrives. What is the satisfaction condition of my condition-dependent desire, prompted by the drama, for the fall of The Prime Minister? If it really is a desire, it should be satisfied by her fall. But we have seen that it wouldn't be.[13] My delight at the play's representation of her downfall disappears when I get the unwelcome news on my phone that she has resigned. True, people sometimes have desires the satisfaction of which leave them unhappy—it might be exactly that way with the tempted non-drinker. But it is not like that with me and the PM: I simply don't want her to resign. Consider also bets. If you and I are watching the drama, and bet on whether my desire (we casually call it that in our conversation) that The Prime Minister resign will be satisfied, the bet isn't decided by what happens when,

---

[13] Thanks to Tyler Doggett here.

amazingly, social media inform me that she has resigned; it is decided by what happens in the play.[14]

I've based my argument on a purported difference between the satisfaction conditions for my desire that The Prime Minister continue in office, and the satisfaction conditions for my theatrically induced 'desire' that she resign. A further objection to my conclusion is that we can explain what is going on in cases like this by invoking only states with conventional satisfaction conditions— conditions that we think of as those possessed by genuine desires. The desire I most saliently have while watching the play, the desire that the outcome of the play satisfies, is that *According to the fiction, the Prime Minister resigns.* That's why I am pleased with the outcome of the play, and disappointed by the news on my phone that the government has fallen.

One thing that should make us hesitant about this solution is that it represents me as too focused on the fact that what I am watching is a fiction. Surely my concern is with the fate of the Prime Minister, not with the fiction which represents her. I don't believe that absorption by fictional stories makes us no longer believe that we are watching a fiction. But it does, surely, push the fictionality of what we attend to towards the backs of our minds. 'It's only a fiction' is what we say when we want to disengage, as we may do if the story is uncomfortably scary.

While this argument should carry some weight there is a stronger one: it is not generally true that wanting P, where P is some event represented in the story, is really a case of wanting it to be the case that, according to the story, P. We see this in our responses to tragedy. I know what will happen at the end of *Othello*; I chose to see it this night partly because it has this tragic ending; I might have chosen a light comedy but that was not what I wanted to see; I believed that the production would follow Shakespeare's narrative faithfully; I would have been outraged if a happy ending had been substituted. All this supports the idea that I want it to be the case that, according to the play I shall see, Desdemona is killed. Does that mean that I want Othello to murder her? No. Like the rest of the audience I am appalled when that happens.

We are now in a position to say something (not everything on this complex issue) about what makes for tragic fiction and indeed for any fiction where Hume's mixture of pleasure and affliction (1777/2008) can be found, which is in just about any fiction. Putting it in the colloquial, awkward, and ultimately wrong way: we want the play, film, novel, or TV soap to have an unhappy ending, but we don't want the unhappy events that constitute that ending. We want the fiction to

---

[14] Doggett and Egan say 'Romeo and Juliet can't survive unless, according to the fiction of *Romeo and Juliet*, they survive' (2012: 285). I leave out of account as irrelevant here some questions: whether the satisfaction conditions for the desire to drink requires that the drinking be caused by the desire; whether desire satisfaction is something which comes in degrees (on which see Skow (2009)).

represent the villain as triumphant, but don't want the villain's triumph. The right way to put it is to say that we desire the fiction to represent the villain as triumphant, but i-desire the villain's defeat. And i-desires are as distinct from ordinary desires as imaginings are beliefs.

Earlier I rejected the view that, in fiction, our attitudes are always directed at the fictional counterparts of real things. I say that Napoleon in *War and Peace* is Napoleon and my daughter in the lion story is my daughter. What is true is that one's attitude to a real thing in a fictional context is an attitude which, while directed at that thing, is not satisfiable in the way that one's real desires would be. Its satisfaction does not depend on what the real thing does, but on what it does *according to the fiction*. To say that one's attitude is directed towards the fiction-alized counterpart of the real thing is most charitably seen as a confused version of what ought to be said: that one's attitude is satisfied, not according to how the real thing is, but according to how that real thing is represented in the fiction.

3.5 Conclusions

I have presented my case as one dedicated to this idea: we need to recognize that, as well as desires, there are i-desires. On that view i-desires are not really desires, but distinct states with certain admitted similarities to desires. Suppose someone responds to the argument by saying:

> I agree with everything you say about the existence, and the nature, of i-desires, but I say also that they are desires and that what the argument shows is that things within the category of desires may have different kinds of satisfaction conditions. Desires are, after all, a somewhat mysterious category and we have no established grip on or consensus about what counts as a desire and what does not. It is less revisionary (and hence better) to say that there are desires with the satisfaction conditions of i-desires than it is to say that things like wanting Desdemona to be saved are not after all desires.

I grant that this line of thought might be powerfully developed. If it is, I won't hang grimly on to the claim that i-desires are not desires. What I do hang onto is the claim that there are i-desires—states in some ways like ordinary desires but with satisfaction conditions quite different from the satisfaction conditions for such ordinary desires as our desire that friends and family members thrive. We will see that a similar issue arises in Chapter 4, where we consider the role of emotion in fiction. I shall ask: Is there a sense (or are there senses) in which it is right to have this emotional response to fiction rather than some other one? The answer will indicate a difference between the emotions of 'real life' and the emotions of fiction, parallel to the difference I have outlined between desires and i-desires.

4

Affective imagining

To learn from fictions we have to understand them—understand them, that is, in the ways they are designed to be understood. Part of that is simply being able to track, within our imaginative project, what happens in the story: we are to imagine that this happens and then that; that this happened because something else happened. I come now to the emotions and how they may contribute to this sort of understanding. I'll argue that they contribute in two ways: by *being the right emotions*, and by *getting things right*. I'll start with the idea of emotions getting things right and, of course, sometimes getting them wrong. If one thinks of emotions simply as eruptions of feeling it is not clear how they could get anything right or wrong. But that view is not widely held. There is currently a debate underway that seeks a unified picture of the functional and ultimately biological architecture of the emotions and their role in rationality.[1] I am concerned here only with questions about the rationality and more broadly the normative constraints on the emotions—itself an issue of some complexity, as we will see. I do accept, though, that theorizing in this region will ultimately have to mesh with the best neurobiological account of the emotions.

My first question then is, what is it for emotions to get things right? In answering it I will make a case for treating emotions as we treated desires in Chapter 3: as subject to a state/i-state distinction.

There is no *one* way for an emotion to be the right emotion to have. *A* way is to get things right, in a sense I will explain immediately. There is a variety of other ways in which an emotion can be appropriate. We must be clear, in all our discussions, about what kind of appropriateness is at issue, and how these different kinds trade off against one another. The issue of trade-offs will be particularly relevant at the end of the chapter when we consider a kind of appropriateness for fictional cases: one that brings in the idea of an *intended* emotional response.

4.1 Norms for emotions

I start with our emotional responses to the real world: we are frightened or delighted by real things, we like some real people and dislike others, we are

---

[1] Important work here includes Damasio (1994) and de Sosa (1987). On the difficulties of reconciling rationality and a modular architecture for the emotions see Jones (2006); see also Linquist and Bartol (2013).

Imagining and Knowing: The Shape of Fiction. Gregory Currie, Oxford University Press (2020). © Gregory Currie.
DOI: 10.1093/oso/9780199656615.001.0001

made anxious by things that may turn out to be real and regret past failures. And these emotions are often appropriate: it is right to fear the fearful, to delight in the delightful, to feel secure with some people and wary of others, depending on how they are and what they do. We have noted significant similarities between our emotional reactions to fiction and to real life: we are frightened by creatures lurking in dark alleys, delighted by romantic unions, and saddened by deaths, whether they are fictional or real. The emotions operate across that divide, and we might expect the constraints on emotions to be the same in both domains. It will turn out that they are not.

A way for emotions directed at the real world to be appropriate is representational; emotions represent their objects as being certain ways, and an emotion is appropriate, in one sense, if it represents its object correctly. Fear *for* someone is associated with a representation of them as in danger, fear *of* something goes with a representation of that thing as dangerous; jealousy is associated with a representation of another as bearing relations to a third party which they ought to bear exclusively to you. An emotion fails to be appropriate (in one sense) when its associated representation misrepresents its object (Gilmore 2011). It is inappropriate (in this same sense) to be fearful for someone who faces no threat, or to be envious of someone who is no better off than you are. Let's call this the *reality test*: an emotion should represent its object as it really is.

I have said there are a number of ways an emotional response can be, or fail to be, appropriate, and failure to be appropriate in one of them does not rule out success in another. Nor is failure to be appropriate in one way always something to be avoided; failing to obey the parking regulations is not a bad thing if it makes it easier for the fire service to get to the blaze. Passing the reality test is neither necessary nor sufficient for appropriateness in an emotional response as we judge it all-things-considered. Rational beliefs are sometimes false beliefs, and one may falsely but rationally believe something which would justify fear or jealousy. An emotion may misrepresent its object and be a required response, all-things-considered; I should have been angered by Smith's behaviour as you reported it to me, given how badly he seemed to have behaved and how reliable you usually are, though it turned out that, surprisingly, your account was misleading (I will have more to say on this topic). Envy might be the wrong emotion to have, even when it passes the reality test; you may indeed have more millions than I do, but envy of one millionaire by another is absurd.[2]

Still, the reality test is not a bad starting point when inquiring into the appropriateness of an emotion; if my information about Smith is wrong, any anger I might have had would have been misdirected, however rationally, and if

---

[2] Perhaps jealousy is something we simply cannot help but feel, irrespective of circumstances. One's obligation in this situation would then be to minimize its duration and intensity and its effects on one's behaviour.

Jones actually does have more millions than you your envy would be free of one defect, though it has others.

Does the reality test apply to fictional cases? It does not, for two reasons. First, many objects of emotion in fiction simply don't exist—there is no truth about them to constrain emotion.[3] Second, where objects of emotion in fiction do exist—as with Prosecutor Garrison in *JFK*—the truth about them may constrain inappropriately, as Stacie Friend (2003) points out. Watching the movie I am moved by Garrison's selfless devotion to truth, even though I believe (truly, as it happens) that Garrison was a conspiracy-fanatic who ruined the life of at least one person in his obsessive bid to prove government complicity in the President's assassination. As far as the reality test goes, any emotion of mine experienced as I sit watching the movie and which represents Garrison as admirable must be inappropriate. But this misses the point.[4] We should ask how Garrison is represented in the film. Reusing a distinction from Chapter 3, it's the film's *representation* of Garrison as devoted to truth which makes my admiration appropriate, not how he really was. For fiction we need, not a reality test, but a *representational correspondence* test: my emotional response to the fictional character or event is appropriate to the extent that the emotion represents that character or event in just the way it is represented as being in the story.[5] This applies to wholly fictional characters like Sherlock Holmes as well as to real people represented in fictions; my admiration for Holmes is (in the sense we are considering now) appropriate just in case he is represented in the stories as being admirable. The test cannot be whether he is admirable, for he (the person) does not exist. A rule of truth constrains aptness for the emotions of life; a rule of representational correspondence—correspondence between how the emotion represents its object and how the fiction does the same—constrains fictive emotions.[6]

There are ways to disguise this difference. One is to argue as follows: the rule of representational correspondence ('rule of representation' let us say) which guides emotion in fictional cases holds also in the real world; it's just that, in the real

---

[3] The ontology of fictional characters is disputed territory; what I think is generally agreed is that there is, for example, no such *person* as Sherlock Holmes, no such *bird* as Tweetypie and no such *place* as Tara. Those who think that fictional characters exist at all don't think that they are people, birds, and places but that they are cultural artefacts of some kind. Being artefacts they do not have the kinds of properties that would make, say, contempt appropriate. The fictional character Karenin does not have the property of being hypocritically vengeful, for the character is an artefact and not a person. On the metaphysics of fictional characters see my 1990, Chapter 4; for a different view see Thomasson (1999).

[4] I will complicate things in Section 4.2.

[5] Fictive emotions I take to be emotions directed at fictional characters and happenings. I am not assuming at this stage that such states are not genuine emotions. That is an issue we shall come to. I do not count as fictive emotions those emotions directed at fictional works, as when one is moved by the superb economy of the story-telling. Fictions are real things and emotions with fictions as objects are appropriate in the same way that emotions which have our friends as their objects are appropriate. Being moved by the superb economy of a story is not appropriate (in our current sense) if the story is not superbly economical in its story-telling.

[6] See Gilmore (2011) for discussion; also Schier (1983).

world, there are two rules: the rule of representation and the rule of truth, and they sometimes conflict. As we have already noticed, there is a sense in which it was right for me to be angry with Smith, given how you represented him in your testimony, though in fact you were, surprisingly, unreliable and Smith had done nothing wrong. So the rule of representation applies in the real world as well as in fictional cases, the difference being that in the real world one's response might satisfy one of these two rules and not the other and so be appropriate by just one of two criteria, whereas for the fictional case the rule of representation is the only rule. So it may be said.

In fact there is nothing that governs real-world cases of emotions that parallels the rule of representation for fiction. The closest things governing real-world cases is a rule of *evidence*—an emotion is appropriate when there is good evidence that its associated representation is correct. And representations are sometimes evidence; if the total evidence available to me, including the evidence of your testimony, suggests that Smith behaved badly then my anger with him is in one sense apt, though it may be that the evidence available to me is misleading and so, in another sense, not apt. It might even be that the only evidence I have is your testimony, and, given your general reliability, that testimony—a representation—makes my anger apt. That is because your testimony is good evidence, not because it is a representation of Smith's behaviour. Merely being a representation of something gives that representation no evidential weight in the real world. The rule of representation that does apply to fiction is not a rule of evidence. In the fictional case, how the story represents the situation is not *evidence* for how things are in the story; it is *constitutive* of how they are. It is what makes things that way in the story. Things are in a story as they are represented to be.[7] In sum, for real-world emotions there is a rule of truth, and for emotions of fiction there is a different rule: the rule of representation. The rule of representation does not apply to real-world cases. What applies there is yet another rule: a rule of evidence, and representations (e.g. testimonial ones) sometimes provide evidence.

At this point we do find a parallel between real-world and fictional cases; we need a rule of evidence for both. Just as it is often far from obvious what is true, so it is far from obvious what is represented in a fiction. A reader can hope to conform to the rule of representation only by weighing the evidence of what is represented. If I decide, at the beginning of the story, that Professor Peacock is the murderer, and it turns out that he is, I have impeccably conformed to the rule of representation; my emotions directed at him—horror, contempt—represent him as the story itself represents him (let us suppose). But my initial reasoning was based on a hopelessly wrong picture of the evidence and my conclusion that he was guilty was simply lucky; I conformed to the rule of representation, but

---

[7] This is a general truth about stories, fictional and non-fictional.

I should have done so *by* conforming to the rule of evidence, which I did not do. I should have attended to the evidence provided by the story.

In all this we need to distinguish carefully between how the story represents its characters and their doings and how the narrator represents them, for narrators can be unreliable, and the representation of a narrator is only ever evidence for how things are represented in the story itself. We cannot coherently say that the narrator was unreliable unless we think that the narrator's account of what happened is inconsistent with what happened according to the story, and what happened according to the story is how the work—the novel or whatever—represents things as happening.[8]

Unreliable narrators mislead us as to what is represented in the story, but we are very commonly misled, at least temporarily, by narration which is selective rather than unreliable. With many kinds of fiction we are under-informed through the earlier stages of the work about a character, being given the false impression that she has this or that character-trait, or performs this or that character-revealing action. In such cases a certain emotional trajectory is, perhaps vaguely, laid out for us by the work, and there is a sense in which it is appropriate for us to experience a range of emotions across the time of narration. A story may ask of us that we experience a warm confidence in one of its characters in order that we be the more disconcerted at the end when they are revealed as the murderer. Or it may be that this change of reaction is not brought about by a change in the presentation of the character's traits, but by a piling up of evidence that their less than admirable characteristics are a product of or an understandable response to hostile circumstances. Perhaps that is how we are to react to the rather calculating Lily Bart in Edith Wharton's *The House of Mirth*, who may seem to have more sympathetic characteristics when we have worked our ways through the catalogue of hypocritical, rapacious, and mean-spirited inhabitants of New York Society ranged against her.

4.2 Truth

It looks then as if truth has nothing to do with assessing the appropriateness of emotions in response to fictions; we thought that it did only because we confused the rule of truth with the rule of representation. But considerations of truth sometimes do and should constrain the responses of the spectator. Doesn't the fact that Prosecutor Garrison was a wicked and/or deluded man make it, in some sense, *inappropriate* for me to luxuriate in admiration for him while watching *JFK*,

---

[8] Which is not to deny the possibility of indeterminacies in the story; where the story is indeterminate as between outcomes A and B, the narrator can be said to be unreliable if her account has it that something other than either A or B occurs.

even though the film represents him as a selfless and committed seeker of truth? There are two reasons to keep truth in mind in a discussion of emotions appropriate to fiction. The first is a well-attested tendency of people to believe that things are as the fiction represents them to be, when the fiction has the kind of real-world basis we find in *JFK*. Indeed, some of the evidence for this general claim is based on responses to this very film: even well-educated viewers have been, it is said, strongly influenced by the film in their beliefs about a wide-ranging conspiracy behind the Kennedy assassination.[9] And it is very plausible that the mechanism of this belief change has something to do with the emotions the fiction elicits. Finding yourself with feelings of admiration for Garrison as represented in the film may make you concerned about your vulnerability to insidious change of belief.

The second worry concerns what I'll call *aesthetic free-riding*. We suspect the film's makers of gaining spurious aesthetic advantage by relying on a tendency in the audience not merely to imagine the events of the film, but actually to believe them and, through believing them, to experience more intense emotions in response to the film.[10] Seen that way, the movie looks like the result of a questionable enterprise: one that aims to achieve its effects *by* misleading people, and not merely something which has, incidentally, this effect. If the makers can call on the extra power of belief, they do not have to work so hard to produce emotional effects that will make the work admired. That can seem to be, and perhaps is, a moral fault, like winning a race on performance enhancing drugs. I now have a reason to stay out of range of the film's emotional influence even if I am rationally convinced that it will not affect my beliefs, and whether or not in doing so I am making a difference to how others react to it. We don't wish to be associated with morally questionable enterprises even when we think we will not personally be harmed by contact with them, or that our disapproval will influence others.

If this is right, truth has not lost all ability to constrain our emotional engagement with fiction; failure to meet the truth constraint, when this is part of a design to boost a work's emotional power and thereby to disguise its artistic weaknesses, gives me a reason (not always an over-riding reason) to resist responding to the work as I am intended to do. How far this constraint extends is difficult to determine and generalizations are hard to make. Worries parallel to those that arise with *JFK* might surface even in a fiction which does not feature—and so does not misrepresent—real people as its characters. We might be uncomfortable with a movie featuring a purely fictional DA who investigates the Kennedy case, if he or

---

[9] See Butler et al. (1995). Since these reactions were elicited directly after seeing the film it is unclear how stable they would turn out to be. See below, Section 9.2.

[10] I don't mean that audiences believe that they are watching those real events, or a filmed record of them. Rather the advantage is gained by having audiences believe that what is represented in the story contains a good deal of truth—much more than in fact it does.

she is presented in something like the way Garrison is presented in *JFK*, on the grounds that the well-attested tendency for people to believe in conspiracies is still being exploited. We worry also about the misrepresentation of ethnic groups even where no real people or incidents are featured. Where fictions are apt, for whatever reason, to generate emotions which misrepresent, worries of this kind arise. We don't, on the other hand, worry much about misrepresentations of Henry V in Shakespeare; time has made that issue seem much less important.

4.3 Emotions and quasi-emotions

There is a difference, I have said, between the emotions of fiction and those of 'real life' in that the former are beholden to a rule of representation and the latter to a rule of truth. The discussion here parallels the one we had in Chapter 3 concerning the satisfaction conditions for desires, which turned out to be rather different from those that apply to i-desires. The upshot of that discussion was the recognition of a kind of imaginative state—i-desiring—which is different from desiring in the way that imagining (in the ordinary sense) is different from believing. It looks as if we now have reason to recognize another kind of imaginative state which we might call i-emotions but which have been influentially labelled 'quasi-emotions' (Walton 1978).

Should we? At this point our discussion connects with an older one. Colin Radford ended his exposition of a puzzle about emotional reactions to fiction in this way:

> Our being moved in certain ways by works of art, though very 'natural' to us and in that way only too intelligible, involves us in inconsistency and so incoherence.
>
> It may be some sort of comfort, as well as support for my thesis, to realise that there are other sorts of situation in which we are similarly inconsistent, i.e., in which, while knowing that something is or is not so, we spontaneously behave, or even may be unable to stop ourselves behaving, as if we believed the contrary. Thus, a tennis player who sees his shot going into the net will often give a little involuntary jump to lift it.   (Radford (1975: 78))

Radford did not doubt that we are moved by fictions and he thought that we are related to them via the same class of emotions that relate us to real things we believe in. On his view we do pity Anna Karenina, but in the 'inconsistent' way that the tennis player tries to lift the ball.[11] Three years after Radford's posing of

---

[11] The involuntary jump of the tennis player may be analogous to the visceral response of Charles the horror movie watcher already discussed, but it is very much unlike a wide range of emotional responses to fictions that depend on reflection. Being moved by the fate of a fictional character, at least when the fiction concerned is worth contemplating, is often a matter of working through a range of

the problem, in a much-cited essay Kendall Walton (1978) denied this. Pity, he says, requires belief in the object of your pity, so we don't, and can't, pity Anna. Of course something is going on that is like pity; we do experience strong feelings, the same as or similar to those we would feel if we really pitied someone. And our having those feelings makes it true, in the game of pretence we play when we read the novel, that we pity Anna. For if we had different, perhaps positive feelings, it would not be true in the game that we pitied her; it might be true in the game that we were delighted by her fate. But the state we are actually in, easily mistaken for pity because of the way it feels, Walton labels *quasi-pity*. I quasi-pity Anna, and that makes it the case that it is pretence or make-believe that I pity her.

Walton's distinction fits nicely with the distinction I have made between two kinds of appropriateness conditions. Fear represents things as dangerous and is appropriate when it represents things as they are; quasi-fear represents things as dangerous also, but is appropriate when it represents things as they are represented as being. No need for talk, *à la* Radford, of incoherence or trying for a magical outcome. Quasi-pity is an appropriate response to what the novel tells us about Anna's situation.

It looks as if we have discovered yet another form of imagining: an emotion-like sort of imagining, something like an emotion but not one, in the way that imagining that such and such is not a kind of belief though it is belief-like. So we end up with belief-like, desire-like, and emotion-like imaginings, all recognized as forms of imagining because of the peculiar nature of their relations to the world. We might call them all *representation-dependent states*. What satisfies my imagining that Anna is unhappy is not her being so, but her being represented in a certain novel as so; what satisfies my i-desire that she be happy is not her being so but her being represented in the novel as so (and so my i-desire never is satisfied); what makes my quasi-pity for her appropriate is not facts about her which make her pitiable but facts about how she is represented as being. Should we say these states are not beliefs, or desires, or emotions, but imaginative counterparts to those sorts of states? I return to this question at the close of this chapter.

4.4 Appropriate emotions, intended emotions

I have said a good deal about how to assess the appropriateness of an emotional response to a fictional situation. If I tell you that I am responding emotionally in some particular way, you can now list for me various ways to assess the

---

possible perspectives on the situation, lighting on one that seems to do justice to the moral and psychological circumstances. This process does not usually derail with us realizing how silly we are being—something Radford surely recognized, at least by implication, given that *Anna Karenina* is his central example.

appropriateness of that way of responding. This leaves unanswered the question: when *should* we respond emotionally? We don't respond emotionally to all the events of a fiction, nor should we. But there are events that we should respond to emotionally, and the question then arises as to what is an appropriate emotional response. Someone who sits watching (a representation of) the murder of Desdemona without their consciousness being disturbed by any emotion is probably not responding appropriately, but they have not violated any of the rules I have canvassed. To violate those rules you have to have an (inappropriate) emotion.

It is tempting to offer a principle like this: the way we ought to respond to the events of the fiction is the way we should respond if those (or relevantly similar) events occurred in real life. One difficulty is that there are many ways to respond to real-life events, including not responding in any distinctive way at all. That, notes Allan Gibbard, is probably what we should do concerning the theft of a stranger's camel far away.[12] Is indifference the right response to a fictional representation of such a theft? Certainly not, if the theft in question is of Antonio's bicycle in *Ladri di biciclette* (De Sica 1948). There is nothing unique to fiction here; a history or journalistic piece, well written, might present a real theft in such detail and with such vividness that, once again, our feelings are stirred. Perhaps the right response to the fictional representation is the right response to the very same representation (same words) now taken to be non-fictional. But this can't generally be true. The appropriate response to a version of *Anna Karenina* one assumed to be non-fiction would be either to wonder at Tolstoy's magical powers of mind-reading, or to rejection of the whole thing as fantastic lies. And while the appropriate response to murder in fiction ranges from horror to hilarity (*The Ladykillers*, Mackendrick 1955), the same range does not seem to be available for non-fiction.

So the problem is this: if we know that it is appropriate to respond emotionally to some event in a fiction, we can, on the basis of what I have said so far, say something about what would make one emotion rather than another the appropriate one to have. What we don't have is a clue about what makes having an emotional response appropriate in the first place.

I have only a partial solution to the problem. It says that in many cases the appropriate response is an emotional one if that is the intended response. When a work is so crafted as to provoke a certain emotion, that is often the appropriate way to react to it. I don't mean by this that the right way to respond to a fiction is to work out what emotions if any it was supposed to provoke and then to adjust your inner life so that you have those emotions. Emotions don't work that way. Rather, our emotional response was appropriate because it was a response to

---

[12] Gibbard (1990: 126). But Gibbard goes on to say that 'It even makes sense to engage one's feelings in fiction from time to time', as if this kind of engagement needs careful rationing.

features of the work designed to elicit that response, and not because the work provides evidence that the response was designed for that response. Elicitation of emotion is not Gricean.

There will not be, for every element of a given work, exactly one intended emotion. Often what is intended is that one responds in any of a certain range of ways, all this being, like most intentions, rather vaguely specified. Fictions vary greatly in the extent to which they guide our emotional responses. Classical realist novels are on the whole quite constraining, though Dickens is more constraining than Tolstoi, while other, more recent genres tolerate much more ambiguity and some works constrain our responses scarcely at all; that is one of the puzzling things about Kafka's *The Trial*. In yet other kinds of cases the author simply takes over what they assume to be the natural emotional inclinations of the target audience, shaping events that they predict will be responded to in certain ways; those emotionally unchallenging narratives fall naturally into the category of the non-literary. A fiction's emotional framing can be ambitious and disruptive, or merely comfortingly affirming.

Why should the, or an, intended response be the appropriate one? It is not always so, and I will discuss cases which contradict this assumption. But there is a reasonable presumption that the intended response is appropriate. It is generally the case with artefacts that the way to use them to best advantage is to use them in the ways they are intended to be used. We do not get the best from our cars by using them as dustbins, or the best from paintings by using them as dinner plates; they were not made with the intention of fulfilling these purposes and it would be a surprising accident if they did fulfil them well. It is the same with stories. Narratives of worth are carefully crafted to convey stories in which certain things and not others happened; those are the things we should imagine, and the careful crafting makes it likely that we will imagine them. Similarly careful crafting makes it likely that we will respond emotionally as we are intended to; the presumption that the intended response is the appropriate one is especially strong in cases where the maker has a reputation for producing work of quality and effectiveness—we can be more than usually confident in such cases that the responses we find ourselves having are the appropriate ones, the ones that will enable us to get the most we can from the works. If not, we are likely to place ourselves at odds with the tone and purposes of the work, to drift away from its themes and to miss the cadences of its storyline.

Paisley Livingston and Al Mele once objected to a proposal of this sort. They cite Baudelaire's poem 'À celle qui est trop gaie' which is expressive, they say, of the '"gruesome hopelessness" of a frustrated misogynist'.[13] Are we, they ask, enjoined to respond to this poem with the ugly feelings it expresses? Such complicity, they

---

[13] Livingston and Mele (1997), see especially p. 164; 'gruesome hopelessness' is taken from an essay by Eric Auerbach.

say, would be 'revolting'.[14] Does my proposal have the consequence that the reader should mirror the narrator's ugly emotions and, if it does, is this a problem for the proposal?

We should agree, first of all, that there is room for an appropriate response which does mirror the misogynist's gruesome hopelessness. There can be layers of emotional responses; one responds in a certain way, and has a judgemental response to that way of responding, thinking 'that [referring ostensively to one's own state] is deplorable'.[15] One may have, and be intended to have, a layered response to Baudelaire's poem which involves, at the first stage, an emotion which is congruent with the troubling response of which the poem is itself expressive. That first response will have the merit of helping us to understand, from the inside, an emotion we find both alien and immoral, without threatening our own moral integrity. Sharing an ugly emotion with another agent is not always a case of endorsing the agent's perspective, and won't be if one fails to identify with that emotion in the way that agent does.[16]

But this appeal to a layered response gets me out of trouble only if the layered response is the intended one. Livingston and Mele say there is no reason to suppose, in the case of this poem, that the intended response involves any such higher-order negative response to the troubling first-order emotion. 'One looks', they say, 'in vain in this poem for evidence of any authorial attitudes of distance or disapproval' (164). Let's assume that is true. The question is whether we always need to locate evidence before assuming that there is such an attitude. I say the answer is no. In some cases we may legitimately take a certain response to be authorially endorsed as long as the author does nothing that we can detect to block that response. In such cases we will 'look in vain' for indications of disapproval, but that is because the author does not need to give any such indications and can count instead on our doing the disapproving without any encouragement. Ring Lardner's story *Haircut* involves a highly unreliable narrator who, we eventually realize, has got the sequence of events badly wrong. That the narrator is unreliable is signalled early by the fact that he makes a series of judgements about someone, Jim, being 'a good fellow' when, from the narrator's own description, Jim is obviously deplorable. One could say about this story that one 'looks in vain' for any indication that the author is urging an attitude of distance from the narrator's

---

[14] Livingston and Mele 1997: 164. Livingston and Mele offered this example as evidence against an earlier proposal of my own concerning appropriate emotions in fiction. I emphasize that I am not seeking to defend here the view I earlier expressed, and I am grateful to Livingston and Mele for their treatment of that earlier and certainly defective account.

[15] This is close to a suggestion of Jerry Levinson, described in Livingston and Mele's paper (n19), though Levinson, as understood by Livingston and Mele, says that this should be a process in which one first has the unpleasant feelings and then, through moral reflection, moves on to an attitude of disgust. In my view it can be possible and instructive to take on some simulacrum of the unpleasant feeling while being *at the same time* fully aware of its deplorable nature.

[16] See Frankfurt (1988), especially Chapter 12.

perspective. But no urgings are needed; the author knows that the audience will be repelled by Jim's behaviour without them. Since he does nothing to avoid or suppress this repulsion we may conclude that it is exactly the response intended. Baudelaire's poem is, I am sure, a more sophisticated and elusive work than *Haircut*. But here to, it may be that the obvious 'gruesome hopelessness' of the voice itself indicates an authorial opposition to the narrator's voice.

Still, not every case will work out that way. There are stories intended to produce emotional effects which we feel uncomfortable with, unredeemed by the thought that the uncomfortable response is one we are intended to be critical of. Livingston and Mele cite 'The Jew among Thorns' from the Brothers Grimm, a story clearly intended to provoke an unpleasant and thoroughly endorsed delight in the fate of the Jew. Cases like this underline an earlier point: there are different ways an emotion can be appropriate. There is a sense in which properly engaging with the Grimm story requires us to respond to the fate of the Jew in the intended way; only by having that response can we fully appreciate how the story works in its own terms, and that is important for understanding a narrative, or any other artefact for that matter. But there are times when the effort of achieving that understanding is not worth the discomfort it creates or the damage it may cause; we may simply find ourselves unable to respond in the way intended. We do often resist going along with fictional scenarios that seem to arise from morally troubling views about the real world, fearing perhaps that going along with them will infect our view of the real world, or simply not wanting to travel in bad company. The debate over 'imaginative resistance' taught us that engagement with a story sometimes requires us to imagine things we don't want to imagine and might think it wrong to imagine; that's no objection to the idea that engaging properly with the story requires us to imagine what we are intended to imagine.[17] It shows merely that engaging with a story is not always the right thing to do. It's the same with emotion: being amused by 'The Jew among Thorns' is best avoided despite its being, in one sense, the appropriate emotion to have.

4.5 Conclusions

There are many ways to be wrong, in one's emotions as in other things. One way for an emotion to be wrong is for it to misrepresent. But misrepresenting takes different forms depending on whether we are talking about an emotional response to a real event or a response to an event represented as occurring by some fiction. Getting things wrong (or right) means one thing for an emotional response to real things and another thing when the state in question is a response to something in

---

[17] The debate goes back to Hume; recent discussion owes much to Walton (1994), and to Moran (1994).

a fiction. For emotions of the first kind it matters what is true; for those of the second it matters what is represented as true. Does truth matter at all for the rightness of an emotion generated by engagement with a fiction? It can matter, in a different way. It matters when we have reason to think that a representation is confusing us about what is true, and getting an emotional free-or-cheap-ride in consequence. And there is yet another sense of rightness/wrongness when it comes to emotions: The Jew in the Brothers Grimm story is represented as deserving of the suffering that befalls him, but an emotional response commensurate with that representation would be, all things considered, the wrong emotion to have.

How should we mark the distinction between emotions directed at the real and emotions directed at the fictional? I addressed the analogue of this question for desire at the end of Chapter 3. The analogous question concerning what I have called belief-like imaginings—imagining that Holmes is a detective—gets a ready answer from most people: these imaginings may be belief-like but they are not beliefs. It may be that recent work on the nature of belief has given grounds for a rethink of that dogma. For example, there is a proposal now to distinguish factual belief from the 'credence' we give to religious ideas, which surely count as beliefs in the ordinary sense; it is suggested that there is an 'in-between' state of belief, where a person is 'not quite accurately describable as believing that P, nor quite accurately describable as failing to believe that P'.[18] Such ideas suggest that belief is a baggy concept with unclear boundaries, though bagginess and unclarity don't immediately win the day for the view that imagining is a form of belief. My preference is to retain an imagining/believing distinction of some rigidity though I have agreed that there may be states with characteristics that put them somewhere between the two.

What, then of the emotion-like imaginings of this chapter—states which have the leading characteristics of paradigmatic emotions except that they represent correctly when they represent, not as things are, but as things are represented as being in a fiction? If we follow Walton and call emotions directed at fictional events and people 'quasi-emotions', should that be taken as implying that these are not really emotions? I don't have enough confidence in any general theory of the emotions to say whether quasi-emotions are 'really' emotions.[19] And for my purposes it does not matter. We can say that they are not emotions but instead 'imaginative counterparts' to the emotions, as imaginings in the familiar sense are counterparts to beliefs. Or we can say that the category of the emotions is a broad

---

[18] Schwitzgebel (2001: 76). We have looked at some other expansions of the conceptual territory: Gendler (2010) Chapters 13 and 14; Schellenberg (2013). See also Neil van Leeuwen (2014); Currie and Jureidini (2004). See also Noggle (2016) for the idea of quasi-belief.

[19] 'It is unlikely that all the psychological states and processes that fall under the vernacular category of emotion are sufficiently similar to one another to allow a unified scientific psychology of the emotions...emotions are not a natural kind' (Griffiths 2004: 233).

one: broad enough to cover both our responses to the world and to the contents of fictions. What matters is that quasi-emotions are very different things from the emotions we encounter when one person loves, fears, despises or admires another; the former belong in the realm of the imagination. It does not matter to me whether things in the realm of the imagination are 'really' emotions. There may even be no answer to the question whether they are or not.

*

The next three chapters, Chapters 5, 6, and 7, make up Part II. They say little about the imagination, focusing instead on belief, learning, knowledge, and on how we ought to approach the question of what we learn from fiction. They are meant as a foundation for the four chapters in Part III that connect imagination and knowledge, starting with the use of imagination to generate conditional beliefs, and the idea that fictions are imaginative thought experiments.

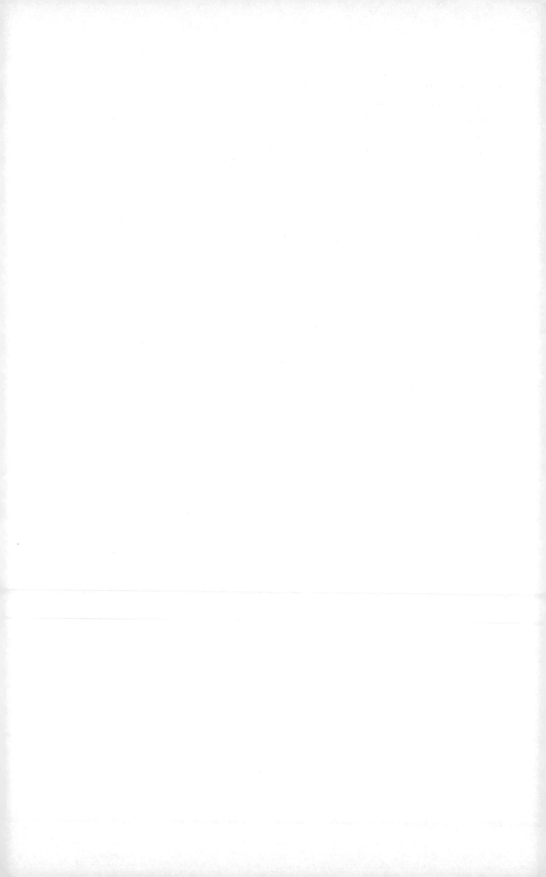

PART II

STARTING TO THINK ABOUT FICTION AND KNOWLEDGE

It's now time to begin an inquiry into the relation between fiction and knowledge. Part II lays some groundwork for the discussion: its first chapter (Chapter 5) reviews some of the radically different kinds of things that fall under the heading 'knowing'; it offers an introduction to aspects of epistemology useful for the rest of this book for anyone who might need it. Chapter 6 asks why we should approach the question of learning from fiction from an empirical standpoint when there seems to be a distinctly philosophical way to answer the question. Chapter 7 introduces one of the great themes we find in fictions of all kinds and one especially celebrated for its treatment in literary fiction; the ways that the beliefs, desires, intentions, and emotions of one agent interact with those of others, especially where conflict and deception are in play. This, surely, is something we learn a great deal about from judiciously selected fictions. I make what I think are some helpful distinctions for thinking about the mind in fiction, and discuss a couple of cases of what we might call the 'foundational literature' of minds in conflict. I conclude the chapter with a warm-up for Part III: offering some reasons to be sceptical about the claim that fiction has emerged and endured because of the selective benefits its focus on mind has produced.

Imagining and Knowing: The Shape of Fiction. Gregory Currie, Oxford University Press (2020). © Gregory Currie.
DOI: 10.1093/oso/9780199656615.001.0001

5

The varieties of knowing

The purpose of this chapter is to give readers who want them some tools for thinking about the cognitive aspects of fiction. I have in mind people—experts, some of them, in their own fields—interested in our topic but not familiar with current problems and theories in epistemology. I will stay as neutral as possible on a range of important issues in epistemology; I don't want to lose much of the audience at this early stage by signing up to some controversial doctrine. And I will draw the net as wide as possible—aiming to capture all the things that might count as learning from fiction. Toward the end of the chapter I'll be more opinionated.

Is knowledge too narrow a notion for our purposes? I'll consider some reasons to reject that worry; later on we will find a reason to think the narrowness objection is right after all. But we should acknowledge right away that knowledge comes in various kinds and does not consist only of beliefs meeting special conditions that philosophers can't at the moment agree on. Knowledge which is a species of belief is propositional knowledge or knowledge-that; there is also knowing-how, and knowing what some experience is like. I will say more about these kinds of knowing later.

5.1 Knowing-that

Asked what we know, we naturally recite facts, or what we take to be facts, thereby calling on a kind of knowledge packaged in the philosophical literature as propositional knowledge, a naming practice I have followed already. Facts correspond to true propositions, and the only propositions you can know are the true ones. Facts and propositions are sometimes objected to on metaphysical grounds, with propositions being particularly hard to fit into a naturalistic picture of the world. That's one of the debates we don't need to enter into. I am content to say that there is a kind of knowledge we express by saying we know *that* such and such; what the metaphysically correct account of that sort of knowledge is we don't need to settle here. If from time to time I call it propositional knowledge or knowledge of facts, please take that as simply falling in with the terminology philosophers find familiar; it is not metaphysically committed.[1]

---

[1] Jeff King's (2014) is a nice introduction to the variety of uses that propositions can be put to if we accept them.

Imagining and Knowing: The Shape of Fiction. Gregory Currie, Oxford University Press (2020). © Gregory Currie.
DOI: 10.1093/oso/9780199656615.001.0001

Discussions of learning from fiction, or from the arts generally, often represent factual or propositional learning as a particularly implausible candidate for what that learning might be.[2] I will not be arguing that this is the only kind of learning we might get from fiction, or that other forms of learning are much less significant. But it is important to avoid a too-narrow construal of what counts as propositional learning. One thing I will not assume is that propositional knowledge is restricted to that which is fully expressible in language, an idea that has allowed critics of learning from fiction to argue that we never actually find interesting knowledge there.[3] It is rare for us to be entirely explicit when we express ourselves in language yet we generally manage to communicate what we wish to communicate. As Robyn Carston (2002a: 830) notes, all of the following, after reference is fixed, are perfectly understandable and (in the right circumstances) appropriate things to say, requiring no elaboration:

a. It'll take time for your knee to heal.
b. Ralph drinks.
c. Emily has a temperature.
d. He's a person with a brain.
e. Something has happened.

But without assumptions about what is meant over and above the literal meanings of the words they contain and which are easily supplied by the hearer, they would be in almost all contexts completely uninteresting. Being more explicit in any of these cases ('I mean a temperature above average for a human being') would be tedious and distracting. Indeed, on one view human language simply *cannot* fully express our thoughts: 'the language system does not have the resources to encode propositions speakers succeed in expressing.'[4] And why should it have them? Given that context does such a good job of disambiguation, why would thrifty nature struggle to provide us with a super-powered linguistic system that does something we don't need?

We can take this line of thought a bit further. The use of demonstratives brings all sorts of stuff into the domain of propositional content that has no plausible

---

[2] 'The view that the business of art is to convey propositional knowledge was always an implausible form of cognitivism'; Morris (2012: 560).

[3] David Novitz said that knowledge of what some experience is like is 'irreducibly nonpropositional, in the sense that it cannot be captured or adequately conveyed in linguistic descriptions' (1987: 120). This kind of knowledge may be nonpropositional, but not because it cannot be linguistically expressed. Stolnitz (1992: 193) gave it as an example of the banalities the learning-from-fiction camp come up with when pressed that 'Stubborn pride and ignorant prejudice keep attractive people apart'. Thomas Rymer suggested that *Othello* teaches wives to 'look well to their linen' (1693: 89). As Kathleen Stock notes, we should not fall into the 'prejudice that the proper objects of propositional knowledge are confined to only those propositions which can be easily or briefly conveyed or assimilated' (2006: 66).

[4] Carston (2002b: 46). Carston lists Austin, Recanti, Searle, Travis, and others as fellow advocates of this sort of radical underdetermination.

linguistic correlate. You want to know what Astaire's dancing was like; I say 'Astaire dances like this', and do some Astaire-like dancing myself. If my dancing is genuinely Astaire-like, and if you have reason to trust my ability to imitate his dancing, perhaps you can come to know what Astaire's dancing is like; it's like *this*.[5] You learned what you wanted to learn only because you had a perceptual experience of what 'this' refers to; no descriptive substitute for 'this' is going to do as well. As a result you come to believe, of a certain way of dancing, that it was the way Astaire danced; if all goes well in this encounter you come to know that. Neither of us could informatively express that knowledge in words. But what we know is propositional and indeed factual. It just is a fact that Astaire dances like this.

So, propositional knowledge makes for a larger class of things than we might suppose if we thought its instances were tied essentially to linguistic expression.[6] But recall that our topic is learning. I'll soon come to the thought that learning is not always a matter of *propositional* knowledge; learning to ride a bike (many of us think) is not a matter of gaining propositional knowledge. But stay for the moment within the bounds of the propositional and ask whether learning is always a matter of gaining propositional *knowledge*. People interested in learning can't afford to ignore everything in belief that falls below the minimum standard for knowledge. Indeed, we have to go wider than belief, for there are many things I don't believe but which I think of as live possibilities. We need to consider *credences*, or rough and ready assignments of probability to propositions. I take my umbrella not because I know or even believe it will rain but because I think the probability of rain is non-negligible. A person's *credence state* is their (idealized) function from propositions to probabilities; the function is defined for every proposition you have an opinion about and specifies your degree of confidence in its truth, which might be zero or one or (more likely) somewhere between the two. One way for thinking to be worthwhile is this: at the end of the thinking your credence state is epistemically better, however that is to be measured, than it was before. Your new probabilities might better reflect the state of the evidence than they did before; alternatively—and this looks ahead to the doctrine of reliabilism which I will discuss later—the thinking was, as compared with what went before it, a more reliable process for generating credences.[7] Thinking that leads to a better credence state in either or both senses would be worthwhile, even if it led to no new knowledge.[8] While I think it is ultimately credence states that matter for learning, I'll continue to talk in more familiar terms of belief and knowledge where doing so won't cause confusion or compromise the argument. The point to

---

[5] For a general account of 'indexical predicates' see Heal (2003) Chapter 9. On the pervasive use of what he calls 'depictions' in verbal communication see Clark (2016).

[6] Here I agree with Gaskin (2013: 119–20).

[7] Some writers on credence combine evidential and reliabilist notions, e.g. Tang (2016).

[8] See also below, Section 9.2.

remember is that our topic is learning and that can be propositional without falling within the domain of knowing-that; learning can take place in the transition from one false belief to another. Learning outruns that which is propositional, and that which is knowledge.[9]

Some will insist that learning is factive: you can't learn something unless it is true, and 'Today we learned that the planets move in ellipses' is false, though it may be acceptable in many contexts, just as 'the planets move in ellipses' certainly is. If our ordinary concept of learning requires that what is learned must be known, then I suggest some conceptual engineering, a project dedicated to finding concepts better suited to our purposes than the one's we have.[10] It is not helpful to think of learning exclusively as the accumulation of knowledge. Think of it instead as the accumulation of better belief, something that comes in degrees.[11] A question that interests us here is whether the imagination, apparently so profligate and irresponsible, is ever capable of improving our epistemic position, and improvements in that position ought to include anything that moves us from a worse false belief to a better one. Not all ways for beliefs to improve are epistemic ways; some beliefs simply make us happier than others do, and that is one kind of improvement. But changes which give us empirically more accurate beliefs, or beliefs that are closer to the truth, are epistemically improving changes, and the transition from the belief in circular orbits to the belief in elliptical ones satisfies at least the first of these conditions. I am using 'learning' here to mean epistemic improvement in belief. The worst you can say about this is that I ought to find another term. I'm sure that could be done.

I just now noted two ways to make epistemic progress; being better evidenced and being closer to the truth. The first way is relatively straightforward: you improve epistemically when you move from a less well-evidenced belief to a better-evidenced one (it might be the same belief). We will note a complication in a moment. The second turns out to be deeply problematic. The idea is that you improve epistemically when you move to a belief closer to the truth. The limit case is straightforward: moving from a false belief to a true one. But the proposal is that, of two *false* beliefs, one may be closer to the truth. It seems that way with the transition from 'the planetary orbits are circles' to 'the planetary orbits are ellipses'; both are false but the second is the closer to the truth. Unfortunately, after heroic effort, no one has come up with a satisfactory way to explain what closeness to truth is.[12] Despite the failures of analysis it is hard not to believe that

---

[9] For general arguments for not give special attention to knowledge when assessing a creature's cognitive competence see Godfrey-Smith (1991).

[10] See e.g. Cappelen (2018).

[11] I'm ignoring here learning which is not belief-related, as some skills-learning may be. We will come to that later in this chapter.

[12] I made this point earlier; see Chapter 1, note 2. The idea of verisimilitude is due to Popper; see especially his (1976).

elliptical orbits represent progress towards the truth over circular ones. Being anxious not to close down areas of interesting dispute, I won't let the history of failed analyses stand in the way of anyone who wants to claim that a certain novel gave them a truer picture of human nature than the picture they had before, though its picture very likely fell short of truth in every respect. We will see reasons to be sceptical of such claims, but the reasons I shall focus on are epistemic, not metaphysical; they are to do with the difficulty of finding evidence for such claims.

For now, let's simplify things and talk about progress towards truth only in terms of the transition from falsehood to truth. How does that kind of improvement relate to evidential improvement? Strictly, they are independent: you can improve on either measure while doing worse on the other. It is possible to go from a poorly evidenced belief in something true to a well-evidenced belief in something false, and from a well-evidenced belief in something false to a poorly evidenced belief in something true. If we combine the two in the right way, coming up with better evidence for a truer belief, do we have the best kind of epistemic improvement? One worry is that this is too local an approach; with certain beliefs already in place, acquiring a new true belief can lead you badly astray. I come to believe that Trump won the election but unfortunately already believe that if that happened it would be because the election was rigged. My new knowledge causes me to believe, falsely, that the election was rigged.[13] We do best, when thinking about epistemic improvement, to take stock of an agent's whole system of beliefs. Here again there are different ways to characterize improvement. We might hope for a measure of overall increase in truth/evidential support for the belief system as a whole. But remember, we have no measure of truth-likeness, and even if we did there is no obvious way to trade off variations in truth-content against variations in evidential support. We can point to some self-evident cases of overall epistemic improvement: I replace a false belief with a true one no less well evidenced than the one I gave up, and no change elsewhere in the system constituted a reduction in either truth or evidential support—a sort of Pareto-optimality condition. But that leaves most real-life cases beyond the reach of anything but the thought 'that seems, intuitively, like a better/worse state to be in'. Clearly, we are a long way from a general theory of epistemic improvement (aka learning). Once again, in the interest of keeping the debate as wide open as possible I won't accuse someone of incoherence if they claim that reading this or that fiction moved them to an overall better epistemic state than the one they previously inhabited. I'll allow that such claims make perfect sense and are even sometimes true. My worries will be connected with the extent to which fictions are ever *reliable* sources of such shifts.

---

[13] I wrote this before evidence of the extent of interference in the election became clear. There may have been a conspiracy but it did not result in a rigged election.

There is one more point to be made about learning. You can learn stuff about the world—that planets move roughly in ellipses or that people are subject to the fundamental attribution error, as psychologists call the tendency to see the faults of others as due to character defects and our own failings as produced by circumstance. You can also learn about representations of the world—what a theory says, how to use the experimental and calculational techniques associated with it, what its relations to other theories in the area are. And we can move up the representational ladder, learning about the historian of science's take on the emergence of Newton's theory, or the historiographer's analysis of Macaulay's presuppositions about the history of England. None of this upward movement takes us, strictly speaking, outside of the domain of 'thinking about the world' since theories, narratives, and philosophies are all things in the world. But in asking questions about learning from fiction, I am focused on learning about thought, action, and human conduct rather than about representations of those things. There is, however, a complication: representations arise from the activity of minds and so may tell us things about the mind if we look at them carefully. The fact that human's produce fictional representations is one of the surprising and puzzling things about the mind and seems to be universal across cultures; the best theory of the mind we could have must explain that. And looking closely at particular fictions can tell us something: exposure to Dickens' novels can teach us things about the mind of Dickens and perhaps about the minds of his readers and other contemporaries; perhaps about minds in general.

I am not going to have much to say about this way of learning from fiction: learning by treating fictions as *symptoms* of mind and of the relations that minds stand in to one another. This is a perfectly good and perfectly conventional way of learning; we learn this way about our human ancestors from their fossil remains and about planets in other systems from the gravitational pull they exert on their stars. I will be more concerned with fictions as the *expression* of mind: devices that, through the reading or viewing process, convey to an audience a picture of human lives and their significance that is partly a matter of stated or implied or in other some way expressed thoughts and attitudes, partly a sense of what certain experiences are like, partly a heightened or refined sensitivity to the value of those experiences. That is enough to be going along with. I think that is what people who have urged the epistemic benefits of fiction have mostly had in mind.

5.2 Knowing-how

We have expanded our discussion from knowing-that to mere change of belief which, I argued, can sometimes count as learning. It's time to move beyond that kind of learning altogether. The natural next stop is knowing-how which, after

Ryle, we so often contrast with knowing-that.[14] Ryle chose to identify knowing-how with the possession of skills or abilities, things highly relevant for our inquiry; someone who thinks that fiction makes us more empathic or more morally sensitive in other ways need not think that this is a matter of our learning moral truths, even ones which lack verbal expressibility.[15] Improvements in moral sensitivity—a kind of learning, surely—seem to many people to be more like improvements in visual acuity.[16] Josh Landy identifies a class of 'formative fictions': 'what they equip us with are *skills*; rather than teaching, what they do is *train*'.[17] Martha Nussbaum urges us, as readers of Henry James, to learn to be people on whose moral consciousness 'nothing is lost'; to be attuned to the exquisite particularity of events and processes in moral life.[18] Coming from a different and more empirically focused perspective, psychologist Keith Oatley and his colleagues at the University of Toronto have argued that fictions educate, not by standing in for lectures, but by providing simulations of social interactions from which we can learn in something like the way that trainee pilots learn from flight simulators.[19]

Before we investigate the connection between knowing-that and abilities let's note that some, called *intellectualists*, hold to the view that knowing-how *is* a species of knowing-that.[20] The proposal is motivated by appeal to a widely accepted view of the semantics of questions due to Karttunen (1977). It says that an embedded question ('where to get a newspaper' in 'John knows where to get a newspaper') denotes the set of true propositions of the form 'Newspapers are at place P'. John knows where to get a newspaper when he knows at least one member of that set of true propositions. So it is natural, say Stanley and Williamson (2001), to think that John knows how to ride a bike (in the sense of 'how he could ride a bike') when he knows at least one member of the set of true propositions denoted by 'how to ride a bike', i.e. the set of true propositions of the form 'w is a way to ride a bike'. So knowing how is knowing that after all.

[14] Ryle (1949), especially 40–7.
[15] The exact nature of Ryle's view of the relation between knowledge and ability is perhaps more complex and difficult to determine than the text here indicates (see Hornsby 2011). Settling this issue will not be crucial to our concerns.
[16] See e.g. McDowell (1979), though he denies that we literally see moral facts. For a full-blooded defence of the idea of moral perception see Wright (2007). See also Döring (2007).
[17] Landy (2012: 10), emphasis in the original.
[18] Nussbaum (1990: 148), quoting from James' preface to *The Princess Casamassima*. See especially Nussbaum's discussion of the scene in *The Golden Bowl* between Adam and Maggie Verver where Adam's formation of an image of her as a 'sea creature' helps him endorse, and not merely permit, her womanly independence (1990: Chapter 5). But see also her endnote to 'Literature and the Moral Imagination' (Chapter 5 again) where she grants that the moral lesson of a literary work may have a propositional expression (though it would be 'very long and probably open-ended'). Landy offers a number of criticisms of Nussbaum; see e.g. his 2012: 30ff.
[19] See, e.g. Oatley (1999), Mar et al. (2006), Mar and Oatley (2008). Some of this material is reviewed further; see Section 11.5.
[20] See Stanley and Williamson (2001). See also Snowdon (2003).

That's not the end of the story. I may know that *this* (pointing at Alice's excellent performance of bike riding) is a way to ride a bike without that justifying my claim to know how to ride a bike. So the intellectualists add that one may know something in different ways. The case of demonstratives is a useful parallel here. John Perry's shopper who sees himself in a mirror knows that *that man* is spilling sugar; he does not know that he (the shopper) is spilling sugar. The case exemplifies two ways to know a single proposition; the shopper knows it in a demonstrative way, and not in a first-person way.[21] These different ways may deliver differences in behaviour: I may know that the meeting starts at 9 am and do nothing; I run out of my office and down the corridor when I realize that the meeting starts now (it being 9 am). To count as one who knows how to ride a bike I need to know, of some way, that it is a way of riding a bike, and to know it in what intellectualists call a *practical* way. Knowing something in a practical way instead of in a demonstrative way ('That's a way to ride a bike') is what picks out the person who really does know how to ride.

Insisting that the relevant kind of knowing is knowing in a practical way is the intellectualist's way of connecting knowing how to do something with actually doing it. Objections to intellectualism range from doubts about the ability of 'knowing in a practical way' to make that connection (it seems to depend on a prior notion of ability) to the accusation that the proposal is out of step with the empirical sciences of human and animal cognition.[22] While this debate has dominated thinking about knowing-how for the last fifteen years I want, having noted it, to simply move on. Let's agree among ourselves that there is such a thing as knowing-how without trying to settle exactly what it is. But a question remains for us: How is know-how related to the idea of having a skill or ability? The question is important, especially for anyone who thinks that the real epistemic value of fiction lies in its power to enable rather than to inform.

A simple answer to the question is: knowing how to do something is a matter of having certain dispositions or abilities: those that enable us to do the thing in question. The simple answer faces difficulties. Someone who can teach me how to win at tennis knows how to win, but they might lack the ability to play at a winning level. And the person who, through injury, loses the ability to play tennis may yet know how to play. Conversely, there are things we have the ability to do—like breathing—which in a very real sense we may not know how to do.

Perhaps the coach does not know how to win, though he knows something: how to get me to win. That's something he is able to do, despite not being able to win himself. So far as that example is concerned, we can hold on to the view that

---

[21] See Perry 1979.
[22] For the first objection see Koethe (2002); for the second see Devitt (2011). For an attempt to explicate the idea of practical knowledge of a proposition see Pavese (2015).

knowing-how and ability go together. What about the person who once could play tennis but, because of injury, can't any longer? No one can play tennis in all conditions—in a gravity free environment, under water, while tightly bound in chains. Being able to play tennis as normally understood means being able to play in a range of conditions considered normal; someone who, additionally, can play under water needs their ability distinguished from the ordinary one. If we relativize abilities to circumstances we can distinguish cases, and also make sense of the idea that the injured player retains both the know-how and the ability. They know how to play in circumstances where they are not injured, and have the ability to play in those circumstances; they never were able to play while injured.[23]

What about the person who has an ability to F they know nothing of? Does she know how to F? Opinions may differ here: perhaps knowing how to F requires, at least, that you know you could F (in the right circumstances). Perhaps you know how to F without knowing you know it. I don't think we need decide this question, but it points us in the direction of an important issue: the existence of learning-from-fiction cases which involve the retuning of sensibilities of which we may be both unaware and over which we may be unable to exercise any direct control. Suppose I am hopelessly unempathic; I then start reading novels, a good many of which happen to be empathy-educating. As a result I become, unknowingly, apt to empathize with people in those situations. I have no idea that this is happening and indeed may never come to realize that this change has taken place (it happens slowly), though it makes a difference to my behaviour over the long run. I have become able to empathize, but I lack the concept of empathy, I am unable to respond intelligently when asked whether I can empathize, and I am unable to exercise conscious control over or to assess the effectiveness of my empathic responses. Have I come to know how to empathize? We need some way, at least, to distinguish importantly different cases. Here are two:

> Francesca reads the great novels of the last two centuries and as a result becomes a bit more empathic without, however, gaining any reflective understanding of this capacity or indeed being aware of it at all; she never seeks to channel her empathy in one direction rather than another, but is simply visited by episodes of empathic emotion.

> Dorit does the same reading which has a similar effect on her. Additionally, she has a lively interest in the extent to which she is empathic, how she can become more empathic and how she can put her empathic feelings to the morally best use. She constantly reflects on her own empathic responses, and tries to direct those responses in ways she considers helpful for moral engagement.

---

[23]   Hawley (2003).

It seems reasonable to say that Dorit knows how to empathize while Francesca merely has some empathic dispositions (not that that is entirely insignificant). What is left when we subtract the first from the second? Dorit has beliefs and desires about empathy that Francesca does not have, but she also has (or is seeking to get) additional abilities: abilities to reflect on and direct her empathic responses. This will be important in Chapter 11.

5.3 Acquaintance

When Robert Pippin speaks of '[Henry] James' brilliant treatment [in *The Wings of the Dove*] of what such an experience would mean for a man like [Merton Densher], and why, under what psychological conditions, it would take place' (Pippin 2001: 3), he suggests a carryover from the literary to the real world, a carryover from what James tells us about the fictional character to what we can learn about the psychologies of people like him. In the person of Densher, James, it is said, provides us with a substitute for a certain kind of experience, a substitute that acquaints us with the experience or some features of it.[24] Empathizing with others may be an ability, but it is said to lead to a kind of knowledge which is not, or may not be, explicable in terms of abilities. Empathizing with you, on one understanding of that notion, I come to feel as you do, and so I come to know how you feel. We might say that I become acquainted with your feelings.

We are often said to empathize with Anna Karenina and other creatures of fiction. What might that teach us? Not, certainly, about how Anna Karenina feels, since there is no such person and so no way she feels. One thing it might teach us is how, *according to the fiction*, Anna feels. The story specifies many things about Anna, sometimes by explicitly stating them, but often merely by implication. Perhaps a way for fictions to indicate what is fictional about their characters is for them to encourage readers and viewers to have certain kinds of empathic experiences which make manifest to us what, according to the story, those feelings are, by recreating those feelings in us. What the fiction won't do is tell us how Anna feels, since she feels no way at all.

The fiction might also teach us something about the extra-fictional world: that this is how someone in that sort of a situation does or would or (modestly) might feel. Those who claim that fictions enlarge our horizons may have this sort of learning in

---

[24] 'To some degree' is the always reasonable qualification to such claims. For advocacy of the idea that fictions provide us with acquaintance see Palmer (1992). Palmer does not really argue for the thesis, but simply asserts that, for example, Alexander Pope 'brought [his audience] to experience [Lord Hervey's] nauseating qualities' without their having to confront them (193). That this is in fact the effect of reading Pope's work is far from obvious. Brian Boyd writes that fiction 'increases the range of our vicarious experience' (2009: 193); see the paragraph before the one I have just quoted from for a range of claims about fiction's capacity to educate; no evidence is offered for any of them.

mind; learning that *acquaints* us with experiences others have and which we might have had if we had not been spared combat, tyranny, or destructive passion.

What sort of knowing is acquaintance? Knowing-that, according to some. Frank Jackson (1982) has claimed that knowing what it is like to see the blue of the sky is knowing a fact or proposition, and that physicalism is therefore false; one can know all the physical facts about colour and still not know this fact. But our discussion of knowing-how at least suggests that not all knowing is knowing-that, and acquaintance may be an example of such knowing.[25] What other kind of knowing might it be? Some have argued that acquaintance is just one kind of abilities-based know-how; when I learn what it is like to see the blue of the sky I am able to do new things: to remember what seeing the sky is like, to imagine the colour of the sky, and more generally 'to predict one's behaviour by imaginative experiments'.[26] But we are not obliged to say that acquaintance is either propositional knowledge or know-how. We may hold instead that acquaintance is a third, distinct kind of knowing.

What kind? We may be convinced, or may suspect, that acquaintance is distinctive without yet knowing what is distinctive about it. But there are suggestions around. Earl Conee (1994) says that it is knowledge of properties. Mary, locked in her black and white room, lacks acquaintance with 'phenomenal blueness', and acquaintance with that property is, according to Conee, given by having an experience of that property. Might fiction give us experience of the relevant properties of some fact or situation, without actually giving us experience of the fact or situation? There are properties of situations such that the only way to experience those properties is to experience the situations: you can experience Napoleon-ness only by experiencing some Napoleon-involving situation. But take the frighteningness or amusingness of a situation: you might be able to experience that by imagining the situation rather than by experiencing it. As Conee says a 'quality can come to be known by being imagined rather than being perceived if the imagining produces an experience that actually has the quality' (1994: 145, note). We will ask (Section 6.2) whether cases of this kind can be assumed to occur as a result of our exposure to fiction and, if they can, whether we can reliably distinguish such cases from cases where the result is a misleading impression of what the experience is like.

5.4 Externalism

Imagine you are in in Fake Barn County, where there are very few barns but many barn-facades, put there as a scheme for rural enhancement; these facades are easily

---

[25] The first use of this idea in relation to literature is due, I believe, to Dorothy Walsh (1969: 96).
[26] Lewis (1983a: 131). The abilities account of Mary's knowledge was first proposed in Nemirow (1980). Jackson is a convert (2011).

mistaken for barns when viewed from the road. Looking at what is actually a barn I form the belief that this is a barn. In a more benign environment, where all barn-like structures are barns, I would, on exactly the same evidence, come to know that this is a barn (Goldman 1976). But in Fake Barn County this seems like a true belief that falls short of knowledge; with all those fake barns around my belief-forming process does not look very reliable. And the difference between these two situations might be one that makes no impact on my inner life; called to account for my claim to know that this is a barn, I would say and do the same in both situations. If these situations differ with respect to my knowledge they don't differ with respect to any grounds I could offer. Simplifying the debate somewhat, *Externalists* think that a knower need not be aware of, or even be able to be aware of, the grounds of their knowledge. *Internalists,* on the other hand, say that the knower must be aware of or in a position to be aware of those grounds.

It is consistent with externalism to think that, in many cases, someone's apparently having no access to the grounds of what they claim to know is evidence against their knowing it. We are naturally suspicious when someone claims to know that interest rates will go up but can give no grounds for their belief; in this and like cases we expect that someone would be able to summons those grounds if they really knew what they claim to. Access to grounds can in this way be evidentially related to knowledge without being constitutive of it. This means that if we ask which view conforms best to intuitive judgement—internalism or externalism—we need to be clear about the content of that judgement: we may hear that X cannot give any grounds for his belief that P, and feel a strong urge to conclude that X does not know P. But that judgement is neutral as between an evidential and a constitutive reading and so does not favour internalism. An intuition undermining to externalism would have to be one to the effect that X not having any grounds for P necessitates their not knowing P; as far as I am able to tell I do not have that intuition and I would be surprised if anyone were confident that they did, intuitions about what is necessarily true being subject to much dispute.

I introduced the idea of externalism through the example of a reliabilist approach to knowledge. But there are forms of knowing where the subject's grasp of reasons is crucial to whether they know or not. The sorts of cases I have in mind are ones where the process of knowledge acquisition essentially involves conscious reasoning. As Jennifer Nagel puts it, reliabilism says that 'knowledge requires thinking in a way that tends to yield true belief' and some kinds of thinking will tend to yield true beliefs only if they involve conscious assessment of the grounds (if any) that favour the proposition in question.[27] Thus a reliabilist, while being an externalist about many kinds of knowledge, could, on

---

[27] Nagel (2016). See also Sosa: 'the epistemic quality of one's belief rise[s] with justified awareness of the reliability of one's sources' (2009: 139 n2).

reliabilist grounds, favour internalism about knowledge acquired through reflective thinking. Relevant here is Ernest Sosa's (2009) distinction between 'animal'
and 'reflective' knowledge; the latter requires an understanding of ground and the
former does not. If that is right, we need not expect that the debate between
internalism and externalism will end with a total victory for one side; these
positions may rather pick out distinct kinds of knowledge.

Another point to note is that the whole set of issues raised by reliabilism and
externalism have no place in discussions of knowing-how. Of course, to know how
to do something one must be able, reliably, to do it. But I may have learned to
bike-ride very well by a very unreliable process: from someone who was wholly
incompetent as a teacher and from whom no one else learned anything about bike
riding. If at the end of the process I can somehow reliably get on the bike and ride
it, I know how to ride a bike. What about acquaintance? Suppose my sense that
I know what it is like to be in prison (despite never having been in one) derives
from my encounter with a prison-set novel or film, and it turns out that the
author(s) had also never been in prison and had never met anyone who had.
Would it follow that I did not know what it is like to be in prison (bearing in mind
that this is a question about something constitutive of acquaintance rather than
about evidence)? Suppose it turns out, just by accident, that the film or novel
got prison life as close to being right as a fictive representation reasonably could.
I am not confident that even in this case we could say that I learned what prison
life was like. But that would not be because the process was a 'lucky' one. To
see that, compare the accidental case just described with a case of a film or
novel produced by very careful investigations that involve the makers getting
themselves sentenced to prison for some time and then taking care to reproduce
the circumstances as closely as possible; nonetheless, this non-lucky film/novel is
scene-for-scene, sentence-for-sentence indiscernible from the lucky case. And
suppose you think, of exposure to the non-lucky case, that it is a case of coming
to know what prison life is like; then you should think the same of the lucky case. If
you agree with that (and so with me) you are not a reliabilist about acquaintance.

How does this debate affect our deliberations about fiction? It is sometimes said
by opponents of internalism that, taken seriously, it would drastically limit the
domain of knowledge; not only could young children and animals not be said to
know anything, but most ordinary people are not in a position to understand what
justifies their beliefs; perhaps none of us are, given the amount of outstanding
philosophical debate there is on this subject (BonJour 2002). Be that as it may, it
seems to me that, for at least some important cases of putative knowledge gained
from fiction, externalism does offer the more promising path for those who claim
that these really are cases of knowledge. A relatively simple case, to be discussed at
length in Chapter 9, concerns the acquisition of straightforwardly factual beliefs
on the basis of reading fiction, as with coming to believe, on reading *War and
Peace*, that Russian aristocrats in the nineteenth century spoke French a good deal

of the time. If this does not count as gaining knowledge from fiction it is hard to see what would. But what justification could most of us offer if pressed about how we came by this knowledge? It might, on the other hand, be possible to tell a story about how you got that belief that identifies a reliable process. When we come to this in Chapter 9 it will be the reliability of process that will occupy us most.[28]

5.5 Understanding

In deciding what we learn from fiction some will prefer to talk of understanding rather than of knowledge. It is not easy to say with any precision what this preference implies. In some cases it represents merely a taste for looser and perhaps more vague terminology; in others, an emphasis on the way that fiction provides a feeling of familiarity with the people and situations there represented. Neither of these motives should interest us; we are not retreating to vagueness, and feelings of familiarity often co-exist with high levels of misunderstanding. It's more promising to interpret understanding in terms of things we have already discussed. One possibility is that understanding is simply knowledge, and contrasts purporting to be between understanding and knowledge are in reality contrasts between adequate and inadequate knowledge. Knowing that Harold lost at the Battle of Hastings is not going to count as understanding the battle but adding a lot more knowledge of the battle's causes, course, and consequences ought to amount, in the end, to understanding it. Understanding is often closely connected with having an explanation: I understand your actions when I can explain them in terms of your beliefs and preferences, and I understand the seasons when I see that they are explained by the tilt of the earth. But then understanding is just propositional knowledge; knowledge of that which explains something, together with the knowledge that it explains. And since explanations can generally be filled out endlessly with further detail, we can see why understanding comes in degrees; some explanations are fuller and more informative than others.

Perhaps this is too swift. Alison Hills (2009) argues that there is such a thing as understanding why such-and-such, and this is not the same as knowing why. One may know why it is wrong to lie by knowing that lying is wrong, along with knowing certain propositions that entail that lying is wrong. But that, according to Hills, is not enough for understanding why lying is wrong. Understanding why P (where Q is why P) involves the possession of certain abilities: being able to do such things as explain why P 'in your own words', to conclude that P from the information that Q, and (perhaps most significantly) to draw an appropriately different conclusion, P*, from slightly different information Q* (2009: 102–3).

---

[28] Stacie Friend is perhaps the first person to seriously consider the relevance of externalist theories of knowledge to the debate about learning from fiction; see her (2014).

If Hills is right, her account introduces no new epistemic capacities into our discussion; understanding is simply a mix of knowledge-that and ability. Such mixtures do seem important and we might even put knowing-what-it-is-like into the mix. What counts as having a really paradigmatic understanding of social life? Perhaps it involves knowing lots of facts about social life, especially those that explain otherwise puzzling social phenomena, as well as being able to negotiate the social world fluently, and perhaps having a good sense (by whatever standards apply in this area) of what other people's experiences are like. It may be very difficult to say what combinations of the various kinds of knowledge constitute understanding (and constitute it to what degree), and the sorts of combinations that count as understanding in one domain may not count in another. But that will not prevent any given case of understanding (to a given degree) *being* a certain domain-relative combination of bits of all these kinds of knowledge. The point to remember is that, on this sort of account, appeals to understanding in the debate about learning from literature do not provide opportunities to bypass or treat as irrelevant questions about whether we get knowledge from literature; on the contrary, someone who thinks that fiction conveys understanding has to think that we get all sorts of knowledge from it. And since it is very hard to say what combinations of knowing count as understanding, introducing understanding into the picture makes the task of someone who wants to articulate a persuasive picture of learning from literature harder, not easier.

There is a broader sense of understanding than that of Hills, where knowledge really does fade into the background. You spend the day reading William James on the emotions; seeking a different perspective that evening, you dip into *The Golden Bowl* by brother Henry. In their different ways, these two works have helped you understand something about the mind—so you think. What do you have to show to support your claim? That you came to know something from both sources? In the serious, philosophical sense of 'know' I think the answer is 'no'. William, I suspect, would have denied *knowing* much about the mind, despite his insightful and diligent approach to it, and modern psychologists rarely claim that they have anything more than plausible working hypotheses with various degrees of empirical support; the current crisis of replication adds to the need for very modest claims in this area. For all that, modern psychology is no epistemic embarrassment; there may be too much emphasis on p-values—one diagnosis of the cause of the replication crisis—but the absence of much that we could confidently call knowledge should not make us think of the project as a failure.[29] Theories with some explanatory power and an ethos of criticism is all we can reasonably ask. When we focus on learning, criticism, and epistemic improvement,

---

[29] Suppose we are testing for the difference in effect between two drugs. The associated p-value is, roughly, the probability that we would get the observed result if there was in fact no difference in their effectiveness.

knowing has not got much to do with it. You can get lots of knowledge and be a very poor learner; and you can be a good learner who knows little or nothing in the relevant area. You might read that article about the fundamental attribution error and simply absorb the views expressed, treating it as the testimony of an expert who knows the facts of the matter; in favourable cases that may get you to the point where you know what the expert knows—testimony is, after all, a reliable source of knowledge.[30] But someone who simply believes everything in the psychology research paper on the basis of authorial testimony is not exemplifying good learning, however much they come to know thereby. Virtuous learning requires an active, critical, and imaginative engagement with the material. We expect (or hope) learners in the sciences will think up possible objections, variations in scenarios, candidates for missing premises in the arguments. None of this need amount to knowledge; rather it is a matter of questions, tentative ideas, constructed scenarios, inarticulate feelings of uncertainty that prevent one from settling on a position. Someone engaged in this way might count as understanding the relevant domain rather well while knowing very little.[31]

Recall Hills' suggestion that explanatory understanding involves not merely knowing that the effect P follows from the assumption of premises Q, but being able to draw an 'appropriately different conclusion', P*, from slightly different assumptions Q*. This condition exemplifies the gradedness of understanding we already noted. There is no particular number of such inferences one is required to make in order to understand; one has to be able to make some, and more will count (in complex ways no doubt) as better understanding.[32] In some domains those different conclusions would be available via a mathematical relation between the cause and the effect; having the formula to hand would be enough for me to generate a new predicted effect from an assumed different cause. But in a

---

[30] For more on testimony see Section 9.5. Of course testimony is not always reliable, but testimony on a topic from a favourably disposed expert on that topic is pretty reliable.

[31] As Berys Gaut says, 'successful teaching is often in part a matter of active stimulation to critical reflection, of getting someone to explore the answers to pertinently posed questions, thinking through issues in her own terms' (2007: 139).

[32] Is being able to make one of these inferences anything more than being able to get yourself to the point where you know *that* Q* explains P*? Presumably we can credit someone with propositional knowledge only if they have certain abilities; you have to have a functioning cognitive system and not merely a 'belief box' with the belief inscribed in it. You have to be able to do things with what you are supposed to believe: infer things from it, recognize its inconsistency with other things you believe. Knowing-that and abilities are getting rather entangled at this point. Also, what about implicit knowledge—stuff everyone agrees you know but have never thought about, such as that there are no purple gnomes in this room now? You have to be able to think about the question when asked, to understand it, to see that it is obviously true. That should not make implicit knowledge a species of know-how, unless all knowing-that is going to turn out to be know-how, as some do claim (see Hetherington (2008)) We need some way to segregate cases where the knowledge in question *is* knowledge-that, but where having it depends on abilities, and cases where the knowledge *is* knowledge-how or ability (for simplicity I am identifying the two). But for the moment I am simply going to fall in with Hills' way of speaking and say that understanding will involve both propositional knowing and the possession and exercise of abilities.

lot of psychological work, especially in social psychology, that is not possible. Consider an experiment conducted by Darley and Batson (1973). Seminarians at Princeton were asked to complete a questionnaire and then told they should go to another location and give a brief talk on the Good Samaritan parable. On the way there a stooge faked a collapse. Willingness to stop and help depended strongly on whether the subjects had been told that there was no hurry, a slight hurry, or a more urgent hurry. Very few in the high-hurry group stopped. Even low-hurriers stopped less often than no-hurriers.

One sensible reaction to the result would be to frame a series of questions about the set up and come to some initial hypotheses in response. Would it make a difference if the authority status of the experimentalist was varied? Suppose it was actually a senior male figure. What would have happened if it had been a less obviously senior female? What about varying ethnicity? Tone of voice? Would more people have ignored the collapsed person if they were not confined in a narrow alleyway with them but saw them from across the other side of a wide street? Asking such relevant questions in an organized way would count towards the claim that one understood the phenomenon in question; it would indicate that one was able to put the research in the context of a broader set of issues about how people are influenced. It would be excellent if those initial hypotheses were right and Hills' approach, with its emphasis on 'appropriately different conclusions', suggests that this is what we are aiming at. But their not being entirely right should not nullify the claim to understanding. And understanding in this sense would be a product of propositional knowledge—in this case knowledge of what the theory in question claims—together with abilities such as being able to spot missing premises or arguments, as well as such imaginative abilities as being able to think through variations in the experimental set up and to have some at least rough expectation about the difference in outcome. Such imaginative abilities are dis-cussed in more detail in Chapter 8.

If we can accommodate understanding within available epistemic categories the same may not be true of wisdom. We have expanded the domain of learning horizontally, starting with knowing-that, and adding knowing-how and knowing what it is like or acquaintance. We may also expand vertically, distinguishing orders of knowing and learning. I know that it is raining, and that I know that it is raining. I know how to ride a bike, and (perhaps) how to learn various skills; just possibly I also know what skills I am most apt to learn and which I will never grasp.[33] As well as, or instead of, getting answers to questions from fiction, we might get an improved capacity to ask questions—to ask the right kinds of questions, to frame them well. And without giving us answers to questions, fictions may help us answer them ourselves, improving our critical, argumentative, and

---

[33] A good deal of what has traditionally been thought of as wisdom is now studied under the heading of metacognition, a fast-growing enterprise started by Flavell (1979).

evidence-gathering capacities. Not all of these claims are equally plausible but they are probably part of what people have had in mind when they have said that we learn from fiction. They are aspects of what we call wisdom. Fiction might help us be wise in other ways. It might help us manage our ignorance: to realize its extent, to see how much there is around that we don't and perhaps can't know, to make fewer unguarded claims to know things or to have reasonable beliefs, to live contentedly and effectively with our ignorance and proneness to error.

How to characterize wisdom is, unsurprisingly, disputed but when it is said that wisdom arises from exposure to certain kinds of fiction the implication is that this is more than an epistemic achievement. We could try to accommodate everything required for wisdom under knowledge-how: the wise person knows how to live well, or at least to live as best they can, and to contribute to the flourishing of others. But in such cases the availability of the phrase 'knows how to' may hide big differences, with knowing how to ride a bike and knowing how to live in such divergent categories of achievement that little is explained by calling them both cases of knowing-how. And someone may know how best to live and not ever live that way, perhaps because they have no desire to do so. Wisdom is partly a matter of having the right desires.[34] Change of desire is sometimes consequent on change of belief—believing there is a beer in the fridge makes me want to open the fridge—so sometimes fictions can change desire just by changing belief. In such cases change of desire is explicable through whatever epistemic powers we end up thinking fiction has. But fictions may also have the power to change desire directly, or at least in ways not mediated by change in belief.[35] So learning from fiction, at least as far as wisdom is concerned, will need to be understood in ways that take us beyond the epistemic tools described in this chapter. But as we shall see, there are several interesting problems to deal with even if we confine ourselves to thinking about the putative epistemic effects of fiction; I postpone an in-depth inquiry into the wisdom that may or may not derive from fiction for some other occasion. However, wisdom will come up again, when we discuss the idea of wise authors, as we will in Chapters 9 and 10.

5.6 Conclusions

There are, we can see, many ways to understand the claim that we learn from fiction, and no particular reason to choose between them; they could all be ways fiction teaches. And many of these do not exemplify a didactic, lecture-like model

---

[34] See Zagzenbski (1996: 22–3).

[35] It would be hard to find a convincing case of a fiction that changed desire without changing any beliefs along the way; a fiction that makes you want to be a priest presumably changes your beliefs about priests, or gives you beliefs about priests you did not previously have. What may happen is that the change in desire is not wholly the product of the belief change.

of learning; few of them suggest that we learn systematic theories or bodies of knowledge which we would expect readers to be able to regurgitate in an exam, should we set them one. They do not even require that the learning be propositional, and if it is, it need not be learning which allows the learner to verbalize their knowledge. We do not expect bike riders to give us useful verbal accounts of their skills, combat veterans to explain to us what battle is like, or Astaire-imitators to describe in full detail his style of dancing (unless we count the imitative dancing as 'describing'). This does not mean that the objection to learning from fiction based on our inability to articulate what we learned is never worth hearing; *some* learning ought to be reflected in a capacity to verbalize what you know—mathematical knowledge is an obvious example. And showing that a piece of knowledge is not articulable is not a way of showing that requests for evidence that someone possesses that knowledge are misplaced; if I know how Astaire dances, I ought to be able to say of various examples of dancing whether and to what extent they are like Astaire's. For other, nonpropositional kinds of learning, there should be other tests. It is easy enough to decide whether someone can ride a bike—get them to ride one. We can't win the argument on behalf of knowledge from fiction by declaring it to be undetectable other than through the assurances of those who claim to have it. Given all this it will be no surprise that Chapter 6 will argue that, whatever learning fiction is said to lead to, we need evidence that that kind of learning takes place and that fiction is the cause of it.

6

An empirical question?

Someone may be worrying about the direction we are going in. Here's their complaint:

> You have prepared us to ask whether we learn from fiction. But that is the wrong question. The philosophically interesting question about fiction is not whether people do learn from it but 'What is there to be learned?' Answering this question requires analytical and interpretive effort, not the provision of evidence, either of an experimental kind or derived from common experience.[1]

This chapter is devoted to the task of undermining the objection. Before that I will develop it a bit. And before that, a couple of clarifications.

A friend of the objection need not oppose the search for evidence of the cognitive effectiveness of fiction; they may (and should) think that looking for evidence in this area is a legitimate and even required activity for someone interested in the sociology or the educational psychology of fiction. But that, they will say, is not relevant to the debate over traditional humanistic concerns with value in literature. These two projects—the humanistic and the empirical—seek to answer different questions, so any indifference of the philosophers to evidential issues is no sign of dereliction on their part. The humanistic project is a normative one, concerned with how the best narrative art might educate us, if we are well prepared by dint of knowledge, attention, and all other necessary things, to meet its challenge. The empirical project, as manifested in current psychological research, is concerned with the sorts of mass phenomena we measure in terms of means and standard deviations, concerning the reactions of the normal, uncommitted, and not especially well-prepared audiences that make up the majority of both consumers of fictional narratives and subjects in psychology experiments.

That does not mean that the philosopher's task can be conducted by pure reflection alone; a philosopher of narrative fiction in all its forms has to engage

---

[1] I don't know of an unambiguous statement of this view in the literature but John Gibson says 'The question is primarily textual: it concerns the nature of the literary, of what we find of worldly significance when we look *inside* a literary work. It is only about readers—about the ways in which their minds and morals can be improved through their encounters with literature—in a secondary, derivative sense' (2007: 24). This is not quite the claim I am considering. If Gibson were making exactly the same point he would have said, 'It is only about readers—about the ways in which their minds and morals *are* improved through their encounters with literature—in a secondary, derivative sense.'

Imagining and Knowing: The Shape of Fiction. Gregory Currie, Oxford University Press (2020). © Gregory Currie.
DOI: 10.1093/oso/9780199656615.001.0001

with a rich and diverse population of narrative fictions. That is a thoroughly empirical enterprise by means of which you acquaint yourself with the highly contingent history of a human activity; that we have the works of Shakespeare and George Eliot is an empirical fact. The task is to understand and interpret these works, in accordance with the best theories of interpretation we can find, and against the background of the best overarching theories of fiction, narrative, value, and whatever else may turn out to be relevant. What we don't need is data on how reading this or that bit of discourse affected the cognition of this or that group of subjects. Let's develop the idea.

6.1 Norms and dispositions

One way to develop the objection is to say that claims about the value of literature should be understood in the way we commonly understand claims about what is right or valid; the widespread occurrence of bad behaviour and of fallacious reasoning does not refute any moral principle or logical law; why should it be different when it comes to the value of literature? There are people who will argue the relevance of empirical inquiry for both the moral and logical case, but let's grant that logical laws are laws of valid inference and not laws of thought, and that at least some moral principles are requirements on the behaviour of any rational being, independent of how that rationality is embodied in a contingent psychology, community, or species. No comparable defence can be mounted concerning the a priori status of claims about the educative value of narrative art. These are essentially claims about the effects of literature on human beings in certain circumstances. They are claims that ascribe dispositional properties to objects of a certain kind—works of narrative art. The appropriate analogy here is not with the laws of logic but with the empirical claim (a rather doubtful one) that thinking logically makes you a more effective agent; the analogy is not with moral principles, but with the effect of belief in certain moral principles on character or personality or behaviour. Those are all empirical claims and their truth values are not obvious to casual observation, though we have often treated them as if they are.

It is true that questions like these, while being empirical, can only be answered against the background of a framework which is at least partly philosophical; we require, among other things, resolution to questions like 'what counts as learning in the relevant area?' Chapter 5 has, in a preliminary way, addressed some of these issues. I am responding here to someone who thinks that the questions philosophers ask about the epistemology of fiction can be answered without reference to the results of systematic empirical inquiry. That response stands.[2]

---

[2] I am grateful here to a reader for the press.

While insisting that the issue is an empirical one we should allow that the connection between evidence and the cognitive value of particular works is somewhat loose. The claim that a certain work has a certain positive cognitive value is consistent with the claim that no one's encounter with that work ever has realized or ever will realize that value.[3] It is no more controversial to assert that there are plenty of works with unrealized educative dispositions than it is to say that many samples of acid never dissolve anything. But why would anyone believe in the possession by certain narratives of wholly unrealized dispositions to educate or civilize? We believe in the disposition of acids to dissolve other substances because we have seen it happen many times. We might, in the case of acids, discover that they have hidden, so far unrealized dispositions. We would do that by examining their essences—their chemical/physical constitutions—and using our best theories of those essences to conclude that in possible but so far unrealized circumstances they would produce a certain effect. But narratives don't have hidden essences, at least not of the relevant kind. If they have educative effects it is not in virtue of the chemical constitution of the ink they are written in but in virtue of the stories they tell, and how they tell them. You can rationally believe that we learn from fictions only if you believe there is evidence that someone has learned from some fiction—though not necessarily the fiction you are currently interested in.[4]

It might be said that all this is irrelevant to the value of literary representations of moral thinking; the value they have is in their showing us how we *ought* to think, feel, and act, not how we often do these things when we are in the grip of debilitating forces. Henry James noted the objection that some of his characters seem too far above the level of real human moral sensibility for their activities to be of any help to the rest of us; he replied that they are 'in essence an observed reality' (1907–9), a view endorsed by Martha Nussbaum when she says that 'there is no better way to show one's commitment to the fine possibilities of the actual than...to create, in imagination, their actualization' (1990: 165). James and Nussbaum seem to be assuming that they have access to a reliable picture of what human beings are capable of, a picture which finds an optimal trade off between the danger of failing because the demands of moral thinking are too hard and the danger of complacency because the standard is set too low. But finding such a trade-off, if there is one, cannot be a matter for armchair speculation or even for the diligent personal observation of one or two writers. Any claim about what is ideal or merely valuable in thinking has to take into account the unobvious difficulties that face us in trying. The best advice about how to get to

---

[3] There may be a Moorean paradox in saying that work W has value V and no one (including the speaker) has experienced V. But Moorean utterances can express true propositions and it is truth rather than assertability that is in question here.

[4] One need not have the evidence oneself; believing, on the basis of testimony, that there is such evidence would usually be enough, in this case as in many others.

Tokyo from here is not to take the geodesic route that joins them, though that will always be the shortest path on the surface of Earth; we must take account of the fact that there is water to cross, restricted points of entry, a train service that runs only along certain pathways. That is why you would not rely on me or Henry James to plan your route. Suppose someone argued for the virtues of formal logic in education on the grounds that the laying out of sound inferences is the bedrock of human rationality. The evidence from psychology suggests that this is not so. The human mind is designed to operate frequently via shortcuts and rules of thumb, and reasoning works best when it is in the service of argument between people, not in isolated, reflective thinking.[5] To the extent that we know these things (or have at least some reasonable belief in them) that is because of systematic experimental work. Instead of putting our pedagogic efforts into teaching formal logic we do better to find out where people actually do go systematically wrong in reasoning—ignoring base rates, observing the law of 'small numbers,' and the rest—and devise ways to guard against these errors when it matters. We cannot do that on the basis of a novelist's conception of how the mind works.

6.2 Evidence and the kinds of knowing

Why isn't it enough, from the point of view of the philosopher's project, that we say what the cognitive potential of the work is—say, in other words, what the work contains? We show that works contain truths by saying what those truths are. That is exactly what we do when we assess the value of a scientific theory; we don't argue for the value of general relativity theory by pointing to the actual effects of reading about it. True, we can't read off the cognitive value of a work of fiction from its text in the way we would hope to do with research paper in physics; works of fiction need to be interpreted in a way that scientific works normally don't.[6] But we might see the project as comparable to (and perhaps of a piece with) the activity of the art critic whose job it is—on one conception anyway—to indicate to the audience what is valuable in a picture. The critic sees what is valuable, is able to identify the features of the work responsible for the various values it exemplifies, and her job is then to help others to see those features in the same way ('see the way that line descends in a graceful curve'). Critical communication is achieved

---

[5] See below, Section 10.1.

[6] Works of all kinds need to be understood and understanding a scientific work can be no easy task. But the effort of understanding is not always interpretive effort; more often what is required is prior subject knowledge. I say this without having a theory of interpretation to support it; I take it to be a constraint on reasonable theories of interpretation that they deliver the result that fictions often require massive interpretive effort while physics papers rarely do. There is a huge literature on relativity theory but not a huge literature on what Einstein meant by his 1905 paper 'On the electrodynamics of moving bodies' which introduced the theory.

when the audience does see those features in those ways. That seems also to be roughly the method of writers such as Nussbaum, who tries to get us to see/read a narrative such as *The Golden Bowl* as having features of dialogue, characterization, and narration which serve to make or suggest substantive points about love and responsibility.

There are commonalities between the project of pointing out what is aesthetically valuable in a picture and the project of identifying the features of a work of fiction that make up its cognitive value. There are significant differences as well, and the differences mean that the latter calls for empirical work in a way the former does not. First, we have already agreed that the cognitive value of literature does not consist wholly in its representation of propositions. Perhaps the work embodies a way of seeing things which is not expressible propositionally, even on the generous interpretation of 'propositional' I have adopted. Its power may be said to lie in its being a source of the kind of experience which enhances our empathic capacities, enlarges our vision, trains our emotions to be more responsive and responsible, or something else which is not purely propositional in nature. In the case of propositional learning, we can distinguish between the thing on offer in the work—the proposition—and the facts concerning whether people know that proposition on the basis of exposure to that work. The claim is that we can see the philosopher-interpreter's project as concerned with identifying the first of these things and not with investigating the second. Can we do the same in the case of other kinds of knowing?

Take knowing-how. Can we identify the know-how that is on offer and leave to others the task of finding out whether people gain that know-how from exposure to the work? We cannot. The claim that the work 'contains' or is at least in some way a source of the know-how amounts to this: that people are apt (in circumstances that no doubt need further specification) to gain the know-how from exposure to the work. It ascribes, in other words, a disposition to the work. And claims that something is disposed to affect other things in certain ways are empirical, and so in need of evidential support: see the argument above.

Precisely what evidence may we hope to get? This is not easy to say. In the case of know-how we can at least point in the right direction: we need evidence that readers have gained or improved a skill, and did so on the basis of their reading of the work. In practice it may be extremely hard to show this. For the moment let's simplify and assume that increments of empathic skill do go with increased tendency towards helping behaviour. Helping behaviour is measurable; experiments have been designed to measure it, including ones that involve exposure to fictions.[7] It is hard, however, to be confident that the change, if there is one, is not simply a very short-lived one. Testing usually takes place immediately after

[7] See below, Chapter 11.

reading and retests later are rare; when they are done there is often no sustained effect visible.[8] But that is the sort of evidence we need if we are responsibly to claim that fiction contributes in some way to knowing-how.

How should we think about the usefulness of evidence in the case where it is claimed that some fiction shows us what an experience is like, that it gives us what I have called acquaintance? While many find it obvious that fictions are capable of this, others suggest that the idea is confused. Richard Gaskin puts it this way:

> The activity of sitting at home and reading an exciting novel does not show you what it would be like to experience the events recounted in that novel; at most it shows you what it is like to sit at home reading an exciting novel *about* those events.[9]

It is true of course that reading gives us the experience of reading about taking part in a battle and not the experience of taking part in a battle. But the idea of acquaintance from fiction was always that a work might enable us to know what an experience is like without our having had that experience, and typically fiction is said to do that by enabling us to imagine being in a battle in such a way that we have, via the imaginative act, an experience like that of being in battle. Gaskin might say that as long as a fiction actually gives us the reading experience it cannot give us the battle-like one, because we cannot have two experiences simultaneously. On some ways of individuating experiences this is false: one can simultaneously have the experience of hearing a noise and the experience of seeing a flash of light. But for the purposes of this argument that ought to count as one experience. Fiction's supposed acquaintance-generating capacity is said to be valuable in providing us with importantly enriched and enlarged perspectives on the world; it is not celebrated for granting us access to the experiences of sounds and flashes, but of battle, slavery, intense commitment, or the daily grind of a refugee life. At least some of this could be given only via the provision of imaginative experiences of considerable richness involving sensory imagining in several modalities along with cognitive and emotional elements. The question is whether that sort of provision is compatible with our also having the experience of reading the book or watching the movie.

A way to argue that it is appeals to the idea of transportation. Originally described by Richard Gerrig (1993), this process consists of the reader (or viewer:

---

[8] There is also evidence for a 'sleeper effect', where a new belief shows up only weeks later (see Kumkale and Albarracín (2004). This seems to occur only where a message is presented along with a 'discounting cue'—information which strongly undermines the credibility of the message. Might the fact that the message occurs in a work of fiction count as a discounting cue? There is, I think, no evidence either way on this interesting question.

[9] Gaskin (2013: 121, emphasis in the original). See also Carroll (2010: 246–8) for opposition to the idea of acquaintance from fiction.

I assume this addition tacitly understood from now on) being 'taken away' from the real world, aspects of which now become inaccessible, and into the world of the story so that he or she is changed in some way on their return. One way the reader is said to be changed is in attitudes: reading a fictional story about a child-murder is likely, if you are highly transported, to lead to you expressing more pessimistic views about the world and urging more constraint on psychiatric patients.[10] Accounts of transportation in terms of movement from one world to another are not very helpful and there is a tendency to exaggerate the extent to which the transported reader becomes detached from reality. Still, the idea that certain kinds of experience with fiction (sometimes called 'immersive reading') substantially reduce our consciousness of the reading process seems reasonable, somewhat in the way that one can be unaware of one's familiar homeward drive, though all the while able to turn the wheel and shift the gears. Anyway, I'll assume that there is not an in-principle objection to the idea that fictions can guide and encourage our imaginings in ways that allow them to dominate our consciousness, leaving us able to recall the episode in some detail.

That granted, what now stands in the way of a sympathetic attitude towards the idea of acquaintance-by-fiction is this: whatever imaginative experiences are generated, stored, and recalled as a result of reading, there is no evidence to help us decide what relations those imaginative experiences have to the experiences people actually have in the situations we are imagining, and hence no evidence to support the claim that fictions can help us to know what experiences we have never had are like. Assertions from the subjects themselves to the effect that they had become acquainted with this experience would be worth little. If I have not had the experience in question how can I tell whether my imagined sense of what that experience is like is correct?[11] We usually take it on trust when someone tells us that they have learned how to ride a bike, but trust would evaporate if we discovered they had never ridden one. I know that I can ride a bike because I have managed to ride one; that's a test I can fail and it will be obvious to us all if I do fail it. What is the failable test you can undertake to show that you have become acquainted with a certain experience?

There might in the end be some sort of positive answer to the question. There might be situations in which someone has an imaginative experience of some kind which they take to be indicative of what it would be like to actually be in the situation imagined; later, they find themselves in that situation and think: 'Yes, this is how I imagined it to be.' Questions would then be asked about how much reliance we could put on such judgements, given the difficulty of comparing an imagined situation with a real one. Subjects would also need to be confident that

---

[10] Green and Brock (2000). For recent work on transportation theory see van Laer et al. (2014).
[11] This sort of scepticism about acquaintance from fiction was voiced some time ago by Putnam (1978); see also Davies (2007: 148–9).

they could distinguish, within the total affective and cognitive state induced by their imaginings, which parts of it were the result of their imagining being in the situation and which parts the result of their spectatorial engagement—fearing *for* a character rather than experiencing the fear which, according to the fiction, the character is feeling. And this sort of evidence, if it is possible in principle, is unlikely ever to be available in a quantity that would fuel a statistically meaningful test. Nor does it seem likely that ordinary practices of engagement with fiction will change so as to require or encourage people to claim that they have learned from fiction what some experience is like only if they can provide that sort of support for their claim.[12]

Perhaps we have gone wrong at an earlier stage, allowing a particular interpretation of 'knowing what it is like' to dominate the discussion. People who claim to know (something about) what slavery is like from engagement with a fiction about it may not be clear in their own minds as between two interpretations of the claim; one is that they have come to be acquainted with the experience of slavery, and the other that they now know certain very detailed facts about slavery—facts important for understanding in a detailed way the moral abomination that slavery is. If that is right then what we have been calling acquaintance may turn out to be certain cases of (rather thickly laden) propositional knowledge: one knows that, in these circumstances—battle, slavery, or perhaps specific historically located instances of these things—this and that would or might happen, where the many thises and thats describe a complex of dynamically unfolding events against a background of more static physical, psychological, and social fact. And recall Chapter 5: the propositions in question need not be fully expressible in language. Film in particular can provide very rich information about the appearances of things, allowing one to think, 'A wartime prison camp in Germany looked like *that*.' I suggest that the best strategy for someone who wants to argue that fictions help us to know what certain kinds of experiences are like is to make this a case of propositional knowing.[13]

In the propositional domain it does seem as if we can distinguish between what is to-be-known, and the knowing of it. Should we say that, at least for propositional knowledge, the cognitive value of fiction is settled by focusing on what is to be known, something we discover by using just the interpretive methods of the literary scholar? I say no, but I'll start by granting something to the opposition. Recall that our interest is in learning and that propositional learning (as I understand it) occurs when we improve epistemically, something that may

---

[12] For more on revisionism about our treatment of fiction see Section 6.4 below.

[13] Murray Smith (2017: 189–90) gives an example where a narrative work enables us to get beyond 'schematic ideas' and have some insight into 'what it would be or feel like to be a particular person in a specific situation', citing Mrs Clutter's 'agonized outburst' (*In Cold Blood*). What seems to me revelatory in this passage is its enabling us to think the proposition 'Those thoughts exemplify the debilitating effects of depression'.

occur without any of the relevant propositions being true. So it won't do to argue in this way: learning requires truth, so the claim that a work is apt to induce learning can be justified only by evidence for the truth of the proposition concerned, and that evidence can be gathered only by empirical inquiry. Still, my weakened conditions on learning don't license us to ignore empirical issues. The claim that learning takes place when you go from believing that the earth is flat to believing it to be spherical requires that we take a view on the relative degrees of empirical support these two propositions get. Going from believing the Earth is flat to believing it is conical is not learning.

It will be said that examples of this kind are misleading; they are not the kinds of propositions that advocates of learning from fiction do or should point to as illustrations of their claims. We do better to look at examples like this from Proust, which others have found it worthwhile to reflect on: 'The whole art of living is to use the people who make us suffer simply as steps enabling us to obtain access to their divine form and thus joyfully to people our lives with divinities.'[14] I grant that this is not an obviously empirical claim; indeed it is far from clear what it means, and whether it is to be understood as an assertion, a recommendation, or in some other way. One might take it as an expression of an ethical stance, perhaps as something one chooses to be guided by in some contexts and not in others. Simply asking 'what evidence is there in favour of the proposition?' does not seem a helpful way forward. Yet the claim that the remark is worth taking account of in one's practical life can't be insulated from empirical inquiry. We need to consider what the most reasonable interpretations there are of it, which will include some discussion of how any proposed interpretation engages usefully with actual situations of moral choice we find ourselves in; we need to connect it in a coherent way with a view about what constitutes flourishing in a specifically human way of life. How we are to do this generally is no doubt a difficult question, and in this particular case I have nothing helpful to say. But a rational approach to Proust's principle must take in empirical questions about character, motivation, and human capacities for forgiveness. Not knowing how to proceed empirically does not license us to proceed non-empirically.

So evidence is relevant to settling many questions, not just to settling the question 'Is this true?' Perhaps you are attracted to an instrumentalist position and want to get away from truth altogether, exclaiming that what matters is not that the propositions are true, or even close to the truth, but that they are empirically verified; you still need to care about evidence—in fact that is all you care about. If you are impatient altogether with the idea of epistemic value from fiction you might focus instead on some non-cognitive value. Perhaps you believe that what matters is making us better citizens or more contented individuals and

---

[14] *Time Regained* (1992: 103–4). See the discussion of this remark in Nussbaum (1994: 940); see also Beistegui (2012).

that matters of evidence and truth don't come into it. The claim that fiction does those things is in no lesser need of empirical support.

6.3 Expert readers

Another way for the philosopher to avoid contact with the empirical literature on fiction and its effects focuses on the way empirical studies are currently conducted. They generally employ non-expert participants, usually undergraduates from disciplines outside literary studies. They generally use brief, 'non-literary' texts, sometimes devised specifically for the purposes of the experiment, rather than works of agreed literary merit. What could such experiments tell us about the cognitive impact of sustained, committed engagement with complex literary works?

Let's agree that questions about the educative powers of fiction or some particular work of fiction are not to be answered merely by examining its actual effects in a range of cases counted as normal or average. Our investigations will have, at some stage, to look at the effects of what we may call expert reading, where subjects are especially knowledgeable of, sensitive and attentive to the material. Literature's (supposed) disposition to educate might be visible, or easily visible, only in unusual circumstances. Nonetheless, the claim that literature has this disposition, however restrictively understood, is an empirical one. It is not legitimate to hold that the educative effects of literature are knowable without inquiry directed at discovering what those effects actually are, even when those effects are said to manifest themselves only in special conditions.

Advocates of the a priori philosophical approach might admit this, pointing out that, since the available studies do not address the relevant special conditions, they are entitled to ignore them. Two things suggest that this would not be a good line of defence. It may be true that, by and large, the experimental results we have so far do not target the conditions philosophers consider most conducive to literary education—those involving highly sensitive and well-prepared subjects and highly valued literary works. But if true this is knowable only by taking an interest in the experimental work being done. More importantly, there are dangers in fashioning a thesis about the value of fiction which, you then claim, holds only in special and difficult to test circumstances. Very often, a psychological effect occurs across a range of circumstances and for a broad class of subjects, though it may be intense, and hence easy to observe, only in some circumstances and for some subjects. And advocates of the cognitive function of literature do often deny that the supposed beneficial effects of literature are available only to the few lucky enough to possess unusual levels of preparedness and attention. They often stress the role of fictional works of varying quality and difficulty in moving people (often young people) towards those conditions of preparedness and attention from which they can benefit from the most demanding works. While hoping for better experiments, sensitive to more subtle effects and involving a more complex set of circumstantial variables, one ought to be interested in the evidence (or lack of evidence) for the effects of literature in circumstances your theory rates as less than ideal.

There is reason enough here to conclude that claims about the educative value of literature ought to take account of, and ought ideally to cohere with, the best work in experimental psychology, though it needs also to be said that psychologists may learn from philosophers about the sorts of effects of literature it would be most interesting to look for and about the circumstances in which they are most likely to be found.

6.4 Revisionism

It seems that claims about learning from fiction require two kinds of evidence: evidence that fictions do (sometimes) change us cognitively, and evidence that these changes constitute cognitive improvements and so amount to learning rather than the accumulation of error and ignorance. So people who want to learn from fiction ought to attend carefully to this second question: as masters of their own intellects they should ask whether what they think they are learning really is learning and not the growth of ignorance. And the best way to do that is surely to regard the fiction in question as part of an information system: a body of interconnected sources which we test against one another. It is starting to sound as if the suggestion on offer here is highly revisionary. Taking seriously the epistemic value of fiction, or of some particular fiction, involves weighing its claims against other sources including the deliverances of science. That just does not seem to be how we naturally engage with fiction, even when we attend to it with exemplary seriousness. We attend to the work, but how many of us seek to check what we take to be its message against, say, research into social psychology?

One might reply that there are other domains where belief fixation takes place without these sorts of rigorous inquiries being made—religious opinion being an obvious one. Two points here: there is currently a lively debate about the extent to which religious ideas, for all their importance in human life, can really be considered as beliefs.[15] Secondly, and regardless of the outcome of that debate, many people seriously committed to the epistemic value of literature would be uncomfortable in placing the literary practices they value alongside those of organized religion which they may have rejected in favour of apparently more enlightened ways of thinking.

---

[15]   See e.g. van Leeuwen (2014, 2016, 2017). See also Rey (2007). Since Rey holds that religious people are (often) self-deceived his view seems at some distance from the pretence view I offer in this section. But there may be a way to bring them closer together: see Gendler (2010: Chapter 8).

It's true in general of course that we do not exercise high levels of epistemic vigilance in forming all or many of our beliefs, especially those where we can rationally depend on testimony: more on that topic in Chapter 10. But where ideas are highly consequential and expertise cannot be assumed we ought to take a (to some extent) more critical attitude. In this respect, the comparison with religious ideas seems apt: we often insist on the importance of what is to be learned from a favoured author, while at the same time treating the work as a source of wisdom isolated from other sources. What follows is addressed to those who, on the one hand, do regard the fixation of beliefs, values, and preferences on weighty matters as requiring some consilience across sources with anything to say on the issue and who, on the other, hope to go on reading Henry James without constant reference to papers from the *Journal of Experimental Psychology*. Anyone who likes the suggestion I shall sketch will be entitled to ignore the empirical issues I have been stressing, but at the cost of abandoning the idea that fiction is an important and rationally defensible determinant of belief.

It is widely agreed that engagement with fictions involves a kind of pretence: a pretence that is carried on in imagination rather than acted out in behaviour. The pretence is that one is reading something seriously asserted and from which you may be able to learn things about the characters and their doings. And there are good reasons for thinking this is pretence: after all, the characters typically don't exist; if they do they have generally not done what the story says they did; we and the author mutually know this. While we are not really learning about the characters and their doings, even by the most relaxed standards of learning, we may be engaged in a pretence of learning. Lewis, citing Kendall Walton, agrees: 'The storytellers pretend to pass on historical information to their audience; the audience pretends to learn from their words'.[16] What I suggest now is that fiction engages us in a further act of pretending: the pretence that we are learning from the story, not just about its characters and their doings, but, in some indirect way, about things which lie beyond the events and characters of its story, which are suggested by them and which may be intended to be communicated by means of the story.

The claim that someone is pretending to do something rather than seriously doing it or trying to do it is an empirical one. Sometimes the claim is easy to test: we can see by casual observation that children are pretending to be pirates rather than seriously being or trying to be pirates. It will be much harder to determine empirically whether people are pretending to learn from fictions. For one thing there are, as I just noted, few behaviours characteristic of such situations: 'pretending to learn' means, in this context, little more than that the subjects imagine themselves learning. We can ask people whether they are pretending and I expect

---

[16] Lewis (1983b: 276), citing Walton (1978).

many will say they are not. But people are often highly resistant to the idea that they are pretending at all in fictional contexts. The idea that readers pretend that Sherlock Holmes is a real person they are learning about is a controversial philosophical thesis and not a platitude of folk understanding; nonetheless I think it is true.[17] It may also be true that readers pretend to learn about the nature of love, time, and memory while reading Proust.

While I have no direct evidence for the proposal I will say two things in favour of its plausibility. The first is this. If we do agree that audiences of fiction engage in a pretence in relation to the characters and events of the story, we can see fictional engagement as very conducive to the further pretence I am suggesting here. I don't mean simply that because we are pretending about one thing we are led to pretend about another; that is not in general a plausible claim. The idea is rather that the basic pretence of the engaged reader—the pretence that we are learning about real people and events—is one that very naturally lends itself to the extension I am suggesting. The basic pretence engages the whole range of our cognitive resources. We make inferences about the characters and events based on our real-world knowledge, and we bring our skills in pragmatic inference to the task of inter-preting the text. We treat the text as if it were assertive utterance constrained by assumptions of conversational cooperativeness and written in the knowledge that we, cooperative readers, will fill out the story in charitable ways from the slender indications of the text. We undertake, in other words, the sorts of interpersonal thinking and inferring that we do when people really are addressing us seriously with some information to impart, as may be when they address non-fictional stories to us. And one of the things we do when people address us seriously is look for evidence in what they say of an underlying motive. Why is this person telling me this, at this time, in this way? Are they trying to convey to me something that is not said and which may be only minimally hinted at in their utterance? Few things are more important to us than the motives and intentions of those around us, and we constantly scan for evidence, even of the most indirect kind, concerning what those intentions are. These scanning devices—sometimes collectively called, rather misleadingly, 'theory of mind'—are not things we can easily turn off when we go into pretend mode, any more than we can easily turn off our emotional reactions when we engage with fictional stories. So the thought is that, in pretending that we are learning about a restricted range of things from the utterances the text presents us with, we are naturally led to include within the scope of the pretence a wider range of pretended learning that takes in the sorts of things we often claim that fiction really can teach us.

The second piece of support for the plausibility of the 'pretended learning' proposal starts with the idea that, as theories of what we might call broadly artistic

---

[17] For philosophical resistance to the claim see Palmer (1992).

engagement go, this is not an eccentric suggestion. Kant said that in the realm of the aesthetic, things have merely the appearance of purpose: 'the form of purposiveness' as he characteristically put it. Richard Miller (1998) suggests a way to develop this idea: think of engagement with a work of art as 'learninglike', though its goal is not, in fact, learning (38). The goal is rather to enjoy the exercise of skills and faculties which the learninglike processes deploy, an activity which, unlike real learning, manages to be both cognitively demanding and secure from 'defeat by recalcitrant reality' (51). This sounds very like the suggestion that serious engagement with fiction—engagement that takes in reflection on the world as well as the content of the story itself—is an exercise in pretended learning, bearing in mind that here there is no suggestion that people know, or know very clearly, that they are pretending. The pretence can be conducted in ways that differ in the extent of the reader's passivity. We may accept, as a basic presumption of the pretence, the reliability of the point of view from which the work is given: the world and the people in it are basically as the work suggests they are. Using the framework, you may then ask questions about the motivations of characters, the aptness of their images and feelings, probing the depths of their psyches in ways you could never hope to do in reality, achieving a high level of self-forgetful absorption in what appears to be learning. That way you get the pleasures—the sophisticated, hard-won pleasures—of solving a mystery, of lighting on surprising implications, of 'the discovery of order in apparent chaos' as Miller puts it (39), without running the risk that it will all be shown to be error.

We can allow the pretence to get more complex. One of the pleasures of fiction is deciding that the author got this character's motives wrong. People can be wrong by their own lights; wrong for reasons they find significant, though they think there is some way round the objection. But we may even challenge the authorial framework, engaging with the author about whether some reshaping of the narrative would better illuminate a motive or an action. Doing this in pretence mode does not put us in danger of having the framework brought radically into doubt by some external authority claiming to know, on the basis of esoteric experiments, better than we and the author do about what motivates people.

Concerned as we were about the revisionary implications of the arguments of this chapter, the present suggestion may not seem to help. After all, it requires us to trade a serious epistemic enterprise for the mere pretence of one. Perhaps that is in the end what is required. But my suspicion is that it is not, and that what we need to change is our opinions about how we think we are dealing with fiction, not how we actually are dealing with it. To say that people who appear to be open to fiction to change their beliefs and practices are 'only pretending' sounds like an accusation of bad faith; it seems we must regard the pretenders as deliberately misrepresenting their cognitive states. But we should drop the assumption of a tight connection between pretence and deliberate aping of belief. Some pretence is like that, some isn't. We are not always in a good position to know when we believe something rather than merely imagine it, where imagining is what goes on in games of pretence. People are certainly capable of being confused about whether they believe something or imagine it; we are prone to claim, in good faith, that we 'remember' something happening to us after we have been asked to imagine it happening.[18] Think also of all the sober people who say they believe what they see on stage at *Othello*, at least while they are seeing it. That doesn't strike me as plausible, and I'm not troubled in this opinion by their confident assertions. Nor do I think they are lying. But they are mistaken about their own cognition. As indicated earlier, I'm not persuaded that all the devoutly religious people of this world really believe what their faiths profess and what they earnestly claim to believe.[19] So perhaps I may be understood as urging a clarification: an acknowledgement that when we engage seriously with great literature we do not come away with more knowledge, better abilities, clarified emotions, or deeper human sympathies. We do exercise capacities that let us explore fascinating and complex conceptions of what human beings are like—ones there is little reason, and little tendency, to believe.

Perhaps this is too neat a picture. Very likely our cognitive stance in engaging with fiction shifts around unstably over time and across individuals. There probably are occasions when readers form genuine beliefs about what we are pleased to call human nature; we dip in and out of pretence mode without fully realizing what we are doing. There probably are times when we learn from fiction; we will see more on this in Chapter 9. There are almost certainly times when what we gain is error and ignorance. I suggest that the mode of pretence is one that readers are in pretty frequently.

6.5 Conclusions

'What's the time?' is about as wholly empirical a question as one could find; you certainly don't need a philosopher to help you answer it. 'What is time?' is a long way down the empirical scale and requires a good deal of philosophical clarification and argument. The question whether we learn from fiction also has a distinctly philosophical aspect; philosophy helps guide us to at least a rough conception of what fiction is and of what counts centrally and what counts marginally as fiction. It constantly pushes us to refine our question, given the improbability that either all fictions do or all do not teach, and teach in the same way. It also helps us think through the kinds of things that can be learned and the

---

[18] See Garry et al., (1996). This effect has been claimed even for such bizarre events as 'Proposing marriage to a Pepsi machine'; see Seamon et al. (2006).

[19] Ryle thought that acts of pretence are on a continuum from 'deliberately...dissimulating' to being 'completely taken in by [your] own acting' (1949: 258).

ways that learning can take place. But the question is surely *more* empirical than the question about time's nature. Beyond meeting constraints of coherence, simplicity and all-round philosophical respectability, theories of time need to comport with our best science, and what counts as best science is an empirical matter. But theories of time don't generally face experimental tests directly. The empirical work done on the question of learning from fiction already establishes a closer connection to empirical results; we can already discuss some empirical outcomes which suggest that learning of that kind has or has not taken place. None of these results are definitive or close to it; it will always be a matter of accumulating and interpreting a mass of data that in the end may shed light on where, if anywhere, the epistemic effects of fiction can be found. On the scale marked 'degree to which this is an empirical question' I rank the question about fiction above the one about time's nature, but way below the one about what the time is now.

Still, the idea that claims about fiction's epistemic credentials need empirical support of any kind poses a challenge to our normal ways of engaging with fiction; it suggests that virtuous epistemic agents should treat fictions as parts of an interconnected informational system, which by and large they do not do. I have suggested towards the end of this chapter that anyone uncomfortable with that kind of revisionism may want to consider another option: to think, in Richard Miller's terms, of engagement with a work of art as 'learninglike', though its goal is not, in fact, learning.

Chapter 7 examines an aspect of fiction highly suggestive of its capacity for providing learning. Something we all want to know about and no doubt could handle better is our relations with others. Those relations depend a good deal on interpersonal understanding. We need to check what we think against the thoughts of others, and our own wants depend very often on theirs. This is not always in the service of a selfless desire to smooth the pathways of our fellows. Sometimes it is because cooperation is a useful strategy for getting what we want, sometimes because competition seems the best or only way. Fictions of all kinds and qualities make this their theme, and it's a theme audiences attend to closely. One thing Chapter 7 will do is look at some ways that the emergence and flourishing of fiction could be explained by reference to this theme.

7

Fiction, mentalizing, and planning

Fiction has a remarkable degree of focus on the mind: the beliefs, desires, intentions, and feelings of its characters, and especially the ways their minds interact, understanding or misunderstanding one another, sharing feelings of intimacy, divided by conflicting desire, united in a common cause. This chapter focuses on the representation in fiction of the ways mental states interconnect and their consequences for action. It ends with a response to the idea that, on Darwinian grounds, fiction's close connection to the imagination makes it likely that it is in some way a good source of knowledge.

7.1 Ways to affect others

I might gain possession of your wallet by knocking you down and taking it. I might, instead, convince you that I have an innocent interest in wallets, persuade you to let me examine yours, and run off with it. These are very different strategies, and while animals of many kinds engage in behaviour like that in the first example, only humans show clear competence with the second.[1] Many of us hold that this competence requires an understanding of inner mental states, the capacity to reason about them, to manipulate them in others, and to take them into account in decision making.[2] In stealing your wallet by strategy rather than by force, I seek to get you to believe something false about my intentions, predicting that this will have certain effects on your behaviour, and consequent effects on my ability to get your money.

My strategy for getting your money may not deceive you for long, and I run the risk of retribution or at least the loss of reputation when the deception is discovered. More subtle techniques seek to gain advantage without ever revealing themselves, and these require complex plans to maintain another's false belief over

---

[1] Sodian and Frith (1992) distinguish between deception and sabotage, with sabotage a matter of disrupting a conspecific's ability to attain some goal without requiring any kind of theory of mind, and deception a matter of deliberately aiming to cause false beliefs. In my (2006), I argue that we can regard some animal behaviour as deceptive even in the absence of any mindreading skills. The general point here is that, however we draw the distinction, the kind of deceptive behaviour that draws on such skills is of a kind distinct from that which doesn't. There is a lively debate about whether any non-human animals engage in behaviour designed to affect the mental states of others; there is no debate about whether humans do.

[2] See above, Section 2.3.

Imagining and Knowing: The Shape of Fiction. Gregory Currie, Oxford University Press (2020). © Gregory Currie. DOI: 10.1093/oso/9780199656615.001.0001

time. I would often do better to get you to *want* to give me your money. This might take some misrepresentation of my own desires, but that can often be achieved without going to the trouble of telling downright lies. Great competence in this kind of manipulation tends to provoke an uneasy mixture of admiration and outrage, and is often taken up in fiction, as with Trollop's Lizzie Eustace and Highsmith's Tom Ripley.

I prefer 'mentalizing' to the more commonly used 'theory of mind'—an uncomfortable term for anyone who denies that understanding the mental states of others and one's self is exclusively a theoretical activity. At least in certain circumstances we try to mirror another's thinking, feeling, and deciding in imagination. But in this chapter I am not taking a stand on how we understand the mental states of others, or asking whether we sometimes use the same methods, whatever they are, to understand ourselves. Nor is that a question that fiction is going to help us answer. There are several plausible theories currently on the books about self/other understanding, and we could write fictions in which agents do it one way, or another way, or a third way, and so on. No one, I hope, thinks that we can settle the question whether the universe is deterministic or not by writing two fictions, one in which it is and one in which it is not, and then see which is more plausible. Why should it be different with psychological causation? You might say it is different because the nature of psychological causation is something we have access to ourselves. But we don't—if we did we could settle the debates discussed earlier between theory-theorists, imagination theorists, and their rivals by appeal to our own experience.[3] I simply take it that we do mentalize, and my interest in this chapter is in the question why fictions which focus on this are of such interest to us.[4]

7.2 Levels of mindedness

We need to distinguish carefully between possession of a mind, and possession of a mentalizing capacity. To have a mind is to have mental states, which may be of various kinds; our discussion will focus particularly on beliefs and desires. It is widely though not universally believed that certain non-human animals, such as higher primates, have beliefs and desires and so would count as minded; it is much more controversial to say that they are able to mentalize.[5] Evidence of mind is

---

[3] See above, Sections 2.2 and 2.3.

[4] What I say here is broadly in line, I think, with Vermeule (2010), which organizes its theme around the literature of the eighteenth century in ways I can't hope to emulate.

[5] The term 'theory of mind' was introduced by Premack and Woodruff in a ground-breaking study of cognition in great apes (1978). Out of this debate emerged the idea of the 'false belief test' as a way of establishing an agent's competence with mental states (Dennett 1978). Jennifer Nagel (2017) urges a re-orientation that would see experimentalists turn away from the false-true belief dichotomy and attend instead to the factive/nonfactive distinction.

generally looked for in flexible and sophisticated behaviour which shows an appropriate sensitivity to a range of features in the environment; evidence of mentalizing is looked for in sophisticated dealings with a particular aspect of the environment—other creatures, particularly conspecifics, already presumed to possess minds. One can have evidence of mindedness without having evidence of mentalizing, since mindedness does not entail competence with every aspect of the environment; lack of competence in dealing with other minded creatures does not entail lack of mindedness.

A mentalizing creature must be sensitive to the mental states of others but need not be a creature able to deliberately affect those mental states. It can, after all, pay to be sensitive to aspects of the world that you cannot do anything about. We and other creatures evolved a sensitivity to weather, and benefit by adjusting our behaviour according to how the weather is. But we are still unable to affect the weather except by the most crude, indirect, and unpredictable means. When it comes to fiction, what seems to interest us most is *change* of mind. Stories in which all we have is one character treating another character's mental states as a given and steering a course round them don't prove very interesting; even where characters have supernaturally powerful minds other characters are generally able to influence them through prayer and sacrifice.[6] Ordinary human agents are generally treated as malleable, and particularly as subject to deceptive manipulation. Intentionally changing minds involves, of course, mentalizing. To effectively alter someone's mental states I need to know where I am starting from: the other agent's current cognitive and conative states.

Attempts to alter other people's mental states are not always deceptive or malevolent: we try to convince those who we love that we care for them; we try to shift their desires when we think they are self-destructive. Fictions sometimes hold our attention by representing these sorts of influences; the first third of *The Winter's Tale* focuses on the honest efforts of various characters to dislodge Leontes' conviction that Hermione is unfaithful; later the emphasis shifts to Perdita's attempts (failed, I think) to bring about a wholesale moral reform of Leontes' character.[7] But the plot here is not so immediately gripping as that of *Othello*, with its representation of extreme, organized, and malevolent deception. And Iago is not merely deceptive; he deceives by misrepresenting his own beliefs and desires. To do that he has to have thoughts about Othello's thoughts about his (Iago's) thoughts. All deceivers have to misrepresent their own mental states at least minimally; they have to hide their deceptive intent. Iago goes much further, misrepresenting in complex ways his own attitudes concerning

---

[6] This perhaps is one reason why Shelley's *Frankenstein* gets more critical attention than Stoker's *Dracula*.

[7] See my (2010a).

Desdemona, Casio, and Othello himself, as well as the facts about the relations between all three.[8]

When agents can manipulate each other's mental states it pays to know the other's mind and to disguise your own. The pressure to misrepresent your own mind accelerates as misrepresenting mind becomes a widespread deceptive tool. An arms race ensues, making us the familiar creatures we are, sensitive to clues from anywhere in the environment about people's mental states, attentive to the evidence of deception in others, prone ourselves to deceptive behaviour. Current evidence suggests that we are much less adept in our conscious judgements about deception than we imagine: on average we are just above chance in judging whether someone is lying, and while detection of truthful statements is significantly above chance, the detection of lies is significantly below.[9] The arms race is preserving a rough parity between the contestants.

When we read literature in which mentalizing is represented we are often prompted to do some mentalizing of our own—working out what this character thinks the other character thinks or wants. And mentalizing on the reader's part occurs even where there is no mentalizing going on in the narrative. Let's say that I'm at level 1 when I believe (hope, fear, suspect) it's raining, and at level 2 when I believe (etc.) that you believe (etc.) it's raining. At all levels I display mindedness. At level 2 or above I am mentalizing. So I will already be mentalizing (level 2) when I follow a story that represents mental states but does not represent mentalizing. And a story that represents mind at level n (C1 believes that C2 believes that ... that Cn is guilty) will require mentalizing from the audience at level n+1. In fact the disparity between the level of representation and the level of reader's activity will be greater than this if we assume, as I do, that working out what is happening in the story depends on the attribution of mental states to the author, even where those mental states are not represented in the story itself. To conclude that the story represents character C as believing it will rain, I may need to decide that the author intends it to be the case in the story that C believes it will rain.

7.3 Mentalizing in fiction

The theme of mentalizing appears early in the known history of fiction.[10] In Homer, gods, heroes, and ordinary mortals wonder about what their enemies

[8] In fact any misrepresentation is, implicitly, misrepresentation of one's own mental states. To claim that it is raining when you know that it isn't is to commit yourself to the proposition that you know or at least believe that it is.

[9] See Bond and DePaulo (2006); for a meta-analysis; Levine (2010). However, there is evidence that unconscious processes are sensitive to lying; see ten Brinke et al. (2014).

[10] For a collection of essays on literature and theory of mind see Leverage et al. (2010). See also Zunshine (2006), (2012), (2015), and Boyd (2009). Authors in this area do not speak with one voice, as is evident from Boyd (2006). Suzanne Keen's (2007) is a valuable, deflationary look at the idea that

think, basing their actions on the best estimates they can make of what those affected by their actions want and believe. Those characters also do their best to affect, sometimes through argument but very often through deception, what those around them think. The ones with superhuman powers are not above short-circuiting the process by inserting thoughts into the minds of those lower down the cognitive chain. Those further down have to make use of other, less direct methods. Agamemnon, believing that the Greeks will be defeated without Achilles, knows he must reduce the shame and anger Achilles feels before he can bring him back to the fight. Priam pleads before Achilles, hoping to weaken Achilles' desire to revenge himself further on the dead body of Hector.[11] And so it has gone. Shakespearean drama focuses on our desires, our errors and their exploitation by others; Don Quixote is the victim of endless scheming by those who would use his deranged beliefs to their advantage or amusement; Pamela cannot hope to extinguish Mr B's desire, but she hopes to domesticate it; Squire Allworthy will, we hope, see the goodness in Tom and the scheming of Master Blifil. Characters who neglect mentalizing and act to achieve a goal by brute causal means are often represented as especially unworthy. In *The Mill on the Floss*, Tulliver physically attacks Mr Wakeham, and his resort to violence is further evidence of his impoverished capacity to deal strategically with other people, already indicated by his disastrous decision to go to law. Mentalizing is equally a feature of less elevated fiction: television soaps, routine mystery stories, and Harlequin romances focus on the interlocking mental states of their characters, the misunderstanding of another's motive being a common engine of plot development.

Do we have a literary universal here—a constancy of focus on strategic themes, visible through the bewildering variability we find in fictional narrative across time, place, genre, and medium? It is not as if every line of every play, novel, poem, or other vehicle of narration is devoted to mentalizing; looking for something universal means simply looking for notable, regular recurrences of the theme across forms, times, and cultures. It's true that in many diverse fictions one person's understanding of another's mental state plays a highly salient role, sometimes serving to win the reader's attention at the beginning of the plot. *Morte d'Arthur* begins with Merlin's plan to deceive Igraine into thinking that Uther Pendragon is her husband, from which follows the birth of Arthur; the *Tale of Genji* begins with the jealous concern of the Emperor's longer-standing wife

---

literature increases our understanding of others. Zunshine denies that fictions are 'instructive' when it comes to mind-reading or, she suspects, anything else (2006: 125, 178; see also 35). But then I don't understand her analogy between reading detective fiction and going to the gym; the latter does not help, she says, with 'everyday activities', but then concedes that it does exactly that for people recovering from injuries.

[11] On the continuity between Homeric and modern representations of mind see Williams (1993).

over his immoderate affection for Lady Kiritsubo and the consequent prospect that Genji will displace the wife's own son as heir to the throne. There are, however, cases where mentalizing is all but absent, or is surprisingly undeveloped. I'll mention two.

Mentalizing figures in both the *Iliad* and the *Odyssey*, but they differ remarkably in the representation of deception. That notable deception, the episode of the Trojan horse, is not represented in the *Iliad*, though a few remarks seem to presage it; in general, the narration of the *Iliad* contains little to do with deception. By contrast, the horse and other deceptive incidents are recalled in the *Odyssey*, which diligently describes the deceptions of Odysseus' journey and return to Ithaca. As if making up for missed opportunities in the narrative of the *Iliad*, Homer gives a hyper-deceptive accounting in *Odyssey* Book 14 of a remembered cold night at Troy where Odysseus helped a comrade get a cloak by pretending to send him as a messenger. In this narration, Odysseus, in disguise, tells the story in the third person, apparently as part of a ruse to persuade the swineherd Eumaeus to give him (Odysseus) a cloak. Here we have deceptive recounting of a tale about deception for a deceptive purpose.[12]

Also puzzling is the so-called standard version of the oldest substantially complete narrative we have, known as the *Gilgamesh* epic. Originating around 2,300 BC, the story is in some form very much older than the *Iliad*, the best date for which is around the middle of the eighth century BCE; though the standard version of *Gilgamesh* is represented in tablets from the seventh century BCE.[13] In the standard version there is a good deal of focus on conflict; what is lacking is deceptive behaviour. The friendship between Gilgamesh and Enkidu begins with conflict: Enkidu hears that Gilgamesh is exercising *droit du seigneur* with young brides and rushes off to challenge him. But the contest is purely physical. When the fight is broken off by Gilgamesh, Enkidu acknowledges the other's kingship.[14] Once united, they go off to defeat the terrifying and monstrous Humbaba, guardian of the Forest of Cedars. If this were the *Odyssey* one would expect victory by trickery. Not here. There is a fight, and Gilgamesh prevails, aided by the god Shamash, who blinds Humbaba with fierce winds (2003b: 609). Once again, the outcome of conflict is determined by agency, but it is agency which produces its *telos* by brute force: 'by your strength alone you slew the guardian' (2003b: 269).

The standard version is not wholly without behaviour that involves mentalizing. Enkidu's desire for the woman Shamhat is used to bring him to Uruk, and

---

[12] On some of the complex relations between Odysseus' stories in Book 14 and the *Odyssey's* perspective on Iliadic morality, see King (1999).

[13] For dating of the *Iliad* see Altschuler et al. (2013). For a translation and reconstruction (on which I rely) of the standard version of *Gilgamesh*, together with the related Sumerian poems see George 2003a. George 2003b, a most impressive work of scholarship, documents, translates and provides an historical introduction to the Akkadian sources.

[14] See George (2003b: 565).

when Gilgamesh and Enkidu are dealing with Humbaba they determine to kill the monster before the god Enlil knows about it; 'the gods could be angry with us' warns Enkidu (2003b: 611). But the first of these examples is not one of deceptive behaviour while the second—involving just the withholding of information—is a rudimentary case, as is the suggestion 'let us startle him in his lair!' (2003b: 199).

It is tempting at this point to suppose that we are seeing, with the standard version, the first thin shoots of mentalizing as a theme in story-telling. Not so. The story I refer to as the standard version of Gilgamesh is recorded in Akkadian, a Semitic language, and known from tablets prepared by the order of King Ashurbanipal (668–627 BCE) at Nineveh.[15] But stories in this tradition are much older. In particular, there exist in Sumerian, a still somewhat obscure language, poems the written versions of which probably originate at the time of King Shulgi (2094–2047 BCE) at the southern Babylonian city of Ur. One of these poems, *Bilgames and Huwawa*, exists in two known versions. Here Enkidu is the servant of Bilgames (the later Gilgamesh) and they, together with the young men of Uruk, journey to the Cedar Mountain to confront the monstrous Huwawa (the Humbaba of later versions), whose strength lies in his possession of seven 'auras', 'the radiant numinous powers that protect him' (2003a: 144). In this story Bilgames tricks Huwawa into giving away all his auras on the promise of a marriage alliance and other gifts:

> 'Give me one of your auras of terror, and I will become your kinsman!'
> His first aura of terror he [Huwawa] gave him.   (George 2003a: 151)[16]

Once relieved of the auras Huwawa is subdued by Bilgames, who, 'like a snake in the wine harbour . . . followed behind him and, making as if to kiss him, struck him on the cheek' (153). Huwawa responds by calling Bilgames a 'deceitful warrior'; in the second less-complete version Huwawa elaborates: 'O warrior, you deceived me, you laid your hand on me, though you swore an oath to me' (160). Bilgames' deception is not very subtle and it's not clear why Huwawa would have believed him, but this is certainly victory by a strategic route.

In another of these Sumerian poems we have an intense episode of attention to the mind of another, where an agent plans victory not by force but by the installation of fear in the opponent. Here the city of Uruk is threatened by King Akka of Kish.[17] Bilgames calls on Enkidu (again in the role of a servant) to 'make ready the equipment and arms of battle'. But the point is not to win a physical struggle. Bilgames wants these arms to 'create terror and a dread aura [auras again] so when [Akka] arrives fear of me [Bilgames] overwhelms him, so his good

---

[15] Nineveh was sacked in 612 BC; the smashed clay tablets were discovered in the 1850s.

[16] Further page numbers in the text are to this volume.

[17] Bilgames and Akka, in George (2003a), especially p. 141.

sense is confounded and his judgement undone' (141). The siege progresses in Akka's favour and Bilgames sends a warrior to speak to Akka and announce Bilgames, whose 'aura overwhelmed the old and the young' (142). Bilgames does prevail over Akka, though what if any deception is instrumental in this is unclear. Awareness of mental states is certainly a central theme here.

Interpretation of these narratives is hampered by incomplete manuscripts and limits to our understanding of the languages, especially the Sumerian. But based on what we have, things are puzzling. We can say that the ideas for a strategically elaborated version of *Gilgamesh* were in place more than four thousand years ago.[18] But the standard version, which seems, from the number of manuscripts discovered, to be the most successful, has very little focus on mentalizing by comparison with the text of a much earlier period.

If evolutionary thinkers are right that the capacity to mentalize was selected for in the highly social and competitive environments of our much more distant ancestors, it is possible that many of the stories those ancestors told around camp fires a hundred thousand years ago were replete with mentalizing. The connection between stories and the evolution of mentalizing is the subject of Section 7.4.

7.4 Explaining the representation of mentalizing

What is odd about the Gilgamesh story is that its evolution seems to show a loss of the kind of content we might otherwise regard as vital: the deceptive manipulation of mental states. Still, mentalizing, and especially mentalizing that is deceptive, is very common in the world of made-up stories. Why? We need the familiar distinction between proximal and distal explanations. An obvious proximal explanation for why mentalizing appears so often in fiction is that readers enjoy fictions with this feature, so fictions, which must compete for a readership, tend to possess it. A variant of this explanation suggests that mentalizing is not itself a desired feature, but is a feature necessary for the presence of other features which are desired. One might argue that it is a desirable feature of a fictional narrative that one be able to understand what is happening in the narrative, and this requires that the narrative must import into its story a great deal of real-world background; the less we can assume that the agents in the story are like real people, the less of a grip we will have on why they act as they do. While the presence of mentalizing in fiction does aid intelligibility, I doubt whether this is the only or primary reason for its presence; there are so many fictions in which one person's understanding of another's mental state plays a highly salient role, often acting as

---

[18]   For other tales of deception in Sumerian see *Inana's descent to the nether world*, http://etcsl.orinst. ox.ac.uk/section1/tr141.htm; for deception in Akkadian literatures see Gurney (1956). Thanks to Andrew George for these and other references.

a way of winning the reader's attention at the beginning of the plot. *Morte d'Arthur* and the *Tale of Genji* have already been cited. We are particularly intrigued by persons currently at odds who, we predict, will come to realize their mutual affection, by seekers of revenge, and by those who uncover hidden motive. We sometimes delight even in agreement, but usually against a backdrop of dispute. *The Spoils of Poynton* hooks us in at first by representing Fleda Vetch and Mrs Gereth as in agreement about the ghastly aesthetic of Waterbath, an agreement that is significant because it signals the beginning of their alliance against the terrible Brigstocks.

There is work to be done at this proximal level of explanation: figuring out which kinds of situations of mentalizing readers are most attracted to, how that attraction informs and guides readers' understanding of character and plot, and how, exactly, one should characterize the pleasures involved. But we will not always be content with a proximal explanation. When people gain a nearly universal satisfaction from some activity—particularly where that activity has no obvious immediate practical benefit—we may ask whether there is some deeper explanation for their preference. At this point we seek a distal explanation for the representation of mentalizing in fiction. It is important to see that several strategies for explanation are possible with, unfortunately, little evidence to help choose between them. One is to look for some adaptive advantage conferred by a taste for fictions which represent mentalizing. In Darwinian terms, such an advantage would be manifested in reproductive success.[19] It has been suggested that fictions of this kind provide opportunities for audiences to develop mentalizing skills, so useful in the management of relations with others. Sarah Worth claims that 'fiction does help to develop theory of mind'.[20] Matthew Keiran suggests that fictions of certain kinds cultivate fine-grained mind-reading capacities:

> We do not just learn that servility can be self-serving but, in doing so, exercise and cultivate the more general ability to see how the tone and nature of particular outward actions can be revelatory of certain character traits.   (Kieran 2013)

---

[19] There is now a literature which connects our interest in the characters, plots, and forms of literature with the circumstances of our evolutionary past. Notable contributions are Boyd (2009); Carroll (2011); Gottschall and Wilson (eds.) (2005). One question thrown up by Darwinian accounts of fiction is what if any evolutionary precursors our attraction to fiction had; Boyd suggests that it developed out of adaptive play in animals; see Verpooten (2011) for criticism. A tendency to be captivated by fiction might be biologically inherited now in our species but have started as something culturally acquired. If fiction started life as a cultural phenomenon but conferred advantages on those who had a tendency to engage with it, there would be a selection pressure to Baldwinize the trait, thereby bringing it under genetic control (see Papineau 2005)

[20] Worth (2017: 183). See also Mar and Oatley (2008). Nussbaum at one point suggests a metacognitive advantage conferred by fiction: 'If Proust is right, we will not understand ourselves well enough to talk good sense in ethics unless we do subject ourselves to the painful self-examination a text such as his can produce' (2001: 2).

If mentalizing skills are important for survival and reproductive success, those who found pleasure in fiction might have improved their reproductive chances by indulging their tastes, thereby contributing disproportionately to the genetic make-up of the next generation, spreading the taste further.

This is a story about how the taste for fiction was selected *for*. Not all selection is selection for. Natural selection gave the polar bear a heavy coat, but nature did not select for heaviness; it selected for warmth and with warmth comes heaviness. Warmth was selected for, and hence was adaptive, while heaviness—a disadvantage—was merely selected.[21] A taste for fiction might have been a similar by-product, selected but not selected for. Isn't that an unlikely scenario, given the current evidence that exposure to fiction improves mentalizing skills? We will see that the current evidence is not very strong.[22] But even if it were, evidence of a present tendency of fiction to improve mentalizing (and that's the only evidence we are likely to get) is not automatically evidence that this had anything to do with the emergence and stabilization of practices of fiction making in the evolutionary past. Heaviness might one day confer an advantage on polar bears; suppose that global warming means that bears have to float from place to place on blocks of ice, and that heavier bears make for more stable floating (this advantage holds until the blocks get very small, and heaviness becomes a disadvantage again). We have no idea what sorts of fictions were available in early prehistory but they were surely very unlike the written or visually enacted fictions which crowd our lives today; we should not expect the effects of fiction to be invariant under such radical change. While much very recent literature does contain complex and often ambiguous representations of interlocking mental states we cannot be confident in projecting this back one hundred thousand years or more and declare it to be the proper function of fiction. Nor does looking at 'ancient' literature like the *Odyssey* or *Gilgamesh* help much; these are, by evolutionary standards, contemporary works.

What reasons are there for thinking that a taste for fiction was a by-product rather than an advantage-conferring trait? I suggest two reasons: (1) there is something intrinsically unlikely in the selection-for hypothesis; (2) there is a plausible account of fiction's emergence that does not depend on the idea of selection-for. Let's take these in turn.

The idea that we needed then, or need now, fiction in order to practice mentalizing sounds odd if we assume that the interpretation of speech of any kind requires the exercise of mentalizing skills. The idea that verbal communication is code-like, with hearers applying only semantic rules and not any kind of pragmatic inference to what they hear is now unpopular, with plenty of evidence

---

[21] The example is due to Jackson (1982) who is thinking about an entirely different problem. For the selection-of/selection-for distinction see Sober (1984).

[22] See below Section 11.5.

around for a role for pragmatic inference not merely in working out what is implicated by what is said, but in working out what is said itself. I have already referred approvingly to the idea that human languages are not built to fully express what speakers mean; given that this almost never happens, building language to meet this specification would be a case of improbable over-engineering.[23] Assuming that fiction did not emerge prior to the development of language it looks as if there were massive and unavoidable opportunities for mentalizing practice available already in the day-to-day environment of any linguistic community. And if, as some suppose, language emerged as a medium for gossip, much ordinary, non-fictive communication in language would have been about matters at higher levels of mentalizing: what that person over there thinks about your recent quarrel with their brother.

It might be that fiction provided a particularly valuable form of practice not otherwise available. We are hampered here of course by not knowing what fiction—stories told round the fire presumably—would have been like at this period and whether indeed they contained a great deal of mental content. If the early versions of the *Gilgamesh* epic are our best guide the conclusion ought to be that while mentalizing and even deceptive content is present its amount and complexity is not great: the story, even in its most deception-focused version, provides no real puzzles to solve when it comes to what agents think and want. Things have become very different by the time of the *Odyssey*; it is extremely puzzling as to why, as noted above, Odysseus is engaging in his lengthy and convoluted deception of the swineherd Eumaeus in Book 14; the same book provides the first known record of irony, the understanding of which is a comparatively complex mentalizing task.[24] But by this stage in literary history we are, as already noted, into recent times by the standards of human cognitive evolution.

But what sort of plausible account could we give of the emergence of mentalizing fiction that is not a selection-for account? Here is one. Just as our highly focused attention to sexual characteristics makes erotica and pornography possible and popular, so our attunement to motive makes for the attractiveness of the literature of love, rivalry, and misunderstanding, which is virtually all the literature we have. Both erotica and mentalizing fiction give easy access to satisfactions otherwise not easily attained. Mind-reading is a capacity we have been granted, in modest degree, by Darwinian natural and sexual selection as a response to the problems of cooperating and competing with others in intensely social environments. But in the wild, mind-reading is hard work, gets limited results, and may fail altogether because our target is cannily deceptive about her intentions. Responding to this thought, one might argue that much of what goes on in literature and in linguistically mediated fiction generally can be understood as

---

[23] See above Section 5.1.
[24] See *Odyssey*, XIV.402–6. On irony and mentalizing see my (2010b: Chapter 8).

providing us with a fantasy of insight: a world in which we are able with ease to monitor the thoughts, and hence the plottings and defections, of others. Many fictions simply tell us, or make it clear in indirect ways, what some character thinks and wants, sometimes presenting what appears to be a direct view of an agent's mental processes. And fiction has the additional advantage that the teller of the tale is not functioning as a mere testifier to events—someone who might be mistaken—but as the agent who determines what is true according to the story. In real life we never meet such helpful and illuminating agents. Fictions, or most of them, provide us with an easily won certainty about mental states that ordinary experience could never provide. This raises the concern that our ability to penetrate deeply into the minds of fictional characters may provide a misleading picture of mind-reading 'in the wild', generating an unrealistic confidence in our ability to understand others. There are similar misleading pleasures available in film and television; though they provide fewer opportunities for the direct display of inner states, their ability to concentrate on visual detail makes them tempting vehicles for another kind of fantasy-of-understanding: the easy reading of expression. As Lisa Zunshine has pointed out, facial expressions are in real life often very ambiguous and are easily misunderstood; visual media of narration often provide us with characters whose expressions are pleasingly but unrealistically revelatory of their inner states.[25]

So it is possible that a preference for mentalizing fiction confers no advantage when it comes to mentalizing and never did, that it is a product of Darwinian forces, but that it is the by-product of some other adaptive development rather than an adaptation.[26] It is also possible that, having emerged as a by-product, it came later to serve adaptive ends; stories are often said to promote identification with a group and encourage sacrifice for other group members. Thinking in this way we might offer an account of the advantages of fiction-reading parallel to the account of religion due to Atran and Henrich, who suggest that while a tendency to religious belief is a by-product of biological evolution, the tendency has been exploited by social groups to enhance and maintain solidarity. Fictional narratives about people sharing, or not sharing, mental states might have undergone the same functional development.[27]

Conversely, it is possible that a taste for mentalizing fiction was selected for, but that this preference is no longer an advantage. Consider the analogous preference for sugar in the diet. It is suggested that this preference was adaptive in the

[25] See Zunshine (2012).
[26] It's very plausible, for example, that the imagination evolved as a planning tool (see below Chapter 8). Once you have that ability you have all you need to enjoy fictions, when available.
[27] Atran and Henrich claim that 'cultural evolutionary processes, driven by competition among groups, have exploited aspects of our evolved psychology, including certain cognitive by-products, to gradually assemble packages of supernatural beliefs, devotions, and rituals that were increasingly effective at instilling deep commitment, galvanizing internal solidarity, and sustaining larger-scale cooperation' (2010: 20).

environment of evolutionary development because small quantities of sugar are desirable for health, and at that time sugar was very hard to come by; a strong preference for sugar therefore drove people to seek out this hard-won and useful substance. But in our sugar-rich environment, this same preference is very disadvantageous. Conceivably, fiction is like dietary sugar, highly advantageous in small quantities and something to which we naturally turn, but also something which, in our fiction-overloaded present, is turning us into mentalizing couch-potatoes who prefer the easy option of understanding characters in soap operas rather than doing the hard work of understanding each other.

Finally, a maximally pessimistic combination of these ideas gives us the suggestion that fiction never did us any good so far as mentalizing is concerned; it was and remains a pleasurable distraction. I don't think there is much we can presently say to help choose between this and the other options.

7.5 Conclusions

While fictions may have locomotives or rabbits as characters, recognizably human minds are always the focus of attention.[28] These minds are usually interacting, often in conflict. The reader, a spectator to the conflict, often gets a privileged perspective, able to explore the thinking and feeling of others in ways that ordinary existence rarely allows. Should we conclude that fiction attracts us, in part, because it helps train our understanding of minds: those of others and ourselves? That need not mean that the prospect of understanding is what drives us to fiction; nature tends to give us an appetite for things that are advantageous without our needing to know what the advantages are. It could be so, and there are confident assertions out there that it is. But there are other possibilities such as 'there is no and never was any such advantage to be derived from fiction' and 'there was but is no longer'. These hypotheses seem to me no worse, on current evidence, than the hypotheses that assert a current benefit from fiction for mentalizing.

With a variety of evolutionary hypotheses at our disposal and little evidence to choose between them, I will turn now to a direct confrontation with some specific claims about what fiction does for our understanding of the world of interpersonal relations. That topic will occupy the third and final part of this book. The next chapter (Chapter 8) starts with a continuation of the evolutionary theme.

---

[28] Nearly always. There are exceptions. *Tarka the Otter* is one, with its resolutely non-anthropomorphizing approach.

PART III

FICTION, KNOWLEDGE, AND IGNORANCE

The four chapters in this part identify some of the problems that ought to concern someone who takes an optimistic view of learning from fiction. Chapter 8 returns us to the workings of the imagination and culminates in a consideration of the idea that fictions constitute or provide imaginative thought experiments not unlike the ones we encounter in science and in philosophy; I am sceptical about that idea. Chapter 9 examines the ways in which the beliefs of an author can be transmitted to the reader via a work of fiction, and the problems of reliability this transmission process generates. Chapter 10 continues that theme of reliability, this time asking what we should make of the idea that certain authors of fiction are to be prized for the wisdom they have and which their works may communicate to us. Finally, Chapter 11 takes a close critical look at what is perhaps the claim now most often heard on behalf of learning from fiction: that it provides opportunities for the development of our empathic skills.

It is easy to characterize the view in Part III as 'disappointingly negative'. Why not argue for something rather than try to knock down the positive constructions of others? Negative theses are often important. How does the atheist argue except by trying to show that God does *not* exist? Atheists will say that they are offering us freedom from an intellectual and emotional encumbrance. And we should not confuse having a negative thesis with the negativism which simply objects to the arguments of the other side. Atheists seek not merely to show that theistic arguments are bad; they offer arguments that conclude with the nonexistence of God. In a small way I think I can claim something similar, though I don't attribute finality to any of my conclusions. And like the sensible atheist I give due weight to the positive arguments of the opposition. I also—and this is a difference between my case and the argument over theism—acknowledge some of the ways in which it seems very likely that we *do* get knowledge from fiction; as I have claimed throughout, a wholly negative insistence that on one ever learned anything from fiction is not plausible. I like to see these chapters as contributing to what we should see as a common cause: helping to distinguish the circumstances that favour learning from the circumstances that make it harder.

Imagining and Knowing: The Shape of Fiction. Gregory Currie, Oxford University Press (2020). © Gregory Currie.
DOI: 10.1093/oso/9780199656615.001.0001

8

Knowledge from imagination

In Chapter 7 we noticed the extent to which fictions focus on thought, desire, and feeling, and particularly on the ways these states in one individual conflict with those in another and on how those conflicts are managed and sometimes resolved. I resisted the idea that in exemplifying these situations, fictions make us better able to understand and to manipulate mental states. I did not there take a stand on how that understanding and capacity for manipulation, such as it is, comes about. In Section 2.3 I argued against the idea that interpersonal understanding is largely a matter of automatic adjustment of behaviour rather than what has been called 'mentalizing'. So I am committed to the view that we manage the interpersonal world by understanding what we and others think and want and feel: understanding beliefs, desires, and emotions. I happen to think, additionally, that this sort of understanding often involves imaginative acts of projection into the situations of others which give us insight into their motives and feelings.

That's a particularly plausible view of how it is that we undertake certain kinds of planning: to see whether a certain course of action and its likely outcome is worth pursuing we sometimes imagine ourselves in the situation of having successfully brought that outcome about and then note how satisfactory or unsatisfactory that outcome seems. As we will see, this has been studied by psychologists under the heading 'affective forecasting'. Such an imaginative project might be called, in some loose sense, a thought experiment and a consideration of the epistemic role of thought experiments is where this chapter is headed. For it has been said that we best understand the role of fictional narratives in learning by seeing them as thought experiments related to those we make use of in philosophy and the sciences.

I start with some ideas about how imagination aids the formation of conditional beliefs which are often important for planning. I then use an example drawn from legal reasoning to illustrate some of the difficulties that this method faces, and to show that the method of imaginative projection has two varieties we will need to distinguish carefully. I then turn to the idea of thought experiments and suggest that they are not, as some claim, disguised arguments, but imaginative exercises of the kind we have seen in action to generate conditional beliefs. Finally I argue that, while we may consider fictional narratives to provide us with thought experiments, there are reasons to doubt that they can deliver the epistemic benefits we enjoy from the kinds of thought experiments we find in philosophy and the physical sciences.

Imagining and Knowing: The Shape of Fiction. Gregory Currie, Oxford University Press (2020). © Gregory Currie.
DOI: 10.1093/oso/9780199656615.001.0001

8.1 Imagination and the updating of belief

Hume said:

> The imagination of man naturally soars into the heights: it rejoices in whatever is
> remote and extraordinary, and runs off uncontrollably into the most distant parts
> of space and time in order to avoid the familiar objects that it has become used to.[1]

The imagination is certainly capable of these things but they are not its most
natural way of operating. Tim Williamson (2016) notes that our ancestors,
walking in the forest, might have set themselves to imagine wolves helpfully
guiding them along the path, but they were better off imagining, as they would
spontaneously have done, the more likely idea that wolves were attacking them.[2]
Those less pleasing imaginings would have put them on the alert for a real and
probable danger rather than absorbing them in a distracting fantasy. Williamson
suggests that imagination was selected for, at least in part, because it helped with
planning, a process that depends on 'leaving the imagination to do its own work'.
And imagination should not merely be a bringer of useful ideas, but a means of
assessing them. We use, Williamson says, the imagination to assess how likely it is
we could cross the stream at this point or climb that tree. Again, this works best
when we let the imagination run free: if I try, I can imagine crossing a stream
which in fact I could not possibly cross; but leave my imagination to its own
devices as I look at the torrent flowing past me and there is a good chance it will
deliver a more realistic answer: me floundering helplessly in the current.

What is happening when you 'leave the imagination to do its own work'? We
might think of the process as a kind of suppositional reasoning. Imagine you flip
the light switch to the on position—what happens next in your imaginative
project? Pretty obviously, the light goes on. You would have to intervene in the
process by making a further supposition (the bulb is blown) to suppress that
natural consequent. Asking what will happen if so-and-so happens, we can
sometimes answer by imagining the so-and-so and seeing what pops up in
imagination. Why is the imagination able to operate that way? Because it enjoys
a free ride on the belief-updating system: the system which helps maintain
consistency and coherence in our beliefs as new information comes in. Belief
updating is a complex business and we don't have a realistic theory about how it
works.[3] One reason for that is what I earlier identified as the 'isotropy'

---

[1] *Enquiry Concerning Human Understanding*, XII, Part 3. Thanks to Peter Lamarque for drawing
my attention to this passage.
[2] See also Langland-Hassan (2016); For the view that reliability in imagining depends on our power
to *constrain* it see Kind (2016).
[3] The most influential theoretical account, though agreed on all sides to be radically incomplete, is
Alchourrón et al. (1985).

characteristic of central rather than modular processing; everything you believe has the potential to change everything else you believe.[4] Thinking about what will happen if I go the party is not a matter of deciding what follows deductively from the single proposition 'I will go to the party'; believing I will go may cause me to believe I will have fun, but only if I believe certain other things about parties in general and this one in particular. And believing I will attend will cause me to cease to believe that I will mark essays tonight, assuming I believe the two things can't be done in the same evening. No doubt limitations of storage and computation mean that I (or my sub-personal processes) can't take into account everything I believe. But belief updating does somehow take cognizance of those of my beliefs more obviously relevant to the new belief.

In some way then, when you get a new belief, change ripples through your system of beliefs, often with results you are not aware of, at least immediately. The mechanisms that drive this process, whatever they are, operate as well on propositions which are merely imagined as they do on propositions that are believed—an unsurprising result given what I said in Chapter 1 about the inferential similarity between belief and propositional imagining. Letting the imagination do its own work amounts here to letting the mechanisms of belief revision work automatically, this time taking imaginings rather than beliefs as input.

This is imagination thoroughly in the service of belief. Indeed, it is likely that a creature with a reasonably sophisticated capacity for belief—one which includes conditional belief—will have the capacity to imagine. We may form conditional beliefs in many ways—via testimony for example. But one likely way is by imagining the antecedent and, as Ramsey put it, adding it 'hypothetically' to our stock of beliefs, then seeing how plausible the consequent looks within that imaginative project.[5] And conditional beliefs are crucial to the process of planning: if I put my foot on that branch I won't be able to get to the branch higher up; if I jump to that stone in the river I'll probably fall in.

It will be as well to emphasize again that this method of planning is heavily dependent on the subject's existing beliefs. If what you believe that is relevant to the conditional is wrong, you are likely to end up believing a false conditional. What will happen if I flip the light switch downwards? My imagining tells me the light will go on. That's because I overgeneralize from my UK experience; as it happens I am in the United States and flipping down will turn the light off. That dependence on prior belief does not make the Ramsey test useless. Does it make it significantly unreliable?[6] Consider a case where getting the answer right is

---

[4] This is not quite Fodor's formulation. See his (1983: 105); see also above Section 2.3.

[5] Ramsey (1929/1990: 143). Jonathan Bennett puts it like this: 'to determine how much credence you should give to (A → C), find out how much credence you attach to C on the pretence or assumption that you confidently accept A' (1988: 517).

[6] We might say that belief updating is conditionally reliable, in the sense that, where the new beliefs generated by the ripple effect are generated via steps that involve only true beliefs those new beliefs will

important and might not be easy. The case is a legal one, an area where conditionals or hypotheticals matter a lot.

8.2 A judgement

In 1936 the Law Lords decided in *Sim v. Stretch* that a libel had not been committed by the sending of a telegram.[7] The plaintiff had persuaded Ms Saville, a cook, to leave a previous employment; the first employers, a couple, turned up one day and, the new employers being out, persuaded Ms Saville to return to them. They then sent a telegram with the message 'E[dith Saville] has resumed her service with us today. Please send her possessions and the money you borrowed, also her wages.' Action was brought by the recipients of the telegram claiming that they were defamed by the suggestion, implied by the statement about wages and borrowings, that they were in difficulty that had led to financial reliance on a servant. The Law Lords, finding against the plaintiff, held that the contents of the telegram did not 'tend to lower the plaintiff in the estimation of right-thinking members of society', this being the new test they set for determining defamation.

How might we make judgements about what right-thinking people will do or believe or feel? The Law Lords did not say. One answer is that we use the belief-updating system to answer the question; we imagine that someone who is right-thinking reads the telegram and see whether, in our imagining, their opinion of the person referred to therein is reduced. Given its heavy dependence on belief, the method is a precarious one in this case. One would need a (largely or approximately) correct theory of how a right-thinking person would react in this situation. I don't know of any evidence that anyone, even senior judges, has such a theory, or indeed any theory on this topic.

Another route would be to ask: If I read the telegram, would my opinion of the person it is addressed to be lowered in their estimation? Perhaps it is more probable that we have a theory of our own likely reactions to the case, than that we have one of the right-thinking person's reaction, though there is too much evidence of ignorance and error of our own psychologies for us to be confident that the theory is correct. Should I make that car journey on icy roads? Yes. After all, I am an above average driver. Most people think they are above average drivers and my belief that I am one is as likely to be false as yours is; conditional reasoning

---

be true. I take the idea of conditional reliability from Goldman (1979: 13), though Goldman does not consider this case.

[7] Sim v Stretch [1936] 2 All ER 1237, 80 Sol Jo 703 (1936) 52 TLR 669. This section is much indebted to Maks Del Mar's 2018; thanks to him for drawing this case to my attention.

is likely to let me down here.[8] So it will, probably, if you ask me whether I will assign equal scores to job candidates whose resumes are equally impressive: very likely if one comes with a name typical for a member of an ethnic minority I will assign it lower marks; no amount of soul searching is likely to tell me that I am subject to bias in this way.

Another route to an answer would be to abandon the belief-updating route altogether and opt for what I will call *immersive* imagining. Instead of imagining *that* I read the telegram (propositional imagining) I might imagine reading it— seeing the words, saying them to myself perhaps.[9] And I might then find that within this imaginative exercise I am starting to feel rather negatively about the person referred to. The suggestion that they borrowed money from a servant is one I feel uncomfortable with; they are, as I would put it, lowered in my estimation. The outcome would not then depend (except in unusual cases) on my having a theory of such reactions, any more than my feeling seasick on a boat depends on my having a theory of seasickness. It is not unreasonable to assume that at least part of what determined the Law Lords' judgement in this case was their having a form of immersive reaction to the case, finding themselves *not* to be disturbed or offended by the imagined news.

Still, this immersive route is no guarantee of a successful outcome, where success means having a reaction the same as that of the right-thinking person. It would have a good chance of success if the Law Lords themselves were right-thinking members of society; their own reactions to the telegram would then give an answer as to what the right-thinking person's reaction would be. If, like me, they were uncaring and negligent or in other ways not right-thinking people they would have difficulty placing themselves imaginatively in the situation of the right-thinking person. You cannot imagine away these sorts of very debilitating traits; you cannot exercise mental powers in an imagined situation that are greater or better than the powers you actually have. You cannot, by imagining yourself able to speak Mandarin, read messages in Mandarin.

Let's suppose the Law Lords in this case to have been right-thinking. A remaining problem is that there might be no one view that all right-thinking people would take, a result that would defeat the application of the proposed test for defamation in this case. The responses of a small number of Law Lords— perhaps resembling each other in ways beyond being right-thinking people— might not have disclosed this disagreement. Also, the Law Lords' treatment of the case makes clear that the relevant right-thinking person is someone with knowledge of conditions local to the community: what might seem lowering to a right-thinking person in one locality might not seem so in another. It is unclear

---

[8] McCormick et al. (1986). For a general overview of these sorts of results see Dunning et al. (2004). I am grateful here to Jonathan Robson.

[9] See above, Section 1.2.

whether the Law Lords had that knowledge, just as it is unclear what that knowledge is. Finally, immersive imagining was supposed to avoid the theory-dependence of the belief-updating route. It doesn't entirely do that, for how we react emotionally depends heavily on what we believe. My beliefs about local conditions (no one round here worries about borrowing money) will be among the beliefs that affect my reaction. The judgement also implied an ability in those making the judgement to distinguish quite finely between the possible intensional objects of their emotional responses. Lord Atkin (presiding) noted that one may react negatively to the telegram because it is an 'exhibition of bad manners or discourtesy', though that is not evidence that it constitutes an 'attack on character'.[10] He did not worry, apparently, that what seemed to him a reaction to the one might actually be a reaction to the other. I will come back to this point.

8.3 The imagination then and now

Amidst this evidence of the fragility of imaginative methods in decision-making we have (what Williamson, I and others take to be) the fact that the imagination is one of those cognitive capacities which emerged under the pressure of selection and so must have made a positive difference to our behaviour.[11] Isn't that a good reason for thinking I over-rate the fragility of imagination? I say no. I don't claim that the imagination is never helpful for decision-making. It may have been particularly helpful for our distant ancestors: members of the species *homo habilis* did not have many exotic options open to them, or the necessity to plan very far ahead or on the basis of little or no knowledge of the circumstances in the imagined situation. If imagination sometimes helped them cross a river, choose a path through the savanna, or climb a tree it may well have paid for itself in Darwinian terms.[12] These are all situations where imagination is likely to be helpful for planning because of strong overlap between the agent's current environment and the situation imagined; the agent does not have to imagine the tree or the river; these things are there visible and imaginative resources may be dedicated

---

[10] The little evidence we have suggests some pessimism about the reliability of imaginative projection in judgements of defamation. Evidence for the 'third-person effect' indicates that people think that messages of all kinds have a greater effect on other people then they do on themselves. Since those making judgements in libel cases are asked to consider, not what they think but what the 'reasonable average person' would think, this result has given rise to concern that there is a systematic tendency to overestimate harm and hence to unjustifiably favour plaintiffs in such cases (See Baker 2008). The third-person effect was first noted in Davison (1983). We see a similar asymmetry in other areas of thinking, as when people assume that their own failings are due to circumstance while those of others are due to defects of character.

[11] That is, we assume that imagination was selected for and not merely selected; see above Section 7.4.

[12] Why pick on *homo habilis*? Living at the time of the transition to symmetrical tools they may have been the first creatures to depend on holding an image of the intended shape in their minds. See Wynn (2002).

to exploring the affordances these things provide. The Law Lords, imagining circumstances that might be outside their experience, did not have that assistance in thinking through *Sim v. Stretch*. It may be that we, with our vastly extended range of options, apply imagination, unscaffolded by perceptual inputs, in ways that are less reliable.

Often of course we do form true conditional beliefs useful for predicting outcomes and planning our own actions. In many day-to-day situations we do have the right kinds of true (or true enough) beliefs to allow belief updating with imagined inputs to form true (or true enough) conditional beliefs ('If I leave the car out overnight it will be iced over in the morning'). And there are many situations where we can trust our own emotional responses to immersive imaginings. Dan Gilbert and Timothy Wilson call this kind of imagining 'affective forecasting' and note that:

> We know that chocolate pudding would taste better with cinnamon than dill, that it would be painful to go an hour without blinking or a day without sitting, that winning the lottery would be more enjoyable than becoming paraplegic; and we know these things not because they've happened to us in the past, but because we can close our eyes, imagine these events, and pre-experience their hedonic consequences in the here and now.   (Gilbert and Wilson (2007): 1351)

Gilbert and Wilson go on to illustrate a range of systematic misjudgements to which affective forecasting is heir. One surprising result is that people are poor at predicting the responses of others, even when they themselves have regularly been in the situation of the other person, in which case one would expect their capacity to put themselves imaginatively in the position of the recipient would be greatly enhanced. Instead:

> Gift-givers expected a positive correlation between how much they spent on a gift and the extent to which gift-recipients would appreciate the gift because gift-givers assume that more expensive gifts convey a higher level of thoughtfulness. Gift-recipients, in contrast, reported no such association between gift price and their actual feelings of appreciation.   (Flynn and Adams 2009: 404)[13]

In general, people tend to over-rate the positive and the negative implications of an imagined outcome, thinking they will be made more happy by a positive outcome and more unhappy by a negative one than is the case. One reason for a general tendency to misjudge responses to negative events is said to be *immune neglect*: the neglect in one's imagining about the future of the coping strategies we

---

[13] Further, 'gift-givers expect unsolicited gifts will be considered more thoughtful and considerate by their intended recipients than is actually the case' (Gino and Flynn 2011: 915).

adopt to insulate ourselves from negative emotion; this may be significant for understanding the widely observed reluctance to disengage from abusive relationships. There is also evidence that the affect we feel (positive or negative) when we experience a situation (and presumably, when we imagine it) 'isn't tied to the representations that produce it' (Carruthers 2011: 136). In other words it is difficult for us to say what it is about a given situation that gives our reaction to it the positive or negative quality it has. People rate their satisfaction with their lives more positively on sunny days than on dull ones, taking what is in fact a reaction to the weather to be a response to other things.[14] Thinking through the case of *Sim v. Stretch*, it might take unusual discrimination to know whether your negative reaction to the telegram was to its defamatory content or merely to it being, as Lord Atkins put is, an exhibition of bad manners or discourtesy.

This last point is important for anyone who cares about learning from fiction. Fictions are, after all, representations, and when we respond to a fiction we are responding to (at least) three things: the events represented, the representation of them and the act of representing them. Fictions which count as literary do so largely because of their representational qualities: their descriptive language, use of metaphor, manipulation of point of view. These qualities serve to foreground the creative qualities of the maker, to which we readers are highly sensitive. Readers end up having hedonically inflected imaginative experiences which are the resultant of three distinct forces: the (fictional) events represented, their representing vehicles, the qualities of the representing agent. Readers cannot then divide those experiences according to the distinct causal histories of their parts and isolate something that is exclusively a response to the events. The often-heard idea that we arrive, through fictional engagement, at an experience which gives us a sense of what some event—unrepresented, owing nothing to authorship—would really be like neglects all this.[15] This point will come up again in our discussion of thought experiments late in this chapter.

What, then should we say about the reliability of the various forms of imagining when it comes to predicting outcomes and our responses to them? We may think about reliability in different ways. We may ask how reliable something is at fulfilling a specific task; imagination is reliable (perhaps) when used to estimate walking-time over a short distance on the flat and without heavy equipment; it is not good at estimating the time taken to walk the same distance with a heavy pack (Decety et al. 1989). Secondly, we may ask how reliable something is across a broad range of circumstances. Taken in an unrestricted form, this is not a useful measure. My car is useless when driven through water, vertically up cliffs or in space, but I don't count this as evidence that it is unreliable. What matters is that it does some good in the environments it was designed for. Perhaps the most useful

---

[14] See Schwarz and Clore 1983. People are able, it seems, to make the segregation if the state of the weather is drawn to their attention.
[15] See above Section 5.3.

generality we could formulate about the reliability of some form of imaginative activity is its reliability in situations Darwinian forces designed it for. Climbing trees, crossing streams and unencumbered walking in open country are plausible cases of actions within that domain.[16] Engaging with the details of a Jamesian plot full of interlocking agents hyper-attuned to each other's mental states may not be.

Now we have some explaining to do. If imagination works well enough only in this narrow range of perceptually scaffolded cases of planning, why are we not disastrous at making much more ambitious plans concerning careers, finance, family and relationships? Perhaps the true extent of our failures in these regions is hidden by our adaptability to circumstance. As affective forecasting research itself shows, people neglect their own adaptability to circumstance and hence over-estimate the negative effects on them of adverse outcomes. If my imaginative planning of the tree climb results in me falling out of the tree when I put the plan into action I know things have gone wrong. But often the failure of a plan evolves slowly enough for us to adjust our behaviour and our expectations. It may be that we are generally bad at planning-by-imagining but adapt, stepwise, to failure, which then does not seem so much like failure after all. Also, a lot of planning is done in other ways. As well as asking how you will feel in this situation you can wonder: What is it morally right to do? What does your spiritual advisor want you to do?[17] What would it be conventionally acceptable to do? Often these questions can be answered without recourse to immersive imagining; one simply asks one's family, or applies some rule of thumb based on experience, testimony or both. We may ask all these questions and settle on a decision that seems the best fit with the various answers. Planning based on these considerations can't be assumed to be infallible, but it may help avoid spectacularly bad outcomes.

For all that, the belief-updating system probably plays an important part in planning, at least over the short term. In helping us to form conditional beliefs it also plays an important role in our treatment of an important tool for knowledge-acquisition: thought experiments (TEs). And the idea of a thought experiment is often said to be the key to understanding how learning from fiction takes place. I turn to this question now.

8.4 Fictions as thought experiments

In philosophy and in the sciences we make good use of TEs. Some of these devices will be familiar to a philosophical audience: the plugged-in violinist of Judith Jarvis Thomson (1971), said to illuminate the case for abortion rights; 'Gettier cases' in epistemology, said to show that mere justified true belief is not knowledge

---

[16] At the other end of the spectrum lie what L. A. Paul calls 'transformative experiences' (see her 2014).

[17] Admittedly sometimes the advisor will need to do some imagining to arrive at the conditionals that will tell her what you should do. But there will also be a stock of rules-of-thumb that are understood to have worked reasonably well in the past.

(Gettier 1963); the variations on the trolley scenario, due originally to Philippa
Foot, highlighting the tension between utility calculations and rights (Foot 1978).
In the physical sciences we have a great many TEs; in very compressed summary
here are three:

> *Galileo's falling bodies*: Aristotle's physics tells us that heavier bodies fall faster
> than lighter ones. Drop a lighter and a heavier body together, connected by a
> cord; assuming the heavier drops faster the cord will tighten and the lighter body
> will slow the descent of the heavier. But the two bodies now constitute one and
> should fall faster than the heavier of the two components. So Aristotelianism
> about falling bodies is contradictory and its negation—rate of fall is independent
> of weight—is true.

> *Maxwell's demon*: A nimble creature opens and closes a door in the wall dividing
> two parts of a container so as to let fast particles through in one direction and
> slow particles in the other; over time the difference in temperature between the
> two parts grows rather than shrinks, contradicting the second law of
> thermodynamics.

> *Einstein's elevator*: A light beam enters a freely falling elevator at right angles to
> one wall; for anyone inside (where conditions are those of special relativity) it will
> move in a straight line across the cabin and pass out through a hole directly
> opposite at the same height. But an observer at rest relative to the light source will
> see the light tracing a parabolic path, since the hole on the other side has dropped
> in the time it takes the light to pass across the cabin. But the same effect must
> occur if the elevator is removed while the gravitational field stays the same. So a
> beam of light in a gravitational field will bend.

My aim in this section is to ask whether the study of these sorts of TEs and their
role in philosophical and scientific knowledge is any kind of basis for understanding the value of those fictions we sometimes point to as the best examples of works
from which we can learn. Some have thought so. Ernst Mach, theorist of thought
experiments and the first to use the expression 'Gedankenexperiment,' said that
'Besides physical experiments there are others that are extensively used at a higher
intellectual level, namely thought experiments. The planner, the builder of castles
in the air, the novelist, the author of social and technological utopias is experi-
menting with thoughts' (1905/1976: 136). More recently Mitchell Green said 'If a
thought experiment in mathematics or physics can be a source of knowledge, it is
far from clear why a work of literary fiction cannot employ a thought experiment
for epistemic purposes' (Green 2017: 49).[18]

---

[18] See also Dadlez (2009: 6): 'literature serves some of the same functions that thought experiments
do in ethics, though often with considerably more effectiveness', and Carroll 2002: 7: '[thought

I am not sure whether Green and I really disagree. His point may be that the success of TEs in science gives us *some* grounds for optimism about the epistemic value of TEs in fiction, thus making a further inquiry into that question worthwhile. All I am doing here then is making that further inquiry. The outcome as I see it is a reduction in optimism.

The extent to which we can claim to gain knowledge from TEs in philosophy and science is unclear and there are strongly divergent views on this topic. There are also strong objections to the idea that philosophy can proceed by way of the sorts of intuitive judgements its own style of TEs brings forth.[19] This ought to be of concern to those who use the fiction-as-thought-experiment argument to support the idea of learning from fiction. While I make no direct attack on scientific and philosophical TEs, I will, at a certain point, suggest that some of the objections that have been raised against the reliability of TEs in philosophy apply with more obviously persuasive force to works of fiction. It is of course agreed that TEs often do not establish anything definitive, at least as originally stated; the right conclusions to draw from Maxwell's demon remain unclear to this day, and considering the violinist's situation was never said to put an end to argument about the morality of abortion. Perhaps the best model for epistemic optimism about TEs is to think of them as steps on a pathway through rational debate, dominated in science by empirical testing and in philosophy by reasoned argument. One worry about TEs in fiction, as we shall see, is that there are no institutions that promote and sustain rational debate in this area and hence no pathway for TEs to be steps along.

One clarification before we get on with the argument. It is common to say that thought experiments are fictions. After all, the ones that appear in science and philosophy are, or seem to be, occasions on which we are asked to imagine a quite specific sequence of events; given what was said in Chapter 1 about the connection between fiction and imagination it would be odd to insist that these things are not 'really' fictions, though they are perhaps not the first things we think of under that heading, and I would certainly not count the larger argumentative contexts in which they occur as 'works of fiction'.[20] And I will not object to the idea that the sorts of fictions this book is focused on—most notably novels, plays, films—are thought experiments, or at least that many are; they do typically invite us to imagine certain specified things and then to respond to those imaginings in ways

experiments] are frequently employed by philosophers to defend and/or to motivate their claims, moral and otherwise. Thus, if these strategies are acceptable forms of knowledge production in philosophy and *if literature contains comparable structures*, then if philosophy conducted by means of thought experiments is an adequate source of knowledge and education, then so should literature be'. But the (by me) italicized clause suggests a reservation on Carroll's part.

[19] See Dennett (1995) and more recently Machery (2017), discussed later in this section. See also Wilkes (1988).

[20] See Section 1.3 above.

that are like the ways it is profitable to respond to the thought experiments in science and philosophy discussed above. So I will not quarrel with the idea that those sorts of thought experiments (the philosophy-science ones) are fictions, and not quarrel with the claim that novels, plays and films are, or provide, thought experiments. What I propose is this: the epistemically exemplary thought experiments we find in science and philosophy have certain features on which their reliability depends, and those features are generally lacking or much attenuated in the kinds of fictions this book is concerned with. What I am questioning is whether the fictions of this book have even the modest reliability we can attribute to thought experiments in the sciences and in philosophy.

I have granted that fictions are thought experiments and vice versa. But I shall be guilty of long-windedness if I constantly compare 'the thought experiments of science and philosophy' with 'the thought experiments of literature'. For ease of exposition I will introduce a temporary stipulation: in the argument in this section I use 'fictions' to denote the sorts of fictions this book is concerned with—novels, plays and films—and 'thought experiments' to refer to thought experiments like Maxwell's demon, Einstein's lift, the plugged in violinist and the various Gettier scenarios. This is just a stipulation, useful for distinguishing between categories of things which are in reality (so I am granting) both fictions and thought experiments. At the end I will dispense with the stipulation and put my conclusion in other, more careful terms.

Views about what happens when we engage in a thought experiment vary widely. One view is that, to the extent that they have any epistemic interest, TEs are to be interpreted as arguments and as such are only as good as the probability of their premises and the degree of support between premises and conclusion can make them.[21] I don't accept this view though it would not be easy to say very briefly why. No matter; we need concern ourselves here only with views about TEs that are of potential help to advocates of learning from fiction. This view—that TEs are arguments—is not helpful; there is little plausibility in the idea that any of us could specify the argument supposedly offered by *Anna Karenina*, and no plausibility at all in the idea that that is how readers have regularly understood it when learning from it, if that is what they have done. The best that could be said might be that if we all treated that novel in a way no one ever has we might learn something from it. This view of TEs is also unpromising from the point of view of helping us understand how fictions might provide knowledge-how or acquaintance, since arguments do not seem to be a good way of acquiring that kind of knowledge.[22] I'll ignore that option.

---

[21] John Norton has developed this idea in a number of publications: see e.g. (2004). Norton's view is generally regarded as somewhat extreme in that he thinks that thought experiments actually *are* arguments (Norton 2004).

[22] Unless the know-how is also a case of knowledge-that (see above, Section 5.2).

In opposition to the TEs-are-arguments position there is a well-known view due to James Robert Brown which will also not detain us: Brown holds that TEs provide us with intuitive insight into laws of nature, conceived as necessary truths; our access to them being the same as the access we have, according to the platonists, to mathematical reality.[23] But for anyone who thinks that fictions provide us with insight into human motivation and conduct this is not a promising pathway, given the difficulty of seeing the truths (at least, the interesting truths) of human motivation and conduct as necessary truths; in any case the appeal to platonic modes of knowing renders this an option not many will take.

There are other views of TEs, too tightly packed in conceptual space for us to be able to consider them individually. We must make do with identifying a rough area of opinion. For a friend of learning from fiction, the more interesting views have it that engaging in a TE is an exercise of imagination from which it is possible to gain at the end ideas which (a) are candidates for knowability—they are not rendered obviously false by the evidence, they seem to be coherent with what we know; (b) are such that the process the TE has taken us through provides some support for them; (c) do not require for their knowability the postulation of philosophically controversial ways of knowing. This third condition is, I grant, more contentious then the other two; you may feel that we can do justice to fictions as TEs only if we go beyond the broadly accepted options; I invite anyone who opposes the arguments below to see whether they can be countered by appeal to more controversial epistemic capacities.

Someone looking for an account of TEs that satisfies our three criteria might draw heavily on what was said earlier in this chapter about ways to get knowledge from imagination. Recall one way: by making an initial assumption, P, we put in motion the process of *belief updating* which makes adjustments in our system of beliefs to accommodate the new member P (though in this case it is not a belief but an imagining). And we can often then find out whether we ought to accept 'If P then Q' by seeing whether Q is an element of the thus updated system. The other way is what I have called *immersive imagining*: we imagine some scenario being played out and are brought thereby to an affective response, perhaps one associated with approval or disapproval of the chain of events being imagined. In the scientific cases briefly described above belief updating seems the natural method; we imagine the demon managing the transfer of particles and simply find ourselves (if things go as Maxwell hopes) imagining the divergence in temperature. For other cases the imaginative immersion account may work better. TEs in ethics may work through belief updating, delivering, say, the outcome 'requiring you to support the violinist would be wrong'. But in some cases, for some people, it seems likely that the process is a less intellectual one. We do get, in the end, to 'it's wrong to require you to support the violinist', but we may get there via a negative emotional reaction that comes when we immerse ourselves in the scenario that involves being forced to stay plugged in.

While both methods are exercises of the imagination, both also involve our actually doing something, where that something has real consequences. As Tamar Gendler says, 'the justificatory force of the thought experiment actually comes from the fact that it calls upon the reader to perform what I will call an experiment-in-thought', something that involves asking yourself 'what would I say/judge/expect were I to encounter circumstances XYZ?' (2010: 38). And for the case of immersive imagining we may add: 'How would I feel were I to encounter circumstances XYZ?'

Gendler emphasizes the way that TEs draw on tacit knowledge—knowledge we do not know we have but which is nonetheless capable of affecting the conclusions we draw—whereas arguments are delimited by their premises and conclusion. How do TEs draw on tacit knowledge? The belief-updating model gives an answer: when we make an initial assumption, P, belief updating takes place and ripples through our belief system; that system of beliefs may then provide an answer to the question whether Q; if we get an answer (we may not) we are in a position to accept or reject 'If P occurred Q would occur'.

But what entitles us to call it tacit *knowledge*? Why not call it tacit opinion? It is one thing to say how TEs work, another to show that their working that way allows them to provide knowledge or, recalling our modest aims for an epistemology of fiction, simply better belief. Gendler's proposal, which she grants is somewhat undeveloped, appeals to a view of Ernst Mach. She puts it this way:

> We have a store of unarticulated knowledge of the world which is not organized under any theoretical framework. Argument will not give us access to that knowledge, because the knowledge is not propositionally available. Framed properly, however, a thought experiment can tap into it, and—much like an ordinary experiment—allow us to make use of information about the world which was, in some sense, there all along, if only we had known how to systematize it into patterns of which we are able to make sense.   (2010: 39)

What reason is there to believe that we have this store of unarticulated knowledge? Mach had in mind an unarticulated capacity to mirror in thought the 'processes of nature in their most general and most striking features' (1919: 28), and we do have a class of TEs which seem to have produced advances in the physical sciences. But it is rarely claimed that fictions give us insight into the world of physics. To be useful to the friends of learning from fiction this idea would have to be extended from the physical realm to that of human thought, feeling, motivation, and interpersonal relations, so often regarded as the area fiction is most apt to illuminate.

I will present a number of arguments to the conclusion that fictions do not perform well in the role of providing TEs in this domain. I start with the weakest, which is no more than a puzzle for advocates of fictions-as-TEs, though I think it is a puzzle they need to respond to. It is this. The flagship cases of TEs that contribute to epistemic progress lie within the domains of moral philosophy and physical science. Suppose someone claims that fictions provide comparably progressive TEs concerning thought, motive, and interpersonal relations. They grant, of course, that there are differences between the TEs of science and philosophy and those we find in the great works of fiction: the latter are much more complex and sustained and in consequence harder to interpret. But if there is a relative abundance of these complex thought experiments in this area why do we not find any of the more elementary kind, more closely paralleling the examples from physics? Academic psychology, which does seriously study human motivation, does not seem to use them. If fictions such as novels and plays functioned effectively as useful TEs, despite all their complexity when compared to the paradigmatic TEs we find in the sciences (often stateable in a paragraph) and despite there being no consensus about where these larger and more ambitious TEs are to be found and what their deliverances are, why do we not find any short, unambiguous, obviously helpful TEs serving as corner stones for thought in social and personal psychology?

Do we not have TEs in psychology? What about Haidt's (2001) imagined siblings who have sex while taking all precautions against pregnancy, having told no one, and suffering no emotional damage in consequence? I grant that this is an imaginative story the point of which is to get from subjects some kind of response. I won't fight over labelling with anyone who wants to call this a thought experiment. But now we need to distinguish two kinds of TEs: the first kind—the ones I have been discussing through this section—are attempts to show us some truth about the relevant domain: that, for example, rate of fall is independent of weight. TEs of the second kind have a different purpose: they are intended to elicit a response which is then in need of explanation. Haight's TE is of the second kind: it purports to show that people stick with their intuitive moral judgement despite the unavailability of any argument to support it, something which Haight explains by offering a theory about the intuitive basis of morality. What I am pointing to here is the absence in psychology of TEs of the first kind, not of the second.

We might call TEs of the first kind insight-providing, and those of the second kind data-providing. The aim of Thomson's violinist TE is to show what is wrong with the inference from the personhood of the fetus to the wrongness of abortion; it aims to provide insight into the nature of an argumentative relation between propositions. The aim of Haight's is to show that people react to a scenario in a certain way, which is then a piece of data that needs explaining. While this distinction between kinds of TEs is a valid one it is also true that categorizing particular TEs as falling into either can be controversial. Thus some have reacted to the violinist TE by saying that there is or may be, after all, an obligation to remain plugged in; if that is true then what most people took to be a TE of the first kind is really one of the second; we need to explain why people say (to the extent that they do say it) that there is no obligation to be plugged in.[24] My argument here does not depend on any judgements about the category to which particular TEs belong. I am simply assuming, for the sake of the argument my opponents want to give, that there are TEs of the first kind in physics and philosophy in order to then consider whether a case is made out for the existence of similar TEs in fiction. If it turns out that all TEs in physics and philosophy are really of the second kind, that project lapses.

The fact that TEs fall into these two kinds should remind us that, like other sources of evidence, their deliverances are open to question. To the extent that we think there are epistemically successful TEs in science and philosophy we should be interested in the features which give them such reliability as they have, and ask whether those features are reproduced in the case of the putative TEs provided by fictions. The rest of my arguments in this section focus on this issue.

My second argument appeals to the notable simplicity that epistemically successful TEs are said to possess and which often helps to generate a robustly convergent response from those exposed to the TE. We would not, for example, think it helpful to add to the Einstein's lift TE a specification of the detailed construction of the lift, the character of its occupant or the motives of the agent who directs the light beam. This is noticed by some who are keen to show we can learn from TEs in fiction. Catherine Elgin says:

> By restricting her attention to three or four fictional families, [Jane] Austen in effect devises a tightly controlled thought experiment. Drastically limiting the factors that affect her protagonists enables her to elaborate in detail the conse-quences of the few that remain.   (Elgin 2007: 50)

Locating success in the smallness of a fiction's canvas would suggest that there is little to be learned from *War and Peace* or other works that create a larger and less well-ordered canvas: not a comfortable result for the friends of learning from fiction.[25] And Austen's method is simplifying only by comparison with these other fictional works, not by comparison with what should be standard for TEs: the brief, much simpler ones that would count as central cases of the genre 'where we are to understand a proposed scenario so that it is as boring as possible' (Unger

---

[24] Peter Singer argues that it would be right to unplug only if the consequences of doing so were better than the consequences of not doing so, which paves the way for an argument that unplugging is the wrong thing to do (2011).

[25] Elgin says that 'in Tolstoy as in Austen, there is a careful selection of incidents, actions, characters and descriptions' (50). But the mere act of selection cannot be proof that what we have is drastic limitation; I can select for your attention the left-hand half of the universe.

1996: 25–6). Her communities are not isolated from external influences such as Frank Churchill, disease, or nationally imposed systems of inheritance. Even fictions on the modest scale observed by Austen generate complexity at least as often and as much as they simplify, presenting the circumstances of social life as more surprising and unpredictable, more packed with incident than they are in reality—witness the improbable marriages of the Bennett sisters to such wealthy and elevated men and the coincidences that bring them all together with Mr Wickham.[26] There are good reasons for that. Fictions of substantial length work by engaging readers, keeping them guessing, having characters act in unexpected ways, subject to conversions of outlook and behaviour rarely seen in the real world, more distinct one from another than real people tend to be, and more resistant to submersion in the flow of events than real people tend to be, their behaviour being often predictable from circumstance.[27]

Concern with complexity in fiction, as I have expressed it here, is a concern with the content of fiction. Fiction's capacity to produce thought experiments is also put into doubt by parallel concerns about the narrative or vehicle of content—my third argument. Writing fiction is an invitation to style: style as authorial voice and as a way of accentuating the response of a reader. We think of style in relation particularly to 'literary' fiction but fictions of any kind with no discernible style rarely gain an audience. And style is an enemy of the kinds of thought experiments that fictions are supposed to offer us: those which explore human thought, feeling, and motivation. As I noted in Section 8.3, we find it difficult to distinguish the sources of our emotional reactions to things: Are we responding to some aspect of the content of the story, or to some stylistic feature of the vehicle of content? Very likely our reaction is to an indissoluble mixture, to content-as-expressed-in-the-vehicle. Philosophical thought experiments that purport to enlighten us on matters of conduct such as those of Thomson, Singer, and others would be regarded with suspicion if they were presented in a heightened style and elaborated over hundreds pages with the artful withholdings of information and garden-path strategies we so often get in fiction.[28] As David Egan remarks, 'None of Thomson's critics allege that the character of the hospital director in her narrative lacks clear motivation or is cliched or two-dimensional.'[29] Fictions can hardly be

---

[26] As Caroline Bingley rightly says, 'with such a father and mother, and such low connections, I'm afraid there is no chance of it' (*Pride and Prejudice*, Volume 1, Chapter 8).

[27] See the literature on situational vs. character-based explanations of behaviour, some of which is discussed in my 2010b, Chapter 11.

[28] For Singer's example of the child drowning in a shallow pool see his 1997.

[29] Egan 2016:146; see also 'the features that make for a good thought experiment often make for a bad story and vice versa' (147). Egan discusses three differences between TEs and fictions which, he claims, undermine what he calls the 'cognitivist' claim that the 'thought-experimental use of literary fictions essentially involves the literary features of the fiction' (142). My argument has a slightly different orientation: I don't understand the cognitivist as one who says that using fictions as TEs requires showing that their literary features (where they have them) contribute to the value of the TE;

expected to function in any way similar to that of TEs when they answer to quite different expectations.[30]

The previous paragraph has already suggested that a strict separation between content-effects and vehicle- or representation-effects in literature is unrealistic: what affects us is content-as-narrated. And while I have granted the narrative innocence of scientific and philosophical TEs, at least as compared with those of fiction, Edouard Machery worries that even the standard philosophical ones induce cognitive errors because we find it hard to disentangle superficial content (which could change without affecting philosophical import) from target (philosophically essential) content, developing this into a point about fiction:

> All philosophical cases have a narrative setting, many of them describe hypo-
> thetical and actual situations in a vivid and lengthy manner, and many are
> presented in a tendentious manner. Just consider Searle's Chinese room
> thought-experiment... the mob and the magistrate case, the last man on Earth
> case, and many Frankfurt-style cases. Incidentally the influence of superficial
> features on judgement shows that it is a bad idea to hone one's moral sense
> against works of literature [footnote omitted]. Their rich narrative content is
> likely to lead judgement astray. Descartes was right to warn us against what we
> may called 'Donquixotism': '[T]hose who govern their own conduct by means of
> examples drawn from these texts ['fables' and 'histories'] are likely to fall into the
> extravagances of the knights of our romances and to conceive plans that are
> beyond their powers'.   (Descartes 1999: 4)[31]

We don't have to agree that philosophical TEs standardly have 'rich narrative content' to worry that the undoubted richness of canonical fiction is an epistemic disadvantage.

Literary works do not always employ these devices; there are works of fiction written in the style of emotionally unengaged journalism. Perhaps these works have the best chance of achieving the sorts of things that ordinary TEs aim at. But

I argue only that such features often compromise their roles as TEs. Still, there is a good deal of overlap between my argument in the three paragraphs above and Egan's and I am indebted to his essay.

[30] Mitchell Green says of Galileo's TE described above that 'there is no reason to suppose that adding literary qualities to this bit of narrative fiction would undermine its epistemic value' (2017: 50). To some degree that may be true, though there are literary tropes (an unreliable narrator, various narrative twists) that would weaken it epistemically. If it is true, I suggest it is because the thought experiment concerns purely physical processes about which we have robust intuitions not easily knocked off balance by aspects of the vehicle of narration. That is a much less plausible claim in the case of TEs that concern moral psychology.

[31] Machery (2017: 119). Machery cites Murdoch and Nussbaum as his opponents, and is quoting from the *Discourse on Method*, trs D. A. Cress, Indianapolis: Hackett Publishing, 1999. Entanglement is one of three 'disturbing characteristics' which Machery says render our responses (including those of philosophers) to TEs unreliable. The others are unusualness and atypicality.

this would be an uncomfortable result for the friends of learning from fiction, casting to the periphery works often cited as paradigms of epistemically valuable fiction: confining ourselves just to writers in English, it would push aside Jane Austen, Dickens, Henry James, Virginia Woolf as well as every dramatist at least since Kyd.[32]

The rejection of style I am advocating here is a limited one. I don't claim that style never aids progress towards knowledge; clarity of style certainly does. The question is whether the distinctively literary styles we associate with canonical fictions make it easier or harder for them to be seen as the epistemically fruitful TEs some claim they are. My answer has been that it makes it harder. Here is an objection to that claim: if thought experiments ask us to imagine things then one thing they may ask is that we imagine something from the point of view of another; and if we are able to do that we may become acquainted with the experiences of that other; be acquainted in other words with what that experience is like. But that requires, or may require, that the fiction present its events from that other's point of view, and stylistic features surely contribute to making such shifts of point of view possible.[33]

The objection is an important one and raises complex issues about the nature and communicability of points of view. At best my response will address the issue partially and superficially. We do sometimes react in a certain way to the scenario provided by a fiction, and think that in doing so we have gained insight into what a certain experience is like. But what should persuade us that this is genuine insight rather than simply our own idiosyncratic response to the imagined scenario? I raised this question in Section 5.3, observing that we can't generally compare our reaction with a reaction to the actual circumstances portrayed. I suspect that, to the extent that people suppose themselves to be having genuine insight in such cases it is because they have confidence in the author's ability to get the scenario right, in the sense of 'leading the reader/viewer to an insightful experience'. But as David Davies notes:

We may find ourselves convinced, in reading a fictional narrative, that the narrator has correctly characterized the affective nature of an experienced situation of a kind that we have not actually encountered. But this may reflect the narrative skill of the author rather than the correctness of our intuitions. Only if the author is, or is rightly believed to be, a reliable source of knowledge as to the affective nature of such an experienced situation—most obviously because she

---

[32] My argument here is similar to Murray Smith's argument that the thought experiments of cinematic fiction are produced for artistic rather than philosophical purposes and that we shall deform and misjudge cinematic works if we conflate these purposes (2006); Smith illuminatingly contrasts the project of Reiner's 1984 film *All of Me* with the philosophical thought experiments of Bernard Williams concerning personal identity.

[33] I owe this objection to Josep Corbi.

has herself experienced the situation in question and is sincere in her communicative intentions—can the claim to derive affective knowledge from the reading
of fiction be supported.   (2010: 66)[34]

I think it is an open question as to whether we can claim to get this kind of
knowledge (what I earlier called acquaintance) from fiction even if Davies'
conditions—the conditions of authorial sincerity and possession by the author
of the relevant experience—is satisfied. But if these conditions are at least necessary for acquaintance (that is all that Davies is claiming here) then TEs surely do
not provide us with acquaintance. For TEs are not supposed to depend for their
persuasiveness on the reliability of their makers. The power of Galileo's falling
bodies TE is exactly its independence from his authority. It is true that Galileo was
a remarkable stylist; with him 'clarity and logic were paramount, but not at the
expense of the explanatory digression, the telling metaphor, the life of the imagination' (Armor 1971: 161). But the force of his tower experiment is in no way
dependent on that style, or any other. Think what you like of Galileo, his literary
genius, his personal reliability, the TE is still a stunning objection to Aristotelian
physics.[35] Certainly, in the sometimes very detailed analyses of TEs in science that
one finds in the literature no appeals to authorial reliability are identified as
contributing to their epistemic force, though one might easily and sometimes
with good reason argue *from* the effectiveness of the TE *to* the epistemic credentials of its maker. And no one has sought to shore up the case for abortion rights
by saying that Judith Jarvis Thomson's views on the subject are reliable.

The theme of authorial reliability is one we will examine in Chapter 9; it will
come up again in Chapter 10 where we will also look briefly at institutional
differences between fiction and the sciences. But there is a point about the
institutional role of TEs that I do not want to delay in making. It begins my
fifth argument. We cannot understand the epistemic value of TEs if we ignore
their role in a larger system of socially organized inquiry. TEs in both philosophy
and the sciences help us to make progress only to the extent that they generate
widely shared and robust judgements about their outcomes. On the assumption
that they do that they are then able to guide a conversation between parties who
share a common purpose: to determine what is a reasonable conclusion on some
clearly defined question such as 'Is a body's rate of fall independent of its weight?'
or 'Is knowledge justified true belief?' While progress in this is never guaranteed it

---

[34] James Young claims that novels can provide 'illustrative demonstrations' of, for example, the
drawbacks of inflexible pride (2001: 69). But illustrative demonstration is a notion he introduces with
the example *showing you the pencil on my table to inform you of its colour*—a process that does not
depend for its effect on your treating me as reliable. The demonstrations in a novel such as *Pride and
Prejudice* are more closely analogous to my drawing you a picture of my pencil.
[35] Are we certain that it is a definitive refutation? Perhaps not: see Schrenk (2004). But attempts to
undermine the force of Galileo's TE do not appeal to his personal unreliability.

is made more likely by institutions of inquiry such as publication in specialist journals, themed conferences, and practices of objection and response within a context of peer-managed argument. For this reason, TEs that turn out not to generate widely shared judgements after all tend to come under suspicion.[36] The situation with regard to fiction seems rather different. I do not know of any evidence for the existence of widespread agreement in response when it comes to the sorts of fictions most likely to be cited as sources of knowledge. On the contrary, my sense is that audiences vary a good deal in their emotional and intellectual responses to fictions of any complexity and that literary scholars focus their attention on developing new and divergent interpretations of literary works rather than settling on some clearly defined question which the fiction might help us answer in a generally acceptable way. I am not offering this as a criticism of fiction or of its audiences and its experts; I am merely pointing out that the practices we associate with fiction do not serve to support the aims we associate with TEs in science and philosophy and that we should therefore not expect to get the kinds of results from fiction that we expect from TEs.

Someone who has considered the institutional aspects of fiction's relation to TEs is Noel Carroll. Carroll emphasizes the importance in fiction of what he calls 'virtue wheels' or artful arrangements of contrasting characters that provoke reflection on desirable and undesirable combinations and intensities of personal traits. He cites the long history, from Greek drama through the mystery plays, the Victorian and Edwardian novels to works of our own day in support of the idea that an educative/clarificatory function is part of 'our literary institution' (2003: 17). I agree that there is a widespread and long-standing practice of regarding certain fictions in this light, one reflected in what Carroll calls 'informal discussions of narrative artworks'. But we need to distinguish between the practice of regarding such works as epistemically valuable—a practice which can perhaps be regarded as an institution—and the existence and functions of institutions designed to see to it that this practice is conducted in an epistemically virtuous way. It is to the absence of institutions of this second kind within the project of literary (or for that matter dramatic and filmic) fictions that I am pointing.

For the better part of this section I have followed my own stipulation regarding 'fiction' and 'thought experiment', using them to refer to distinct classes of things, the one centred around items like *Anna Karenina* and the other around items like Galileo's falling bodies scenario and the plugged-in violinist. We could have called those two classes 'A' and 'B', though that would have made the dialectic harder to follow. Now the arguing is done, let's use the neutral 'A' and 'B' in just that way (A

---

[36] See for example attempts to undermine the power of Gettier cases by showing that intuitions to the effect that these are cases of justified true belief but not cases of knowledge are not invariant across cultures: Weinberg et al. (2001). The Weinberg et al. study has been criticized (see Kim and Yuan 2015) and I take no stand on the facts of the matter. But it is widely agreed that if the evidence for cultural variation is robust there is a problem for the Gettier TE.

for *Anna (Karenina)*-like and B for (falling) body-like). I've argued that there are some reasons for doubting that the epistemic role of things in A could be anything like that of things in B. As I said earlier I am not arguing against the view that fictions are thought experiments and that thought experiments are fictions. All I say is that B-things have epistemic powers within their home institutional context that A-things do not have in theirs. The right conclusion then is not that we cannot learn from fictions, or even that we cannot learn from them by means of their provision of TEs. All that I am claiming is that anyone who argues that fictions are epistemically valuable because they provide TEs cannot use the example of those TEs we regard as unambiguously valuable as support for this claim. They will have to show how it is that the A-things deserve to be called epistemically valuable thought experiments when they are in so many ways different from the B-things which are antecedently agreed to be valuable.[37]

If it is right to think that A-things provide thought experiments with the capacity to give us knowledge—or, more, guardedly, that they are as helpful in moving us in that direction as B-things are—then something is badly wrong with the institutions of knowledge. One of the functions of those institutions is to bring together the various sources of knowledge in ways that enable us to make rational judgements about how well supported any given view is. In academic psychology this is achieved through such measures as the insistence that research papers review the relevant literature, and are themselves subject to peer review. But there are no institutions that help us unite in our thinking the deliverances of, say, social and personal psychology with those of literature; we do not find that reviews of the state of the evidence relating to some psychological question take into account the deliverances of fiction. Nor do we think that writers of fiction who aspire to inform us need be steeped in that psychological literature. This adds some weight, I think, to the earlier suggestion (Section 6.4) that talk of learning from fiction is a kind of pretence: children pretending to be pirates don't bother with the hard work of steering a ship in stormy seas.

In all this we should agree that there are simple messages effectively communicated by fictions which overall have a complex structure and which exhibit many, perhaps all, of the epistemically compromising features discussed here.[38] Despite all the artful distractions of *Madama Butterfly* it is not difficult to draw the conclusion that behaviour like Pinkerton's is wickedly exploitative, while viewers of *The Third Man* will probably come away with the feeling that while Anna Schmidt's loyalty to Harry Lime is to some extent understandable, Holly Martins' betrayal of him was

---

[37] In addition to the idea of fictions as TEs we might have considered here the less-often developed idea that fictions are or provide 'models' somewhat like the models we find in physics, chemistry, biology, and economics. This would have resulted in a rerun of virtually all the arguments I have raised concerning TEs, so in the interests of space-saving and reader fatigue-avoidance I have left this for another occasion (for a preliminary assessment see my 2016).

[38] Thanks here to Manuel García-Carpintero.

justified and indeed required. Conclusions like these are hard to argue with once stated and do not require much support from imaginative engagement. We should not discount such effects entirely, despite the obviousness of the principles involved; as some have argued, the works in question may serve to focus us on an important principle and to provide vivid markers of memorability, though the extent to which they effectively do this and go on to impact behaviour in positive ways is not clear from current evidence. It is when fiction claims to give us signposts to less obvious, more complex and more contestable areas that the arguments I have offered gain their significance. If it is said that the *Golden Bowl* traces a pathway through the complexities of a father–daughter relationship to show how a morally adequate mutual recognition might be achieved, we may worry that artful construction makes the channel of communication unreliably noisy.

8.5 Conclusions

I began this chapter by asking whether evolutionary considerations suggest that fiction's dependence on the imagination gives us grounds for optimism about fiction's ability to deliver knowledge. I say not. We can agree with the evolutionary assumption, and still say there is a world of difference between the uses of imagination prominent in our deep past and the imaginative scenarios provided by the kinds of fictions we have become familiar with. The problems our ancestors faced a million years ago were probably dealt with (to the extent that they could be dealt with at all) by modest imaginative exercises which involved short time scales and high levels of support from perceptual experience: problems to do with hunting, foraging, tool-making, and avoiding predators. Fictions, particularly literary ones, ask us to engage in imaginative enterprises for which the skills of our distant ancestors are entirely unsuited. They provide no perceptual input to go with the situations they describe; they concern the circumstances, activities, and personalities of agents often designed to be attention-grabbing in their distinct-ness from the folk we come across daily; they are representations crafted by agents whose story-telling successes and failures we respond to emotionally, leaving us open to confusion between a response to the situation represented and a response to its manner of representation. It may be that even in these unfavourable situations we are capable of learning from our fiction-guided imaginings. I think the burden of proof lies with those who claim it is so, not with those who deny it.

Chapter 9 starts with an easy win for the learning from fiction hypothesis; there are readily available circumstances in which fictions provide a conduit to transmit the beliefs of an author to a reader, and in many of those circumstances the process will be reliable and may even generate knowledge. But as we move from purely factual beliefs to those with a significantly evaluative component that reliability declines steeply.

9

Fiction, truth, and the transmission of belief

That testimony is a source of knowledge is not in dispute.[1] Historians, journalists, friends, and passers-by offer us testimony; if we take up their offers we acquire new beliefs; if things don't go badly wrong (they sometimes do) we get to know things. Very often what we come to know is exactly what they have told us.[2] We would go badly wrong if we treated fictions in the same way. Someone who took the Holmes stories as the reliable testimony of a certain Dr Watson would end up with some very false beliefs. But we don't have to be making that mistake to think that fictions are sometimes a reliable source of truths. It's a mistake to assume that when Conan Doyle begins *A Study in Scarlet* with:

> In the year 1878 I took my degree of Doctor of Medicine of the University of London, and proceeded to Netley to go through the course prescribed for surgeons in the army

we are being informed by someone of the facts of their career. It would not be a mistake to conclude from Conan Doyle's utterance of the sentence just quoted that the University of London existed in 1878, at that time awarded medical degrees and that Netley was a place where one may be trained to be an army surgeon. None of these things is asserted by Conan Doyle; nor is any of them a consequence or a presupposition or an implication of anything asserted by Conan Doyle because Conan Doyle did not assert what is said in the words I have quoted.[3] He was, roughly speaking, inviting us to imagine that we are hearing from someone who tells us that he did these things and who is, we soon learn, called 'Watson'. The puzzle is how this invitation to imagine should make it reasonable to acquire beliefs about the University of London and about army medical training.

---

[1] This chapter contains some material from a paper written with Anna Ichino (see our 2017).

[2] As indicated above, what they have told us may not coincide with the words they speak; those words may require pragmatic enrichment: 'There's a petrol station round the [next] corner [in the direction you are currently travelling in and within a practical walking distance].'

[3] Here I take 'what is said' in the weaker of two senses identified by Wilson and Sperber (2002, especially Section 2), that is as 'merely expressing a proposition'. In the stronger sense it means 'asserting or committing oneself to the truth of the proposition expressed'.

Imagining and Knowing: The Shape of Fiction. Gregory Currie, Oxford University Press (2020). © Gregory Currie.
DOI: 10.1093/oso/9780199656615.001.0001

I will be particularly concerned with the ways audiences can draw reasonable conclusions, not from what is said but from the saying of it. There are many things I can conclude from your saying 'I have two children'. One, which Grice called a generalized conversational implicature, is that you have only two children; if you had, say, thirteen children it would (in most contexts) have been appropriate to make that clear; since you didn't I assume it is just the two. That is something you intended me to conclude. There is plenty I can conclude that you probably did not intend: that you are alive, that you speak English. I may conclude from your lecture that you know a lot about quantum mechanics, and from your speech to the electors that you value honesty above position. In the former case it won't matter to my concluding this whether I think you intended me to conclude that; in the latter case it will.

These implicatures, so called, are generally studied as part of an inquiry into assertion; on the standard view implicatures are licensed inferences from the making of an assertion which provide us with information (intended or not) that goes beyond what is said. I am pointing out that there are implicatures associated with verbal acts of fiction-making like the one we just noted from Conan Doyle. One of the things we will do in this chapter is to see how they work.

9.1 Beliefs from fiction

It is an obvious truth that fictions affect the beliefs of those who come into contact with them. I am probably not alone in having *War and Peace* as the source of my belief that Russian aristocrats in Napoleonic times spoke French. Systematic studies also reveal this kind of effect, showing that television viewers acquire from the medical drama *ER* enduring beliefs about medical issues, and that readers' beliefs are influenced by statements made by characters in stories—even statements as implausible as 'Chocolate aids with weight loss'.[4] The literature on Transportation indicates that absorbed readers are influenced by the evaluative opinions fictions implicitly suggest, with viewers' opinions on capital punishment influenced by whether they saw an episode of *Law and Order* that focused on successes or failures in the justice system; the effect was more evident for viewers who empathized strongly with characters.[5] Debates ignite occasionally on the responsibility of historical fictions for forming beliefs about the characters and actions of agents such as Thomas Cromwell.[6] Critics and philosophers also speak

---

[4] See Brodie et al. (2001); Gerrig and Prentice (1991); Marsh et al. (2003). Misrepresentations in *Silent Witness* have been said by one pathologist to be 'quite damaging' (http://www.theguardian.com/culture/2011/jan/09/stuart-hamilton-silent-witness).

[5] Mutz and Nir (2010); see also Dal Cin et al. (2004). See above, Section 6.2.

[6] See http://moreintelligentlife.co.uk/blog/maggie-fergusson/wolf-hall-effect#. According to friends of Mantel's project, *Wolf Hall* goes some way to undo the damage done by an earlier fiction: Robert

on behalf of learning truths from fiction, sometimes as part of a more general claim. Iris Murdoch said that 'Great art is able to display and discuss the central area of our reality, our actual consciousness, in a more exact way than science or even philosophy can'.[7]

How should we assess such ideas? Elizabeth Fricker has said that 'looking for generalizations about the reliability or otherwise of testimony...as a homogeneous whole, will not be an enlightening project...[W]hen it comes to the probability of accuracy of speakers' assertions...testimony is not a unitary category' (Fricker 1994: 139). I similarly deny that we can hope for a general account of the reliability of beliefs derived from fiction. Fictions, and the beliefs derived from them are of many different kinds. Moreover, the relations between the fictions and the beliefs are various; they are not all testimonial relations and while some have similarities to testimony others are of an entirely different kind, as we will see. The best I can hope to do here is to examine a few pathways: ones that strike me as commonly implicated in the generation of beliefs from fiction, and to move in an orderly way from cases where the propositions in question are purely descriptive to those where they are, at least in part, evaluative.

In distinguishing pathways from fiction to belief, I'll have in mind the idea that some are more apt to support learning than others. Here I give particular attention to pathways which depend on readers' assumptions, often tacit, of the author's reliability; these are the pathways that are testimonial or related to testimony. Such pathways are, in favourable circumstances, epistemically benign—apt to provide beliefs which are true, justified to varying degrees, and sometimes deserving the title 'knowledge'. They are pathways to belief particularly appealing to the philosophers and critics who have made a case for literature's cognitive value. Before that however, I briefly discuss pathways that are more prominent in the psychological literature, and which are less likely to support the humanistic belief in learning from literature. Before that, some preliminaries.

9.2 Belief change

We have already seen that learning may fall short of the conditions for knowledge; it may even fall short of truth.[8] A better understanding of yourself is not necessarily a true one, and people who come to believe the earth is spherical rather than flat are learning something. *Better* belief is what interests us. If the better beliefs

---

Bolt's *A Man for all Seasons*, with its unrealistically positive representation of Sir Thomas More. While the examples here are taken from a variety of fictional media, I avoid disjunctions like 'literary, filmic, televisual, or theatrical fictions' and refer simply to 'literature'.

[7] Murdoch (1998: 240, from a paper written in 1972).   [8] See above, Section 5.1.

that fiction gives us rise to the status of knowledge, that is to the good. But for our purposes knowledge is not essential.

Some are sceptical that learning from fiction involves change of belief. Noel Carroll emphasizes fiction's capacity to reconceptualize what we already know/ believe, or to make us see its significance.[9] On that view fiction has effects *on* belief but does not produce change *of* belief. But both reconceptualization and enhancement of significance do involve belief-change. Assuming beliefs are propositionally individuated and that propositions have conceptual structure, reconceptualization gives us new beliefs; notably so if it sharpens previously vaguer understanding. Since belief is not closed under deduction, drawing out the consequences of what we believe is similarly belief-generating, while seeing the significance of what we believe involves linking it with known propositions to derive new conclusions. I grant that fiction has effects on belief which don't amount to belief change, such as reminding us of what we believe. But it is hardly deniable that fictions sometimes affect *what* we believe.

As we recognized much earlier, fictions might affect things other than beliefs. There is fiction's supposed capacity to enlarge our skill or know-how; many deny that this enhancement of practical knowledge need involve change in belief (Nussbaum 1990). I'm happy to grant that change in empathic abilities is possible without change in belief, but it is often likely to result in changed beliefs: your sharpened empathic powers are likely to lead you to new thoughts about the lives of others. So fictions that affect empathy are likely to affect belief as well. It is often said that *Uncle Tom's Cabin* brought about significant change in reader's capacity to empathize with slaves. If that is true it is surely in part due to changes in readers' beliefs (in some cases by way of refinement or reconceptualization) about the conditions that slaves endured.[10]

While the claim that fictions produce change of belief is hardly controversial, it can be unclear in particular cases whether we have change of belief rather than some other kind of change. In the next section (Section 9.3) I'll argue that some behaviours elicited by fictions which seem to indicate belief change may be misleading. And something that is highly controversial is the nature of the mechanisms by which fiction affects belief. Belief change may not be the most important cognitive change that fiction is capable of producing, but it may be the most tractable and it is important enough to be worth knowing more about.

For all my emphasis on belief change, there are ways fiction changes belief which I ignore: effects that don't take us far from the fiction itself, or that belong to

---

[9] See e.g. Carroll (1998: 142). See also Gibson (2007: 101–2). Carroll, I think, has in mind only evaluative propositions here; I don't think he would deny that readers of *War and Peace* may form the belief that Russian aristocrats spoke French on the basis of their reading of Tolstoy. For more on evaluative learning see Section 9.6.

[10] For an account of the history of reading the novel through to the early twentieth century see Hochman (2011).

other explanatory projects. We come to believe that it is true according to the story that Holmes lives in Baker Street, because that is what the text says or implies. How beliefs about what is true-in-a-fiction are gained on the basis of reading the fiction itself is a rich topic, since many fictions make these judgements difficult by introducing plot twists and unreliable narrators. But our concern is with the acquisition of beliefs about the real world beyond the story itself. And if reading a fiction causes us to imagine P, we may well form the belief that we imagine P; how we monitor, with some reliability, our own imaginings is a problem I leave to inquirers into metacognition.

Finally, we must recall our discussion in Section 5.1 on what counts as belief change and how it can be identified. To measure the effects that a stimulus S has upon a belief P, psychologists sometimes probe for an estimate of agreement with P, seeking differences in confidence before and after the exposure to S. If a subject moves from a very low confidence-point to one slightly higher, we say she has a raised degree of belief in P, or now believes that P is more likely, and not that she has come to believe P. My talk of belief change covers all these cases: change from not believing to believing and vice versa; change of belief concerning probability; change of credence (where the greater degree might still be very small).

9.3 Murder in the Mall

Psychological studies of transportation, the experience of becoming deeply absorbed by a story, have been taken to indicate fiction-induced belief-change.[11] Psychologists Green and Brock had subjects read a short story about the murder of a girl by an unrestrained psychiatric patient. They found a shift towards agreement (or increased agreement) with propositions suggested by the story: 'The likelihood of a death by stabbing in a shopping mall is quite high'; 'Psychiatric patients who live in an institution should not be allowed out in the community during the day', and 'The world is violent and unjust'.[12] This tendency correlated with self-reported transportation, but—surprisingly—was independent of whether subjects thought they were reading fiction or non-fiction (Green and Brock 2000).

A number of explanations for this and similar results are available, not all involving the assumption of belief-change of any kind. Since a follow-up test was not carried out, one may ask how long-lasting these effects were; other experiments of this kind have found reversion to pre-test attitudes within days or hours, and readers' responses may have been indicative of temporary changes in mood

---

[11] On transportation see Section 6.2.
[12] For the last of these the trend towards agreement was below significance.

rather than of belief-changes.[13] On the other hand, beliefs are sometimes of brief duration.[14] Suppose, then, there was change in belief. One explanation appeals to the *availability heuristic*: a process by which we form beliefs concerning the likelihood of a given event on the basis of the ease with which vivid examples of that kind come to our mind (Tversky and Kahneman (1973)). This is a hard-to-suppress mechanism with distorting effects on belief since it causes us to weigh examples within our own recent experience heavily, when what is really needed is broadly representative data. It is also, as Kahneman and Tversky noted, blind to the distinction between real and imagined cases: people rate nuclear war more likely after having seen a movie depicting it. Readers of *Murder at the Mall* may similarly have raised their estimates of the incidents of violent attack on the basis on the vivid though fictional example the story presented.[15]

Green and Brock do not consider the explanatory value of the availability hypothesis, developing instead a theory of Dan Gilbert's: we believe everything we hear/read, and disbelieving means ridding ourselves of a belief already acquired, something that takes effort; for various reasons that effort is not always forthcoming. Engagement with a story is one such reason: the story absorbs the reader's attention, and the absence of an assertoric voice makes us less prone to critical assessment; epistemic vigilance is lowered and appropriate processes of belief rejection are not activated.[16] On this model belief-acquisition is relatively automatic, and belief-acquisition from fiction is notable for the absence of the second, reflective, process of assessment. So the argument goes.[17]

Even if it were true that, as Gilbert puts it, 'we cannot *not* believe everything we read', this wouldn't explain why subjects came to believe that psychiatric patients should be confined, since no such statement occurs in the text of the story. In many such cases the relevant propositions are not even directly implicated, but only loosely suggested by the story; that is how it is with *Murder in the Mall*. How then does the reader hear in the story the implication about confinement? An obvious answer is that readers are inclined to infer that the author believes that patients should be more closely controlled, because the story is more plausibly a product of someone with that view than of someone without it. Readers may go further, concluding that the author intended them to understand that he or she

---

[13] See Hakemulder (2000). Mutz and Nir (2010: 211) say, 'We can provide no evidence as to the longevity of the effects that we have observed.'

[14] Sullivan-Bissett and Bortolotti (2017) argue that the burden of proof lies with those who deny that such short-lived states are beliefs (167). I say there is no generally applicable burden of proof; a case where there is reason for thinking that new evidence has become available should be treated quite differently from a case where the state has come and gone without any such evidential change.

[15] Heuristics are also appealed to as explanations of the effects of television viewing on people's overestimations of the occurrences of crimes, marital discord, etc. (Shrum et al. (1998)).

[16] See Green and Brock (2000: 703), citing Gilbert et al. (1993).

[17] For other uses of the Gilbert model as an explanation of belief from fiction see Prentice and Gerrig (1999); Marsh et al. (2003), Marsh and Fazio (2006).

held this view and that the story was a way of making that intention succeed. They might also take the author's belief in the proposition to be evidence for its truth, and come to believe it themselves. It might happen in this way or some other, but it can't happen via Gilbertian belief acquisition. And anyone who thinks it does is going to have a hard time explaining why readers don't end up believing all the things actually said in the fictional stories they read (like Watson's having trained at Netley) where absorption of attention and lowering of epistemic vigilance are in place as, according to the argument, they normally are. People are not so credulous.

Perhaps Gilbert's model works better to explain cases of fictions' influence where readers come to believe general factual statements explicitly presented as true according to the story and providing background information on geographic, historical, or scientific facts. Even here I take Gilbert's model to be implausible, given the pragmatic processing generally required to decide what proposition to believe when we read general statement which, like others, are rarely if ever fully explicit (Sperber et al. 2010). 'Everyone cheered the Emperor', said in a novel set at the Battle of Austerlitz, will not provide you with the belief that every person in the whole world cheered on that occasion. You might acquire from this the belief that most people (perhaps within some vaguely specified group) present on that occasion cheered. But if that's what you believe you must have done some pragmatic processing of the utterance 'Everyone cheered the Emperor' *before* the new belief was acquired. In general there must be a system of pragmatic processing involving inference about mental states prior to the insertion of any proposition into the belief box: before such pragmatic processing takes place, we don't know what proposition to insert.[18]

I've argued against Gilbert-style automaticity of believing. If I am mistaken about that it would be no victory for believers in the cognitive value of fiction. Recalling what was said in Section 5.5, a sensible advocate of learning from fiction will emphasize fiction's role in creating a thoughtful, critical, and imaginative attitude rather than simply being a mechanism for drip-feeding beliefs into the mind. Pathways to belief opened by such things as the availability heuristic and failure of vigilance are thus not likely to appeal to the literary and philosophical advocates of learning from fiction. Those advocates do not seek to show that cognitively valued works of literature depend on reason-defying heuristics or on the suppression of opportunities for rational reflection. The humanistic tradition holds literature to be cognitively valuable on account of its (supposed) capacity to promote a reasoned and reflective exploration of our moral, social, and psychological worlds, where part of the material for that reflection is our affective

---

[18] See Origgi and Sperber (2000). On some of the complexities involved in making inferences from what is true-in-the-fiction to what is factually true of the real world, see below Section 9.4.

engagement with fictional characters and situations.[19] I will focus in the rest of this chapter on pathways that allow rich opportunities for reflective thought, the elaboration of reasons, conscious engagement with the details of plot, narrative, or style, and with the personality which lies, or seems to lie, behind it.

As indicated in the discussion of Gilbert above, my particular interest is with cases where the reader's acquisition of a belief depends on their view of the author's reliability. We often form our beliefs by taking people's behaviour as indicators of their opinions, which we then embrace. Beliefs thus formed do not always depend on assumptions of reliability: your assertion that life is meaningless may simply bring this idea to my attention, with me then finding my own reasons for believing it. But often, when we come to believe a proposition that someone else believes, it is partly because we have confidence in her opinion. Plausibly, this is true also in some cases of fiction: readers take the way the work is written to indicate something about the author's serious beliefs, they have some confidence in the reliability of those beliefs and hence some confidence that the propositions believed are true.

I treat two sub-cases separately, distinguished by their subject matters. In Sections 9.4 and 9.5 I examine the acquisition of beliefs concerning purely factual and relatively uncontentious aspects of the real world such as the location of London landmarks and the outcome of the War of the Spanish Succession. After that I examine beliefs concerning at least partly evaluative and often controversial matters such as the nature and value of loyalty and obligation, love and friendship.

9.4 Truth, and truth in fiction

I earlier expressed my own conviction that I gained knowledge from *War and Peace*. The possibility is, it seems, officially recognized; the *Katie Morag* stories by Mairi Hedderwick are used in some junior schools to teach island geography. While learning of this kind is common it is not obvious how it happens. It is not generally the case that authors convey factual information by moving out of the pretence-mode of utterance they occupy when they tell us about the thoughts and doings of the characters; if an author writes of her fictional character:

Walking across Trafalgar Square to The National Gallery, Jane realized that she did not love Manuel

she is not asserting anything about London geography any more than she is asserting that the character was walking, thinking or existed; the proposition in

---

[19] I do not claim that processes of belief formation that bypass rational reflection are universally to be deplored or that they never result in knowledge (for a particularly strong defence of the respectability of such processes see e.g. Gigerenzer and Gaissmaier (2011). See also below, Section 11.2.

question is offered as something to be imagined.[20] Yet readers with no inclination to believe in Jane or Manuel may well come to believe (truly) that The National Gallery is on or near Trafalgar Square. For works in some genres, readers would be justified in believing this, and would regard the author as at fault to some degree if it turned out to be false. Readers might even be justified in believing it if the statement was put in the mouth of a character. Readers of Iris Murdoch's *Under the Net* may come to believe (not unreasonably) that there is such a place as the Wallace Collection in London and that it possesses a portrait by Hals on the basis of what is said by the character-narrator Jake Donoghue, though Jake shows signs of unreliability on other matters; 'money means nothing to me' he says at one point.

I start from the assumption that ideas about London geography, Scottish islands, and Russian history are established by the author in the first instance merely as *true-in-the-fiction*, and that there are processes of plausible inference available to suitably prepared readers which enable them to infer from 'P is true-in-the-fiction' to 'P is true', for some propositions P and some fictions.[21] A complete taxonomy of such inferences would be hard to provide. I describe here one inferential pattern I take to be common and important and where the ascription of serious beliefs to the author plays a key role.

It is uncontroversial that what is true-in-a-story and what is true tout court typically overlap strongly, though different genres have different rules about where overlap with real-world truth is to be expected; fantasy stories allow magical forces but discourage (to some extent) psychological unrealism, as well as extreme coincidence.[22] Here, briefly, are some (increasingly speculative) suggestions about why this is.

The first, most obvious and least controversial is *communicative economy*: authors could not make explicit everything that is true-in-their-stories and do not need to as long as they can count on readers assuming that, where there is no good reason to think otherwise, what is true is also true-in-the-story. That way authors do not have to tell us that their characters have arms and legs, breathe air, and depend on food and rest for survival. The second is *creative economy*. If Elster (2000) is right that creativity is a matter of maximizing value subject to constraints, insisting on a large measure of conformity to real-world truth is a natural and effective way of constraining, and thus encouraging, literary creativity. A third

---

[20] It may be fictional that the author is asserting these things. Lewis says that 'Storytelling is pretence' (1978: 266). Perhaps we should think of authors as creators not merely of the fictions they tell, but as creators of fictions about their telling of it.

[21] As a reader reminds me, the reverse inference is common: we infer that it is true in *Bleak House* that London is in England because it is true that London is in England. Such inferences, in both directions, are defeasible.

[22] Arguably many fantasy stories are psychologically unrealistic. Perhaps we should say, more guardedly, that they are not generally less realistic by the standards of ordinary opinion about what constitutes psychological realism than other genres.

is that by so conforming, writers increase the likelihood that readers will be imaginatively and emotionally engaged ('transported') by their work. The imagination, I have assumed, is an evolved capacity which throve because it enabled us to survive and reproduce.[23] It is then unsurprising that the imagination is highly tuned to scenarios which are in significant ways plausible; we find it easier and (perhaps in consequence) more satisfying to imagine the unfolding of physical and psychological processes of kinds we do or might encounter than we do processes which are ecologically deviant. There are spectacular exceptions to this with tales of magic and the supernatural and our attraction to these ideas is itself the subject of much theorizing. Our facility with imagining such things is presumably a product of the ever-expanding stock of imaginative memes created by culture and retained through human imitative tendencies; in the environment where imagination evolved imaginative activity was probably much less inflated.[24] And studies of folk-conceptions of religion and related phenomena indicate that these ideas are highly constrained by features of the natural world; deities officially conceived of as all-powerful are represented in normal thinking as limited to managing one task at a time (Barrett and Keil 1996); trolls, goblins, and witches have very limited supernatural powers and their motivations are explicable in folk-psychological terms. Finally, a preference for a high degree of conformity to truth would be explicable if fictional stories emerged and flourished partly because they were a way of conveying factual information. The way last week's hunt, with all its confusions and mistakes, was conducted might not be the best guide you could provide for trainee hunters, and anyway no one is now certain about exactly what happened. An invented episode may do a better job, as long as it respects the likely behaviour of prey and the real efficacy of weapons. A general preference for verisimilar fiction would then help to make verisimilitude an adaptive feature of fictional stories, and a cause of our having fiction as an enduring feature of social life.[25]

Note that once it is in place, and for whatever reason, the expectation of conformity to truth will be strongly reinforced because gratuitous violations of it will have communicative costs. In fiction there is something similar to the Principle of Relevance in Sperber and Wilson's neo-Gricean approach to communication. Sperber and Wilson (1995) argue that communication is governed by

---

[23] See above, Section 8.3.

[24] Paul Harris (nd) maps a developmental pathway from the highly reality-constrained imagining of young children to the more fantastical imaginings of older children and adults, doing much to undermine the popular idea that young children are spontaneously attracted to magical ideas.

[25] Note that these reasons for fiction's conformity to truth need not be reflected in the thinking of readers or writers. Perhaps neither group understands all or any of these principles; perhaps some are understood to a degree but are hard to articulate. They are meant as explanations for why people expect fiction to conform to truth, and why they prefer that it does so, not as reasons people would or could give to justify their preferences and expectations. (See also remarks on the reality-orientation of imagination in Williamson (2016: 114); on the pedagogic role of narrative in hunter-gatherer societies see Sugiyama (2017).

the assumption that the cognitive value to the addressee of a communicative act will be such as to make worthwhile the effort of processing it; the greater the processing costs the greater the presumed value to the hearer of the information intended to be communicated. Similarly, deviations from truth are to be expected in fiction but they are expected also to pay their way in terms of what I will call *narrative values*: all those values that make the fictional story worthwhile paying attention to. Obvious among these are the development of interesting characters and situations, the creation of an arresting mood, a narrative we want to pursue to the end. If something in the fiction is known or suspected to deviate from that which is known or assumed to be true it will create the expectation that there is some narrative payoff to be revealed. If the author moved the date of that battle or the location of that railway station, a reader who knows this will think that something in the narrative is consequential on that decision, and will expend attentional resources on finding out what that is. If it was just a slip her attention has been misdirected and the author is guilty not merely of failing to minimize deviation from truth but of miscommunicating, as a speaker would (in most contexts) be miscommunicating if they said 'I have two children' without intending the implicature that they have exactly two children. The principle guiding the construction and interpretation of stories in this way may be formulated like this:

Narrative value (NV):   Deviations in fiction from truth are expected to be justified by their narrative payoff.

It should not be supposed that this principle can be applied mechanically. There will be disagreement in particular cases as to whether there was payoff, or sufficient payoff, to justify a given deviation. That is one aspect of the irremediable contestability and indeterminacy of literary interpretation, something we have to acknowledge in our theorizing rather than seek to eradicate.

9.5 The author's beliefs

The reader who is misled in situations where the fiction deviates from truth without narrative payoff is someone who knows that something true-in-the-story is not true; she is misled because she thinks that its being not true is an indication of some available payoff, and her search for the payoff will produce no legitimate result. On the other hand, a reader who wants to learn about the habits of Russian aristocrats does not yet know the relevant facts and looks to the fiction to provide them. How it is that, having recognized that some particular proposition P is true-in-the-story, such a reader is sometimes able to conclude that P is also true? One simple way is to consider P and judge it to be true on the grounds that it coheres well with what else one believes; given what I know about the standing of French culture in nineteenth-century Europe the idea that Russian aristocrats spoke French has a certain plausibility—but not enough, probably, to make me confident of the proposition without finding further support for it, for I am ignorant enough to think it equally likely they spoke English or Italian. Another way is for the details of the story to reveal a way for the proposition to be true. The credence you give to a proposition may rationally depend partly on seeing how it could be true; we raise our credence in the theory that the Polynesian Islands were populated by people from South America when Heyerdahl's expedition shows that the journey could have been undertaken with then-available technology.[26] Fictions sometimes offer didactic projects of this kind, without living up to standards comparable to those we would expect to be observed by Heyerdahl-type investigators. The movie *Fail Safe* purports to show how nuclear war could start, but only by making unrealistic assumptions about the level of security in the US bomber command system at that time. Would we give any credence to Heyerdahl's theory of migration between South America and Polynesia if he had made a fictional film about people undertaking the voyage?

Another way to support the inference from P is true-in-the-fiction to P is true emerges when we ask whether Tolstoy *believed* that Russian aristocrats spoke French. There are many ways to know what an author believed; after reading *War and Peace* one might come to know that Tolstoy believed that Russians of the relevant period spoke French because he said so in a letter. But we are interested here in learning *from* fiction, and so focus on cases where the fiction itself provides us with evidence that the author believes the proposition in question.[27] More particularly, I am interested in cases where the work is *expressive* of a belief. Tolstoy's way of writing the novel—his lexical, grammatical, and narrative choices—is expressive of certain beliefs, and *War and Peace*, being the result of that activity, is expressive of Tolstoy's beliefs in those propositions. The test of this claim is that an appropriately prepared reader, though one with no specialist knowledge of Tolstoy's opinions, could reasonably infer from their reading of the novel that he believed these things. Here is how such an inference might go.

Someone who wrote a vast and admired novel of the Napoleonic wars would be likely to have true beliefs about at least the more general, salient, and verifiable aspects of relevant events, the linguistic habits of Russian aristocrats at the time being one; the work gives all the appearance of being in the genre of the realist novel, creating a general presumption in favour of adherence to historical

[26] If that is what it does show. It does not matter for present purposes that the theory is almost certainly wrong.

[27] There are many cases where the fiction is only part of the source of learning. Readers of Ngaio Marsh's *When in Rome* may wonder whether the story's church built over a temple to Mithras is real, and might by inquiry discover that it is, under a different name (Basilica di San Clemente al Laterano). Some of what they have to that point been imagining about the church then gets converted to belief, along with detail added from other sources.

actuality; that presumption might be violated if there was a good deal of narrative value to be had by having the characters speak French rather than some other language. But there does not seem to be any such additional value—the story would not be less exciting or the characters less convincing if they were represented as speaking English or Italian. It is likely therefore that Tolstoy had his characters speak the language he believed their real counterparts spoke at the time, and it is likely that his belief was correct. It is likely therefore that Russian aristocrats did speak French, in the circumstances roughly indicated in the novel, at the time the novel is set.

There is an important distinction between a narrative *being (merely) expressive of* the author's belief and the author *expressing* that belief through the work, just as there is a distinction between a person's unintendedly slow walk being expressive of their sadness, and their expressing their sadness by deliberately and openly walking slowly.[28] Tolstoy's writing that 'Anna looked out of the window and saw Alexey Alexandrovitch's courier on the steps, ringing at the front door bell' is, presumably, merely expressive of his belief that door bells were used in nineteen century Russia; we may infer from his putting it that way that he believed that door bells were so used, since he is unlikely to have invented a novel way for the courier to make his presence known. But it is also unlikely that he would be actively expressing this uninteresting belief. By contrast, readers of Solzhenitsyn's *One Day in the Life of Ivan Denisovich* probably have the impression that he wished to communicate news of conditions in Soviet labour camps to an ignorant audience, and was not merely placing his characters against a realistic background in conformity with genre expectations. Where the proposition in question is less morally significant, less controversial, or more widely understood, that proposition is more easily seen as merely expressive of belief rather than as something the author is expressing.

So a work of fiction may be expressive of the author's beliefs in two ways: it may be expressive of them because the author uses the work as a means to indicate or suggest that she has the belief, in which case the author expresses her belief through the work; it may provide unintended evidence that the author has the belief, in which case the work is *merely* expressive of the belief.[29] And the class of cases where the author expresses a belief is itself highly differentiated. Some of these cases will involve outright assertion, as when Herman Wouk breaks off the narrative of *The Winds of War* to list the names of pilots killed at the Battle of

---

[28] The distinction between expressing and being expressive of is explored in Vermazen (1986), though Vermazen is there concerned with the expression of emotions rather than beliefs. My epistemic version of this distinction is close to one made by Stacie Friend (2014): 'authorial testimony' vs. 'comprehension-based beliefs'. Friend argues convincingly for the possibility of testimonial transmission via fiction.

[29] Kim Sterelny has an evolutionary perspective: 'Agents leak information in their everyday activities' (2012: 26).

Midway. In such a case the author's expression of their views amounts to the provision of testimony, which is often understood to require an explicit statement or assertion from the testifier.[30] Most cases of authors expressing their beliefs in fiction are not of this clearly testimonial kind, just as a good deal of ordinary communication is not testimony; the tutor who writes that Smith's handwriting is excellent and his attendance at class punctual is not testifying that Smith lacks philosophical talent even though this is clearly part of what is meant. Fictions' more evaluative messages (something I discuss in Section 9.6) are often not stated by anyone, author, narrator, or character, but are rather suggested very indirectly by the content of the story or tone of its narration. It is best to see testimony as the high point of the expression-spectrum, points along which vary in the extent to which the utterer is manifestly committed to that which they express. The fact that the expression of belief in fiction is usually below this high point has consequences for the reliability of beliefs derived from fiction, as we will see immediately.

Should it matter to readers whether authors are testifying to their beliefs, or expressing them in some less explicit way, or not expressing them at all, while their work is merely expressive of them? It may matter, and there are competing reasons to prefer one practice to the other: favouring subtlety and indirection, readers will prefer a muted voice which does not actively broadcast opinions; favouring reliability they will prefer the committed stance of the testifier, because more open commitment to a proposition means a higher cost of being wrong, and so greater likelihood of being right. We feel able to blame those who testify falsely, especially if their failure is negligent, but less entitled to complain if their commitment to the proposition in question was less than explicit, and even less able to complain if we merely noticed their behaviour and drew a conclusion about what they believed, even though we suffered by adopting the belief ourselves. Blaming people, we are likely to trust them less, to spread distrust about them, and to punish them by withdrawing cooperation; knowing you will be blamed for a mistake makes you more careful and hence more reliable.[31] Suspecting that you can get away with it by avoiding explicit commitment will make you less careful, and some authors may practice the following deception: deliberately writing in such a way that their story is merely expressive of a belief while hoping at the same time to convert readers to a belief they could plausibly disown if pressed. And making one's narrative merely expressive can be a particularly effective method of propaganda because work which is merely expressive of opinions the author is (apparently) not intending to communicate can easily seem to contain opinions so well established that communicating them would be pointless. That way, one may

---

[30] 'To accept testimony is to take someone else's word for it' Owens (2006: 105).
[31] See Friend (2014) for an important discussion of the reliability of (putatively) factual information transmitted by fiction.

persuade people to believe what you believe by convincing them that what you believe is very widely believed and hence likely to be true.

Still, moderately rational people can be misled by fictions the authors of which are neither deceptive nor especially irresponsible. Reading *Our Mutual Friend*, I acquired the false belief that there was in Victorian London a recognized form of employment which involved collecting dead bodies from the Thames; the novel opens with an episode of this kind, which I took to be based on fact. It seemed unlikely that Dickens would invent this form of employment, such things normally constituting the 'realistic background' against which such novels are set; had the novel been a futuristic, dystopian novel I would not have drawn this conclusion. On reflection, I should have been more careful. The episode does present a dramatically effective opening for the novel and would be tempting, in accordance with principle NV, for the author to invent. Similarly, sensible viewers of Schiller's *Maria Stuart* will be wary of concluding that Elizabeth and Mary met, given the obvious dramatic advantage of having them together on stage. The sensible course, as in many other cases, would have been to withhold judgement while making further inquiries.[32]

I have so far said nothing about the role of imagination in this sort of belief transmission. There are different ways for the imagination to be implicated in learning. One, examined in Chapter 8, is for an act or instance of imagining to be part of the mechanism that generates a new belief and for that mechanism, under certain circumstances, to be reliable. When it came to the idea of fictions as imaginative thought experiments, my suggestion was that any reliability we might hope to find in the familiar thought experiments of philosophy and the sciences is unlikely to be found in the case of fictions. What is the role of imagination in the process of belief transmission via fiction? A reasonable answer is that it will depend on the particularities of the case. But here is one general thought.

Someone might approach a work of fiction entirely from the point of view of one interested in mining it for knowledge of one kind or another: knowledge of Russian history, human agency, or whatever. Suppose they approach it as the kind of thing focused on in this chapter: a conduit for belief. And suppose the reader decides to stay resolutely outside its influence on the imagination, treating it in an entirely forensic way as a document carrying evidence for what the author believed. Perhaps such a reader could identify certain propositions as 'exportable' in this way.[33] But I don't think such a reader will get very far. For one thing, the reader will not be able to make the kinds of judgements I spoke of earlier, as when

---

[32] As with Frank Kermode, reviewing McEwan's *Atonement* (*LRB*, 1 October 2001). Noting the orderly march of the Guards against the chaotic flow of retreating soldiers towards Dunkirk he asked 'Did it, in fact, happen?'

[33] On exportation from fiction see Gendler (2010: Chapter 9).

one judges that at this point truth-in-the-story corresponds with truth, because no narrative benefit would have accrued to the reader by moving away from real world truth. Unless one is imaginatively engaged by the story one simply is not in a position to know whether there is any such narrative benefit accruing. For another, one cannot simply read off from the text what is supposed to be true-in-the-story, for what is written may be metaphorical or ironic or in some other way non-literal. One cannot make judgements about how the text is to be interpreted without engaging with it in the way it is supposed to be engaged with—imaginatively.

9.6 Evaluations

While we may get historical and other kinds of purely factual knowledge from fiction, this is not what the humanistic tradition emphasizes. Talk of learning from Tolstoy or Proust brings more naturally to mind insights into human character, motivation, and moral values. In such domains we often treat the author not as a transmitter of information that might be available from other authorities also, but as a source of wisdom: someone with valuable insight and a perhaps unique perspective on the human condition.[34] The kinds of propositions involved in such cases have features which make for greater difficulty in accounting for their role in learning than we found in the case of straightforwardly factual beliefs acquired from fiction. The difficulties are of (at least) three kinds:

Epistemic: Unlike the historical, geographic, and other kinds of purely factual information one might learn from fiction, these propositions are typically controversial or at least not widely agreed to, even by experts (assuming there is expertise in the relevant area).[35]

Interpretive: The propositions in question are not usually made explicit in the text nor obviously implied by it, they may be the subject of extensive and perhaps unresolvable interpretive dispute and we may never articulate their contents with any precision.

Conceptual: Concerning, as they often do, such things as the complexities of duty, the nature of a caring relationship, the dangers of rigid morality, these propositions deploy thick concepts combining evaluative and descriptive elements not easily separated.[36]

---

[34] On wisdom and its relation to knowledge see Section 5.5.
[35] For scepticism about expertise in the relevant domains see below, Section 10.3.
[36] For a defence of the inseparability of descriptive and evaluative components of thick concepts see Dancy (1996).

This last feature raises difficult questions about the connection of such propositions with expressive acts, with desires, and with values, questions which are likely
to reinforce the earlier conclusion that learning in this area is not simply a matter
of belief change. Surely learning in an evaluative context involves changing one's
desires as well as one's beliefs and, perhaps by doing those things, changing
one's emotional dispositions, coming to feel hostility to things one previously
felt comfortable with, or vice versa. Our discussion in Part I of what I there called
i-desires and the emotions of fiction suggests that there is a parallel with what has
been said in this chapter about belief. In engaging with a fiction we take up the
invitation to imagine its contents but in the process we may recognize among
those contents propositions the author believes, and which we may come to
believe also. As well as inviting us to imagine that Anna Karenina falls in love
with Vronsky, the novel offers us an imaginative and emotional perspective to
adopt (very likely encompassing a range of perspectival options, as literary fiction
tends to do). That perspective (or those perspectives) may in turn suggest the
availability and indeed the value of really desiring certain things, of really responding in certain emotional ways rather than others. Chasing down the complexities of this process would be a lengthy, complex business; for now I am going
to concentrate on belief. Belief maybe the most tractable attitude to consider in
this context, and it is sensible to start with that. We will, however, try to take some
notice of the epistemic and interpretive problems as we proceed.

At this point we have particular need of the distinction between authors
expressing their beliefs and their works being merely expressive of them.[37]
While fictional works are often merely expressive of historical and geographic
beliefs, evaluative propositions are more naturally seen as expressed (sometimes
ambiguously and indirectly) by their authors. One reason for this is that evaluative
beliefs are, in the context of storytelling, more salient than descriptive ones
because they are more likely to be controverted. A storyteller may conform the

---

[37] A reviewer asked whether this is a sharp distinction or whether there are two extremes connected
by a continuum of points, with no clear demarcation between regions. As it turns out neither of these
alternatives is right. Take *S expresses P* and *S's behaviour is expressive of P*. There is a clear distinction in
the sense that the one does not blend into the other; things which are borderline for expressing P are
not automatically borderline for being expressive of P, any more than people who are borderline for
being tall are automatically borderline for being thin (though of course they may be both). But both *S
expresses P* and *S's behaviour is expressive of P* come in degrees. Someone may clearly and emphatically
express their sadness, and they may only marginally express it. And someone's behaviour may clearly
and emphatically express their sadness, and the behaviour may only marginally express it. In both cases
there is no absolute point where expression ceases. Now consider the relation between *S expresses P* and
S's behaviour being merely expressive of P, which means 'being expressive of P while the relevant person
is not expressing P'. When is something merely expressive? When it is not something the person
expresses but is something their behaviour expresses. But we have agreed that there is no particular
point on the scale of diminution of expressing at which we can say a person is no longer expressing, and
hence no point at which something becomes merely expressive. But that is not because *S expressing P*
and *S's behaviour is expressive of P* are on a single continuum.

events of the story to the facts of London's geography without much reflection on or even awareness of what they are doing. An author who conforms the plot to a personal vision of the value of love and friendship is likely to be aware of this, to be aware of the controversial nature of their opinion and the interest that will be taken in it, and likely therefore to craft a narrative which shows their perspective in the best light. A narrative designed to communicate that perspective is likely to *seem* designed to communicate it, and correspondingly unlikely to seem designed to communicate propositions about the layout of London streets. In this section I focus mainly on fictions in which the author expresses their belief in the relevant propositions, though they may not do that by uttering those very propositions.

How might readers of a novel understand that the author wished to communicate propositions about love, fidelity, and happiness when such propositions are not explicit in or directly implied by the story text? How—to go back to a notably unliterary example—might readers of *Murder in the Mall* conclude that the author wished to communicate to them that unrestrained psychiatric patients are dangerous?[38]

However readers arrive at these conclusions, they must be based on a sensitivity to details of the work itself. Readers start these sorts of inquiries, John Hospers noted, 'by observing carefully which passages contain the greatest passion and intensity, which themes are most often reiterated, how the plot is made to evolve, which characters are treated with the greatest sympathy.'[39] Neither Hospers nor later commentators have been able to say much about the inferences involved, and some have concluded that nothing much can be said.[40]

There is, indeed, no single form which such reasoning takes, any more than there is a single way for a detective to infer the identity of the murderer from the accumulated clues. But it is tempting to think that reasoning from the assumption of conversational cooperativeness will often be involved, since such reasoning is

---

[38] Perhaps the effects on belief (if any) of *Murder in the Mall* were mostly due to processes such as the availability heuristic. But note that participants were told that the story was written by a 'prize-winning author', which might have had some effect on estimations of the author's reliability (for evidence that people are influenced in their willingness to rely on argument by the perceived competence of the person communicating see Orosz et al. (2016). How might we discriminate between the effects of such processes as the availability heuristic and apparently more rationally-based mechanisms such as testimony? One way would be to assume that the latter kinds of processes are more extensively cognitively penetrated than the former. We would then see whether subject's (apparent) change in belief was affected by the presentation of information emphasizing the fictional nature of the story, suggestions of unreliability, etc. The less these interventions affected the change of belief, the more confidence one would have that something like heuristic-based belief acquisition was involved.

[39] Hospers (1960: 41). Hospers speaks of careful observation, which is what one would look for in the most responsible interpreters. But audiences that take little care may still come away from many works of fiction with a strong sense that something has been communicated and have at least an outline understanding of what that is.

[40] See e.g. Lamarque and Olsen (1994). For a review of philosophical opinion on this over the last half century see Mikkonen (2010).

often thought to play a significant role in coming to understand what people mean in their acts of communication.[41]

In cases where a fiction is presented as a contribution to a conversation, we might apply the conversational maxims in straightforward ways. According to Luke's Gospel, Jesus tells the story of the Good Samaritan in response to the question from 'a certain lawyer': Who is my neighbour? Jesus' response, taken as a literally meant assertion, violates various conversational rules, notably 'be relevant', since the story, taken that way, manifestly fails to answer the question. Casting around for a way of preserving the assumption that Jesus is maintaining conversational cooperativeness, we conclude that he is offering a set of merely pretended assertions, the content of which can be easily understood to exemplify the proposition that people to whom one owes the obligations of a neighbour include those who are culturally distant and even antagonistic, this now being understood as his serious answer to the question.[42]

But the parables are not typical cases of fiction. Fictions are much more commonly produced and put forward outside of any immediate conversational context. While they frequently pick up on matters of current public concern, they often seem to answer questions we would not otherwise have thought of asking. In this they are, like many non-fictional texts, isolated from any conversational context: texts which create a standard of relevance of their own, with relevance in later parts constrained only by the contents of earlier parts. Nor do we normally apply conversational rules to work out that what we are reading is fiction rather than asserted utterance; we know that the work is fiction because it is advertised as such. Fictions generally contain a good deal that is false, but we do not derive conversational implicatures from their telling by exploiting this fact, for a work's being fictional acts to suspend rules like 'do not say what you believe to be false' rather than to violate them.[43]

Sensitivity to conversational cooperativeness will not, I claim, get us far in understanding what beliefs are expressed in fiction. Fortunately we have other resources to appeal to. Humans are highly attuned to each other's mental states even outside of conversational contexts, capable of grasping them on the basis of exposure to a vast range of behaviours, from facial and bodily expression to such affiliative choices as dress, food, and mode of transport. Traces of behaviour can

---

[41] See Grice (1989: Part I).

[42] Perhaps it is a substantive historical question whether a contemporary audience would have taken the story-content of Jesus' parables to be true and known by Jesus rather than as fictional. Even if they would have, it does not seem to be essential to the testimonial effect of the parables that they be so taken.

[43] Assumptions of conversational cooperativeness play an *internal* role in fiction, helping to guide us to the right imaginings: if the text of a realist novel says that 'Smith was invisible' we understand that what is true-in-the-story is that Smith made little impression on others; that way we avoid supposing it part of the fiction that the narrator is violating the requirement that one does not say what is obviously false-in-the-fiction.

be equally informative: the content of your diary, wardrobe, and credit-card purchasing record all tell a good deal about you. These sources vary on a number of relevant dimensions: the strength of conviction they convey in the idea communicated or manifested by the agent; the specificity of what is communicated or manifested; the degree to which an audience can be confident that something is communicated or manifested. I may end up suspecting that you strongly believe that P; strongly believing that you suspect that P; suspecting that you suspect that P, or something with similar content to P. Assuming our contact with the author is exclusively through the work, the range of available behaviours is limited; we as readers are confined to what there is in the work which seems to be expressive of this or that opinion, given relevant background knowledge. But fictional works are in another sense especially rich sources of clues as to the mental states of their makers. The narrative of a fictional story is guided less by requirements of fidelity than are history and journalism; more in a fictional text represents a choice, and what people choose to do, rather than what they are obliged to do, is often a good guide to their opinions.[44] Just as plot is chosen, so is the mode of representation for plot. At this point Hospers' remarks about passages of passion and intensity, the reiteration of themes, the evolution of plots and the portrayal of characters are especially relevant. Such details in a fictional text may indicate very precisely the author's choices, helping to make certain hypotheses about the author's communicative intentions more probable than others: precise details about what Albertine and Marcel say and do make a difference to any conclusions we draw about Proust's perspective on love.

9.7 Trust

When readers learn from fictions by taking on the beliefs of authors expressed in their works, they often do so because they treat the author as a reliable believer.[45] This does not mean that they trust authors. We treat thermometers as reliable without trusting them, and we may do the same with people; my threats to murder your family give me grounds for treating your assertions about where the money is as reliable though my resort to threats indicates a complete lack of trust. We may treat an author of fiction as reliable on, say, geographic matters simply on the grounds that we believe she has the requisite expertise, has no particular reason to deviate from truth in presenting the story, and that she dislikes readers complaining that she got background wrong. Trust need not be a factor.

---

[44] Much we have said earlier should make it clear that these choices are still highly constrained.

[45] Recall that exceptions to this occur when the reader notices the proposition in question and finds their own reason for believing it.

Still, trust often is a factor in settling our judgements of people's reliability. What is required for trust, over and above the assumption of reliability?[46] Without seeking to adjudicate between fine-grained competing accounts of these notions, I assume that a crucial difference is affective. For Karen Jones trust is characterized by an emotional attitude of optimism towards the goodwill of the other, while Annette Baier and Richard Holton emphasize, in different ways, the feelings of betrayal that disappointed trust provokes.[47] Are we more likely to be wrong in trusting someone than in simply relying on them? You might say that reliance is clear headed while trust, being affectively tinged, is apt to miss signs of unreliability. But trust in testimony (rather than mere reliance on it) is not always the more risky policy. A tendency to trust may be supported by iterated verification of the other's reliability. Trust is likely, if broadcast, to call forth feelings of obligation on the part of the one trusted, thereby improving their reliability (Pettit 1995: 24). And trust enables the one who trusts to dispense with high levels of vigilance, which are cognitively expensive. But is an attitude of trust likely to be warranted in a fictional context?

There are reasons to think not. The lowered vigilance induced by a trusting attitude raises the likelihood of forming unreliable beliefs, and this increase is not, in fictive contexts, much constrained or compensated for by the factors just mentioned. First, our relations with authors generally lack the reciprocity required to form a mutually trusting relationship. Perhaps this can be overcome in the case of an author with a long and public literary career (Dickens comes to mind) who may be aware that his readers trust him and who feels an obligation to live up to that trust; such cases are unusual. And trust, being in part an emotional attitude, can be induced by factors that do not correlate well with reliability. Appearance and demeanor can affect our tendency to trust people, while failing to track expertise in difficult areas of inquiry such as moral psychology. Authors whose work we enjoy, who we admire for their uses of language, their inventiveness with plot, their vivid character portrayal, who become (we imagine) our best narrative friends, are likely to generate feelings of trust in their views on moral psychology when, in this complex and specialized area, one ought to seek unusually strong evidence of reliability.[48] Nor could we be confident that the rewards of past trust in a given author justify future and perhaps more extensive trusting. The authors we read rarely address the details of our own present concerns and it would be

---

[46] Perhaps one can trust a manifestly unreliable loved one. Here we consider only the difference between trusting reliance and untrusting reliance.

[47] Baier (1986); Holton (1994); Jones (1996).

[48] On authors as best narrative friends, see Booth (1988). It's striking how personal a relationship readers can feel they have with authors they know nothing about, apart from their fiction. On the author Elena Ferrante, whose character and even identity were until recently unknown to her readers, one enthusiast commented: 'But ... Elena is my friend! My private relationship with her, so intense and so true, is one that nobody else can fully know!' (http://www.theguardian.com/books/2014/oct/31/elena-ferrante-literary-sensation-nobody-knows).

difficult to show that whatever lessons we took from their works contributed materially to such good fortune as we enjoyed. Nor is it clear how we could find independent sources to check on the reliability of favoured literary perspectives on moral psychology. We might appeal to psychological research or the deliverances of moral philosophy, but this sounds, once again, like a recommendation to replace the familiar stance of absorption in literature with a quite different and antithetical practice.[49] It is not part of the humanistic belief in the cognitive value of literature that readers need to treat their favoured texts as pieces of evidence to be weighed against the deliverances of scientific and analytical thought. Whether trust in authors is widespread is unclear, but we can say at least that a desire to trust them should not easily prevail.

Some of these concerns extend beyond trusting and bring into question the weaker stance of assuming reliability, notably the lack of confirmation for the propositions in question other than the subjective conviction of readers. To the extent that literary artists generally do not openly assert those propositions, there is a corresponding danger that what they communicate will not be the product of responsible inquiry. I said that it is common for the evaluative implications of a literary work to be arrived at only by subtle methods of interpretation applied by academic critics, and to be themselves the subject of complex and sometimes unresolved dispute. While authors may worry that factual errors will be brought to their doors, they rarely have reason to fear that their views on love will be identified with enough precision to be refuted, or, if identified, that hard evidence against those views will be found.[50]

The same concern extends to propositions which are thoroughly descriptive in their content, but likely to be favoured because of their proximity to evaluative beliefs. The clear evidential value of Tolstoy's French-speaking Russian aristocrats contrasts with Proust's remark that the Dreyfus affair had the effect of making Jews less welcome in the upper parts of French society.[51] For someone with any knowledge of the case this proposition will be very plausible. But Proust's expression of it should not raise its probability much for the attentive reader; even Dreyfusards are not epistemic saints, and Proust may be generalizing casually and in a favoured direction from a very small number of known instances.

Back in Chapter 5 I made the point that an emphasis on reliability as a condition for knowledge is not automatically an endorsement of externalism about knowledge because some processes of knowledge acquisition depend for their reliability on the subject's ability to reflect on and understand the grounds for

---

[49] See above, Section 6.4.   [50] See below, Section 10.1.
[51] *Within a Budding Grove* (revised translation by D. J Enright of *À l'ombre des jeunes filles en fleurs*, 1919, Chatto and Windus, 1992), pp. 103–4. This is the first reference in Proust's novel cycle to Dreyfus.

what is said to be known. There I mentioned Sosa's distinction between animal and reflective knowledge, which he describes in this way:

> Animal knowledge does not require that the knower have an epistemic perspective on his belief, a perspective from which he endorses the source of that belief, from which he can see that source as reliably truth conducive. Reflective knowledge does by contrast require such a perspective.   (2009: 135)

If we are to have propositional knowledge derived from fictions conceived of as conduits between authorial opinion and our own, the difficulties outlined above mean that this is more likely to be reflective than animal knowledge. For reflection on the reliability of the source, especially but not exclusively in cases of evaluative knowledge, is surely required if the process of knowledge acquisition as a whole is to count as reliable. Such reflection, however diligent, will not be a sufficient condition for the case to be one of knowing, but it will often be necessary.

9.8 Truth as a value in literature

It is one thing to say that fiction changes beliefs, sometimes even giving us knowledge and so true belief. It is another to say that this capacity constitutes or contributes to the literary value that the fictional work may have.[52] Indeed there are people who grant the first proposition and deny the second. Lamarque and Olsen argue that while literature may speak to serious human concerns, it 'is the *content* of the proposition [expressed], what it is about, not its truth as such, that confers interest' (1994: 330). If correct, this would allow us to celebrate literature's bearing on humans concerns while avoiding the argument about the truthfulness of its claims altogether.

The words just quoted from Lamarque and Olsen seems to imply that in some cases there is no interest to be had in finding out whether an interesting claim is true or not. Surely, the truth value of an interesting claim is always of interest. But Lamarque and Olsen need not (and probably do not) deny this. Their claim need be only that, *so far as literary criticism is concerned*, the question of truth is of no interest. They may think, and probably do, that truth is always of interest from some point of view—but not from this one. Even that more moderate proposition strikes me as extremely implausible, contradicted by the deliverances of reflection and counter to the views often expressed by critics, theorists, and practitioners of

---

[52] For excellent arguments, applicable across the arts, for aesthetic cognitivism—the view that 'the cognitive (or, equivalently, epistemic) merits of works of art are, under certain conditions, aesthetic merits in those works or condition their aesthetic merits' see Gaut (2007: Chapter 7).

literary fiction. It is a highly revisionary doctrine and one we would need very great confidence in before it persuaded us to rethink our approach to literature.

Here are some examples of a much more conventional view of truth in literature from practitioners of the art. Prefacing a late novel, Storm Jameson said, 'The situation in the book is an invented one, but might, at some time, in some place, among people of one nation or another, occur. The events related are a vehicle for an account of the workings of that strange organ, the human heart.'[53] It would have been odd if she had added 'and of course it does not matter, from a literary point of view, whether the account is remotely correct'. Conrad, a more obviously literary writer, said (also in a preface) that writing *Under Western Eyes* was 'an attempt to render the psychology of Russia itself'. It was a novel, he said, by which he hoped to 'express imaginatively the general truth which underlies its action'. Again, I would be surprised to hear that Conrad thought his success or failure in this enterprise was completely irrelevant to the value of his novel as literature. Entirely unambiguous opposition to the Lamarque and Olsen view comes from Henry James, reviewing *Our Mutual Friend*: 'It were, in our opinion, an offence against humanity to place Mr. Dickens among the greatest novelists. For, to repeat what we have already intimated, he has created nothing but figure. He has added nothing to our understanding of human character.'[54] For James it was part of the novelist's duty to add to that understanding, and many of his readers have thought that he, at least, was successful in discharging this duty. He also, as the quotation indicates, thought that this duty is a literary one: the great novels add to our understanding, and that is part of what makes them and their authors great and it is what, according to James, denies greatness to Dickens. James' view is not an eccentric one, at least for his period. Turgenev said of *War and Peace* that:

> French readers not put off by certain longueurs, and the oddity of certain judgements, will be right in telling themselves that *War and Peace* has given them a more direct and faithful representation of the character and temperament of the Russian people, and about Russian life generally, than they would have obtained if they had read hundreds of works of ethnography and history.[55]

He would have been puzzled, I think, by the idea that this is not a *literary* judgement. Nor have writers and critics stopped saying these things. 'My aim as a novelist is, by examining these themes, to see what they can tell us about all of humanity and the way in which all our minds work in sickness and in health', said

---

[53] *Last Score: The Private Life of Sir Richard Ormston* (1961).
[54] *The Nation*, 21 December 1865.
[55] Quoted in Bartlett (2011: 179). See Engel (2016), for the collection of a number of similar statements.

Sebastian Faulks in a BBC interview.[56] Speaking about the novels of Natalia Ginzburg, Rachel Cusk says she 'separates the concept of storytelling from the concept of the self and in doing so takes a great stride towards a more truthful representation of reality'.[57] A vast army of other writers have aimed at truth, and it is hard to deny that they and their commentators saw this as integral to the literary project they were embarked on.[58]

And truth matters to us as readers, often in ways that influence the judgements we make about the work's literary merit. Literary judgement depends on framing the work in the right way, and that's partly a matter of getting its genre right. Knowing a work's genre is partly a matter of knowing where we can expect the story to deviate from truth, with naturalistic novels, magical realist ones, fantasies, and works of science fiction deviating in different ways. And truth matters not just because it is an indicator of genre. In *Saturday* McEwan describes an operation to remove a clot from the brain of a man who, hours before, had invaded the surgeon's home. The account of the operation is central to the book: an economical, detailed description taking us through an astonishingly skillful act of repairing the body. McEwan went to some trouble, apparently, to get the medical details right, here and elsewhere in the novel. This matters to the work's literary quality; if McEwan had simply made up medical and anatomical detail to match the rhythm of his description this would be much less of a literary achievement.[59]

It is true that among theoreticians of literature we can find statements or implications that agree with Lamarque and Olsen. A number of deconstructive and postmodern theorists fall into this category, offering a future free from the irritating need to think about how texts instruct us about reality; the thought that there are relations of correspondence between the personal traits of fictional characters and those of real people has come in for particularly hostile treatment, attacked as both philosophically incoherent and ideologically backsliding.[60] The very idea of the kind of stable, explanatory profile of character traits so often represented in fiction 'seemed quaintly moralistic, redolent of a world of backbones and stiff upper lips, of Victorian rather than modern or postmodern thought'.[61] But as Lamarque and Olsen note, these forms of scepticism about truth in literature derive from a more general scepticism about the notion of truth and indeed about the idea of referential language. Lamarque and Olsen go to some

---

[56] http://news.bbc.co.uk/1/hi/health/4220290.stm. From an interview in 2005.

[57] *Times Literary Supplement*, 20 April 2018; under the section heading 'Literary Criticism'.

[58] There are dissenters from this view; Shaw, in a letter in support of Tolstoy and included in Crosby 1906, speaks of the 'emptiness of Shakespeare's philosophy' (166) calling on the support of Voltaire who 'as he grew older [was] less disposed to accept artistic merit as a cover for philosophical deficiencies' (168). See also below, note 65.

[59] For other arguments favouring the connection between truth and literary value see Harcourt (2010), and Gaskin (2013: 43–9).

[60] See e.g. Cixous (1974).

[61] Felski (2011), though she concludes that we ought now to see that the representation of character in fiction 'offers otherwise unattainable insights into the historical inflection of personhood'.

trouble to distance themselves from these views and wish to be aligned with those who think that there is nothing conceptually wrong with the idea of truth, in particular truth from fiction, and nothing wrong with valuing truth.[62] Indeed, as I remarked, they may think that there is as a matter of fact a good deal of truth to be had from fiction. They rightly do not claim it as an advantage of their view that it is supported by theorists in the no-truth camp.

Undeterred, Lamarque and Olsen say that there is no place in literary criticism for 'debate about the truth or falsity of general statements about human life or the human condition' (1994: 332). This prohibition is part of their more general project of ruling out, for purposes of reflection on literary values, questions about the truth value of statements made or implied in literature. Indeed they claim that, as a matter of fact, 'debate about the truth or falsity of the propositions implied by a literary work is absent from literary criticism'. If this is true, someone who claims that such debate has a rightful place in criticism would have some explaining to do; they would be claiming that something is an intrinsic part of criticism but has never shown up in the history of critical practice. That would certainly be strange. I'll spend the rest of this chapter considering this claim. While I don't think it gets Lamarque and Olsen where they want to go, there is something to the idea. It will help to motivate a line of argument about the value of literature according to which the practice of literature is deeply flawed in one respect: a literary work's capacity to provide learning is intrinsic to its literary value, yet the practices of literary creation, consumption, and criticism contain no mechanisms that exercise effective quality control or even quality assessment in this domain.

One person who has been struck by the power of Lamarque and Olsen's claim is Peter Kivy, who agrees that 'there is, most of the time, no true-false evaluation in [criticism] of the general thematic statements [in a literary work]'.[63] But Kivy is not on the side of Lamarque and Olsen. He goes on to argue that, while evaluation is not visible in criticism, it does not follow that it is irrelevant to the evaluation of narrative fictions. Evaluation, he claims, is part of appreciation, and appreciation is the job of the reader, not of the critic. The job of the critic is to make available to the reader 'whatever hypotheses the fictional work may, directly or indirectly, propose' (1997: 125). It is then up to the reader to evaluate those hypotheses.

As responses to Lamarque and Olsen go, this strikes me as a weak one. Kivy's distinction between criticism, which makes the content of the work available, and appreciation, which involves evaluation of that content, does not correspond to anything we find in critical practice. Critics regularly have appraised literary fictions on various grounds, especially moral ones. For example—and there is a

[62] See Lamarque and Olsen (1994: Chapter 8).
[63] Kivy (1997: 123). For discussion of Kivy's view see Carroll (2002).

vast array of examples—James Gould Cozzens novel *By Love Possessed* was attacked on its publication by critics Irving Howe and Dwight Macdonald because of what they saw as its racism, snobbery, and general conservativism. Macdonald's review in particular was responsible for the almost total destruction of Cozzens' literary reputation.[64]

This example and many others are not, it will be said, examples of criticism which focus on psychological truthfulness; they are cases of ethical criticism.[65] But such cases do involve, at least implicitly, judgements as to psychological verisimilitude. Much of the fictional literature of morality is an investigation of the fit, or lack of it, between moral precepts and psychological reality as the author sees it; Jane Austen and Henry James are novelists with an interest in morality, but they are not authors of abstract moral treatises; they focus on the *psychology* of moral— and immoral—behaviour. The troubling implications which critics claimed to find in Cozzens' treatment of Jews, African Americans, and Catholics were 'thick appraisals' involving factual propositions that function to support evaluative ones.[66] The claim was that characters from these groups were represented as morally inferior in virtue of certain traits of character or disposition which—the critics suspected—we are invited to 'export' to the real world (Gendler 2010: Chapter 12). And the critics were, in their turn, rejecting those factual claims, at least implicitly. These critics did not then set about *arguing* that Jews, African Americans, and Catholics did not have any of the status-reducing characteristics which they took Cozzens to be implying they did have; they simply took it as evident that they did not; I will return to this. But their objections to the novel would have little force unless it was an at least implicit part of their critique that the novel was based on, and expressed, false assumptions about people belonging to these groups. A similar outlook is maintained by today's most influential critics. James Wood said, of Jon McGregor's *Reservoir 13*, 'Novels aspire to be social documents, group portraits, measurers of time, renovators of the ordinary, but few come close to achieving those ambitions. This entrancing book does.'[67] Presumably Wood does not think that the novel was a substantially false or misleading social document, or that in general a novel's documentary status has nothing to do with truth.

---

[64] Macdonald (1958).

[65] Tolstoy combines ethical and psychological criticism of Shakespeare; see especially his analysis of King Lear ('in Shakespeare there is no language of living individuals', Crosby 1906: 55).

[66] No one in this debate need be claiming that these views are explicitly asserted in the work itself. Various things are said by characters supportive of them, though this could be explained as simple faithfulness to the realities of opinion among the kind of people Cozzens was writing about. There are also passages not explicitly ascribed to any character but which could be understood, generously, as free indirect discourse. Where Macdonald is certainly wrong is in claiming that Cozzens is unaware of the priggishness of his own central character.

[67] 'Four books that deserved more attention in 2017', *The New Yorker*, 20 December 2017. Wood is said to be notable for leading a turn in criticism *away from* political and other realism-oriented concerns.

Kivy could, I suppose, argue that cases where critics depend on the truth of psychological claims are ones where they overstep the boundary of their responsibilities as critics and make pronouncements which they either should refrain from making or which they make only when speaking as readers rather than as critics. In that case Kivy could not claim to find the distinction he makes between readers and critics displayed in the historical record; he would be imposing on the record a distinction which he thinks people have failed to be aware of; critics generally do not preface their psychological remarks by saying, 'I am now speaking as a lay reader rather than as a critic.' One would not want to rule out such a strategy a priori, but it would need a good deal of arguing for. Of the many arguments against proceeding in this way, I will mention here two. The first is simply that the question 'What is the proper domain of the critic as opposed to that of the private reader?' is so contested and contestable, that the idea that we would find a preponderance of evidence in the history of critical practice for one view rather than another about the limits of the critic's duties and entitlements—as Kivy implies we do—is very implausible indeed.

The second argument is more complex. Its central premise is that much of the best and most celebrated criticism could not be understood without assuming that the project of criticism is, in part, the project of assessing the work and its characters against standards of presumed truthfulness, notably with respect to motive. The most obvious examples here come from the literature on Shakespearean drama, much of which is concerned with the psychological plausibility of Leontes, Othello, Lear, Macbeth, and, most notably, Hamlet. In all these cases, a great deal of speculation and debate goes on about the extent to which these characters are motivated from within—by plausibly human models of deliberation and feeling—or from without, by dramatic necessity, by poetic inclination, by the need to make the always difficult fourth act work.[68] It is only if we find Hamlet's delay difficult to explain psychologically that we invoke some dramatic reason for slowing the progress of the plot; it is only if we think that Hamlet hasn't really got a good reason—a reason that makes sense within the boundaries of the plot—to go to England that we say that Shakespeare was following the ur-Hamlet too closely at this point. A. C. Bradley (1904) argued that Iago acts as he does because plotting enhances his sense of power; Empson (1951) agreed, supporting the claim with the observation that this is a common explanation in real life for 'apparently meaningless petty cruelties'. Bradley's explanation, he says, is to that extent more plausible than Coleridge's postulation of motiveless malignity, which he, Empson, thinks of as a literary conceit. Psychological credibility is often the first test, and if a character's behaviour passes

---

[68] This returns us to the internal/external distinction of Section 2.3.

that, there is less pressure to look for explanations that invoke the dramatic texture of the work.

That is not to say that psychological realism is always where the critic starts; whether it is or not depends on genre and other considerations, many of which invoke the intentions of the work's maker. Psychological plausibility is sometimes given little significance because of the perceived anti-naturalism of the work in question, or simply because a sacrifice of naturalism here makes for a gain in some other value. In Max Beerbohm's *Zuleika Dobson* the characters' speech and actions are absurd in about equal measure, but one would be missing the point to see this as the key to deeper motives. But it is rare for verisimilitude to be given no weight at all; if characters behave in ways that have absolutely nothing to do with the ways we think real people behave (and what would such behaviour be like?), a critical discussion is likely to ensue about what might justify such a dramatic deviation from the path of truthfulness. Ideas of truth and truthfulness are woven into the fabric of a kind of criticism that is widespread now and comes with a long and distinguished history. A critic may—and some critics do—reject the idea that truth plays a role in criticism; she may pursue such strategies as deconstruction. I shan't argue that such people are not true critics; all I ask is that they and others not argue the same about those who are guided in their criticism by notions of truthfulness; the critics with whom Lemarque and Olsen are naturally aligned are so guided.

Lemarque and Olsen may point out in response that what is at stake here is not psychological truthfulness but presumed truthfulness: we expect the default position to be something like 'the folk understanding of human psychology' which may in fact be far from the truth.[69] There are two ways to understand this response. One is as claiming that folk understanding counts because it is what we think is true, and changes as what we think is true changes. Thus understood the response is weak: it grants that what matters is truth and merely points out that, in seeking to apply truth as a standard for judging fictional representations of human psychology, we can only go by what we take to be true. But on another reading the claim that folk psychology counts is the claim that folk psychology, as it actually is (at least roughly) is the preferred standard for judging fictional representations of human psychology, irrespective of whether it is true or not. Thus one might argue that there is something uniquely 'fitting' between the way (or some way) we intuitively understand human motivation and the ambitions of any serious fiction. For example, it might be claimed that serious fiction could not thrive if required to conform to an eliminativist account of human motivation: an account which eschewed belief-desire psychology in favour of neuroscientific

---

[69] This objection was put to me by David Davies.

explanation. If eliminativism is true we had either better not know it or we must ignore it when producing and consuming fiction.

This is an interesting response. In reply I say that while there may be limits to how far we can move away from current folk-psychological thinking and retain the project of constructing fictional characters which will be interesting, it would be an exaggeration to fix on our current conception of motivation in all its detail and insist that it is the standard fiction must conform to. Folk psychology has changed; it changed in the recent past as Freudian ideas started to permeate common thinking. I for one would be pleased to see it change again under pressure from the recognition that the Freudian picture is fundamentally wrong. The point is that some changes to our understanding of human motivation would both retain the possibility of constructing engaging fictional characters and change our judgements about what counts as plausible in fiction. It is said that someone now painting in the style of Giotto would be judged very differently from the way we judge Giotto, given all that has taken place in representational art between the two times. Similarly a modern writer who adopted Homeric ways of thought, having her characters be motivated by gods, would count as self-consciously archaic—something we would not say of Homer. We might judge the result a success, but our view of it would be coloured by our view of what is, and what is not, true in human psychology.

Lamarque has said something more recently which might be seen as countering my insistence on the literary importance of psychological truthfulness. His comment returns us to the two-perspectives on literature—internal and external—that we discussed in Chapter 2:[70]

> Realistically drawn characters, like Anna Karenina, are indeed similar in certain respects to real people. We imagine them to be real people and in filling out the narratives of their lives we make inferences based on common assumptions about what people of that kind are like. But the notion of 'understanding character' is equivocal; it can mean understanding characters as imagined people and it can mean understanding them as elements in a literary work...It is the second sense that concerns the critic attending to the works as literature or as art.[71]

The distinction Lamarque draws is a real one but it does nothing to undermine my claim about the literary importance of psychological truthfulness. Things which are distinct are not always independent and these two things are not, as I argued in

---

[70] See above, Section 2.3.

[71] Lamarque (2014: 239). I am grateful to a reader for the press who brought this passage to my attention. It should be noted that in this passage Lamarque is not responding to my claim but to a claim of Jenefer Robinson's about the role of emotion in literary understanding.

Chapter 2. There are not two disjoint activities you can engage in: understanding Anna as a(n imagined) person, and understanding her as an element in a fictional work. Her place in the work is that of a character with certain specific traits and properties; if Anna was a Zuleika Dobson-like woman, or a man, or a horse, or (somehow) an armchair the critic would need to say entirely different things about her (his, its) role in the work. Influenced by certain aspects of literary structuralism one might develop a notion of literary functional role (sometimes called an 'actant') according to which the same literary role might be played by a woman, a man, or possibly an armchair. But this would be to operate at an extreme level of generality not remotely corresponding to how we think in critical terms about literary constructions; serious criticism depends in exquisite detail on the characteristics of the occupants of these roles.

So literary understanding depends in good measure on person-understanding. What we say about a character's psychology constrains what we may say about their literary role. In particular, a character whose thoughts, feelings, and motivations are deemed psychologically true, realistic, or plausible will generally be assigned a role that is in some way different from a character who is none of those things.

So I reject both Lamarque and Olsen's claim about the irrelevance of truth to critical practice, and Kivy's attempt to rescue truth by making its determination wholly the responsibility of the reader. And yet: Lamarque, Olsen, and Kivy have noticed something important. There *is* something odd in the practice of humanistic critics who appeal to notions of truthful representation in their criticism. Critics who make quite startling claims about the psychological truthfulness (or otherwise) of authors hardly ever argue for these claims.

Perhaps it is this absence of reason-giving which prompted Kivy to say that in criticism there are no true-false 'evaluations'. If evaluation requires explicit argument I agree with Kivy here, though what he says does nothing to support his contention that critics merely make explicit 'whatever hypotheses the fictional work may, directly or indirectly, propose', leaving it to readers to evaluate those hypotheses. If critics ascribe truth values to these hypotheses they cannot be said to be leaving evaluation entirely up to readers; they would then merely be inviting readers to provide arguments in favour of those hypotheses. Lamarque and Olsen are right (more or less, there are exceptions) to say that 'debate about the truth or falsity of the propositions implied by a literary work is absent from literary criticism.' They are wrong to infer from this that truth is not a value in literary criticism.[72]

There is further support here for the revisionist proposal of Chapter 6. There I suggested that we might make sense of critical practice in terms of pretence: the

---

[72] For other commentary on Lamarque and Olssen and on Kivy's intervention see Davies (2010).

pretence that there are things to be learned from the work and that the diligent reader is learning them. Later, in the discussion of thought experiments I noted the absence of institutions within the world of fiction that promote rational agreement about what is true and what is not, likening the 'search for truth' in literature to the play of children pretending to be pirates who don't bother with the hard work of steering a ship in stormy seas. Something else we don't find among those deeply and sometimes professionally committed to discerning truth in literary fiction is argument. This topic will be prominent in Chapter 10.

9.9 Conclusions

I began this chapter by distinguishing two quite different ways fictions might serve to transmit beliefs between author and reader. One was by taking advantage of those quirks of cognition sometimes labelled heuristics and biases which bypass mechanisms of rational assessment; the other was via the processes that generate and manage testimony, along with 'sub-testimonial' processes that depend on the reliability, if not the trustworthiness of authors. To the extent that the beliefs in question have an evaluative component reliability is likely to be lacking: many such beliefs are inherently unreliable in that we find no convergence of opinion about their truth values, mistakes are hard to identify and anyway not strongly sanctioned, and it is often hard to know even roughly what proposition is in question. For all that, fictions can be powerful vehicles for the expression of evaluative perspectives and their capacity to make us vividly and imaginatively aware of such perspectives can be considered a contribution to understanding.

Finally I asked how much a debate like this one, concerning the transmission of propositions between agents where truth is important, might matter not merely because truth is important in itself but because truth is a contributor to literary value. I argued that it is a contributor to literary value. However, the practices of literature do not function to take that value seriously. This supports the revisionism of Chapter 6 and it is a theme continued in the next chapter (Section 10.1). There I will look again at those practices and how they and associated institutions of literature differ from the practices and institutions of science designed to foster truth and truthfulness. After that I turn to the reasons we might have for thinking that literary creativity is generally or often accompanied by a high level of understanding of the mind, and of relations between minds. If that were so it would be reasonable to look to the works of talented authors for insight into these things.

10

Wise authors?

This chapter continues a theme of Chapter 9: the reliability of authors of fiction on topics we think we are able to learn something about from reading or watching their works. One might see this as a matter entirely to do with the qualities of authors themselves: their knowledge, their honesty, their reliability, and—perhaps—their trustworthiness. But I will emphasize a social or institutional dimension to this. To the extent that we rely on the deliverances of science, that is not because we have a personal faith in the integrity of the individual scientists responsible for the results in question: very likely we know nothing about them and it is only in those thankfully exceptional cases where deception is suspected that questions about these personal qualities arise. So I will say something about the contrast between science as an epistemic institution and the world of fiction-makers and their audiences. I will then turn to more directly personal matters, raising some questions about the psychology of artistic creativity and its relation to that great theme of literature and quality fictions of all kinds: the mind. Here my conclusions will be especially tentative, given what has already been noted about the paucity and sometimes the weakness of relevant evidence. Additionally, much of the evidence I will cite here bears only indirectly on the question of authorial reliability. I will, however, discuss the evidence in some detail; evidence is always to be valued even when rather weak, and close attention to it can help us to see how more relevant and finely tuned data might be got. Finally I take a look at the general idea of expertise, asking where we can expect to find it and where it is more likely to be illusory. I suggest that the idea of the 'wise author', able to see further into the depths of moral psychology than the rest of us, is one we have reason to be suspicious of.

Is the idea of authorial wisdom too outdated to be worth considering? The British Council recently declared its belief in 'Shakespeare's awesome human insight, recognized by every commentator since Ben Jonson'.[1] There are deniers, but they are rare exceptions to an opinion Emerson expressed when he said that Shakespeare was 'inconceivably wise' (1850/1996: 5). While academic writing is now less given to such enthusiasms the idea that literary works derive from and are evidence for the greatness of the mind that created them is, for most people who take an interest in the question, very plausible. And for those who have some

---

[1] https://www.britishcouncil.org/research-policy-insight/insight-articles/shakespeare-lives.

Imagining and Knowing: The Shape of Fiction. Gregory Currie, Oxford University Press (2020). © Gregory Currie.
DOI: 10.1093/oso/9780199656615.001.0001

conviction in literature's power to educate, this idea naturally provokes the thought that we learn from literature because its makers know something we don't; in learning from fiction we are learning from the author. We have seen that this is very plausible for the case of factual knowledge gained from fiction; you could not expect to learn anything from *War and Peace* about the conventions of Russian society or the practice of warfare at a certain time unless you thought that Tolstoy knew about these things; a scenario in which Tolstoy is very ignorant about these things but happens, by accident, to pass on to us something correct would be a good case of the kind of luck that defeats a claim to knowledge and is anyway not likely to happen very often.

There are qualities of mind besides knowledge or wisdom that are indicated by the production of remarkable fiction, most obviously creativity. Wisdom and creativity are often taken to go hand in hand in the world of literary production. Is that true? Might there be a case for saying instead that there is a certain tension in the idea of their being possessed in high degree by the same person? There is no a priori reason to think so, but there might be evidence that it is, in fact, difficult to combine them. The evidence I will consider is at most suggestive. But it is evidence of some kind and a focus on evidence in this area is long overdue. It cannot count as the generation of genuine insight merely that people have the feeling that insight has been generated; being insightful is not like being funny or creepy. Nor can we say that literary insight is attained when we arrive at truth, or at something that enhances the reader's moral and interpersonal capacities and leave it at that. We must offer some standards, no doubt fallible, by which to tell when people have arrived at whatever form of enlightenment is at issue. We are good at creating and implementing such standards for various forms of knowledge: physics students sit physics exams; plumbing apprenticeships aim to produce good plumbers, and we check their effectiveness by seeing how well the apprentices fix plumbing problems. There is such a thing as getting it right in physics as well as in plumbing, lion-taming, and other respectable practical skills. In all these domains there is such a thing as confirmation that the learner has gotten it right. The sensitivity training purportedly offered by literature cannot be a glorious exception to this.[2]

Creativity is often discussed alongside imagination, a major theme of this book. What is their connection? For all that has been written about it creativity remains a mystery and focusing on the imagination will not unlock that mystery. When people imagine in the various ways outlined in Chapter 1 they may do so creatively or uncreatively: I can no more form creative mental images than I can paint creatively. Imagination provides us with representations (creative or not) of things not present and which may never occur, and that seems at least a necessary

---

[2] For more on this theme see above Section 6.1.

condition for creativity. We might say that having a more powerful imagination is apt to make one more creative because it provides more options to choose from in problem solving. But having many options can overwhelm and paralyse cognition rather than aiding it, and humans don't play chess by working through astronomical numbers of options. The connection between the two gets to sound closer than it is because 'imaginative' means little more than 'creative'; as I just noted, we can imagine creatively or uncreatively and so we can imagine imaginatively or un-imaginatively. Understanding imagination captures little in the domain of creativity. But not understanding creativity won't stop me (as it does not stop others) from talking about it, in Section 10.2.

10.1 Institutional constraints

Before we turn, as we will, to the psychologies of authors we should note an institutional dimension of the problem, something I started to discuss at the end of Chapter 9 and which was mentioned briefly in Section 8.4. We need not agree with those who think that literature is essentially an 'institutional practice' in order to think that there are, as a matter of fact, things which are in some loose sense institutions of literature: patterns of behaviour, mutually acknowledged expectations, sanctions, inducements.[3] The same is true in science; it is not essentially institutional, since it can be practiced by a lone individual who happens to come up with a theory about the world which makes predictions which she seeks to test. But there are, as a matter of fact, some very strong institutions associated with science and which support such goals as explanatory success. We want theories with high degrees of confirmation; accordingly, the institutions of science constrain the behaviour of scientists in ways that make it more likely that they will come up with well-confirmed theories. We expect them to put forward highly testable theories and to conduct carefully designed experiments that will test them, and to find their theories confirmed (to some degree) in the process. We reward scientists well if they do that, and less well or not at all if they don't. If there are indications, as there sometimes are, that people have tried to avoid the constraints by cheating, professional ruin is likely to follow. Sometimes there is evidence that failure in testing regimes is systematic, as with the current reproducibility crisis in the behavioural sciences. While there are questions about why this was not recognized sooner, the fact that it has been recognized and is the subject of intense discussion indicates how much 'getting things right' matters in

---

[3] Peter Lamarque (2010) suggests that there is explanatory mileage in the idea of literature as an institution. But I am puzzled (as is Blackburn (2010)) why the idea that reading literature as literature requires a distinctive kind of attention means that there are 'conventions' of literary reading.

science.[4] It is the existence of very real constraints of these kinds that makes it sensible to talk about science as an institution, though not essentially or necessarily one, just as the president, whoever she is, is not essentially or necessarily the president. Can we say the same thing about literary institutions?

I say no. First of all, literature has a very weak institutional structure. There are patterns of association, influence, and antagonism in literature, but these do not really amount to institutions. Funding, other than via sales of the literary works themselves, is negligible, and organizations like PEN have virtually no influence on the activities of their members or the upshot of those activities. Indeed, the goal is to free writers from constraints on the content of their work. Were it ever suggested, PEN would surely oppose the introduction of assessments of the psychological insights that literary works provide. What literary institutions there are do not set or constrain epistemic goals, and the idea of introducing them strikes everyone as absurd—partly because this would be an unreasonable constraint on creativity.

We do, it is true, possess institutions of criticism which to some extent regulate or at least influence the activities of writers: literature departments, prizes, journals, reviews, and newspaper columns.[5] But they are not designed to promote, nor are they connected in any systematic way with, epistemic reliability. Indeed, it is noticeable that the last forty years of academic criticism have seen a great deal of enthusiasm for the rejection of such ideas as truth, knowledge, and objectivity; no comparable movement has gotten far in the sciences. And when truthfulness is invoked in criticism, it often seems to mark the achievement of some vivid effect, with no very obvious connection to the idea of being right about anything in particular. A reviewer says of Thackeray's *Barry Lyndon* that 'the narrowing of the gap between voice and ventriloquist allows Thackeray to achieve a profound truthfulness about his protagonist's inner life.'[6] It would be odd and probably unprofessional for a reviewer within academic psychology to declare a piece of research as profound truth with no further specification or argument. This same ideology of free-floating truthfulness is found in Nobel Prize citations, describing an *oeuvre* wherein 'beauty and truth are closely allied or completely fused together'.[7]

This tendency is not new. Johnson said of Shakespeare that 'he has not only shewn human nature as it acts in real exigences, but as it would be found in trials,

---

[4] 'An energetic thinker with some original ideas may understandably rebel against the oppressive demand to get it right, especially when the demand comes, as it often does, from cautious and conventional colleagues. In responsible subjects such as the natural sciences, such people rebel against the demand only at their peril—or rather, their ideas will succeed only if the demand is, in the end, obeyed, and the colleagues turn out merely to have been too cautious' (Williams 1989: 3–5).

[5] Though this does not make criticism an institutional phenomenon; criticism can exist without them.

[6] J. D. Taylor, *Times Literary Supplement*, 15 July 2011, p. 15.

[7] Nobel Prize for Literature citation speech in honour of Patrick White, 1973.

to which it cannot be exposed' (1765: xii). Perhaps Johnson knew from experience how human nature acts in real exigencies; it is less clear how he could be confident that people would act this or that way in circumstances he admits no one, including himself, has experienced—or even could experience. And should Johnson have been confident that Shakespeare has shown how human nature acts in real exigencies, when he, Johnson, carried out no surveys or carefully structured experiments to find out whether it really was so? When Leavis (1948: 257) says, rather grudgingly, that *Hard Times* does not give 'a misleading representation of human nature', it is tempting to ask how he could possibly know something that not even the greatest psychologist would think of claiming: what human nature is. This tendency of critics to imagine themselves able to survey human nature, as well as its literary representation, may help to make understandable the postmodern revulsion against humanistic criticism.

Communities that aim to increase knowledge or merely spread it around have audiences, and the responses of an audience can be institutionalized to make them significant contributors to truth and truthfulness. Here, once again, the contrast between literature and science is stark. The relevant audience in the case of science is the scientific community itself: highly trained, highly critical, and with a professional interest in showing up a proposal's weaknesses or elaborating on it if it shows promise. In contrast, the audience for a piece of narrative art, however knowledgeable and well versed in the conventions and techniques of the genre, is simply not tuned to the issue of truthfulness, and is likely to be swayed by powerful emotional forces unleashed by the work itself. It's worth underlining these points with some recent ideas from psychology about the emotions and belief formation.

Emotions affect beliefs in somewhat the way perceptions do. When things are observed to be inconsistent with what we believe, our beliefs tend to shift accordingly. And when our emotions are in conflict with what we believe, there is at least some tendency to bring the two into harmony by adjusting belief, at least when emotion does not easily give way (Clore and Gasper 2000). That is often to the good; neurological patients in Damasio's gambling experiments did badly because they failed to get the right kind of aversive emotional cues from high-risk strategies and did not rethink the options for their play; participants with intact orbitofrontal cortices were guided by their emotions, adopted more sensible strategies, and avoided big losses.[8] But emotion is course-grained and provoked by representations of events as easily as by events themselves; the emotions aroused by manifestly fictional representations of events may have quite strong effects on beliefs, although there is no guarantee or even much indication of a correlation between the fictional representation and the real events themselves.

---

[8] See Bechara et al. (1994). For criticism of the experiment and the conclusions drawn, see Dunn et al. (2006).

Even well-educated viewers of Oliver Stone's rather unreliable *JFK* turn out to have been highly influenced by the film in their beliefs about the likelihood of a wide-ranging conspiracy behind the Kennedy assassination.[9] And we are strongly affected in our beliefs about a represented situation by emotionally arousing features of the representational vehicle that have no bearing on the question of whether what is represented is true; we see this in the care taken to aestheticize religious practices and state ceremonies.[10]

Belief formation is susceptible to other influences that blunt the receiver's critical faculties. Recall first a theory due to Dan Gilbert that makes the problem seem particularly acute.[11] In one of Gilbert's experiments, subjects read an account of a crime; at the end, they were asked to recommend an appropriate sentence for the crime. Within the narrative were certain false embellishments to the descriptions of the crime that, if taken seriously, would make the crime seem worse. These 'fictional' passages were not disguised; they were clearly indicated to the reader as false, being printed in red, while the rest was in black. Nonetheless, the results indicated that subjects who were distracted while reading the account by a digit-search task (and hence less vigilant) were influenced in their decisions by the material in red, tending to give more punitive sentences than were given by people who were not exposed to the false material.

Gilbert's explanation was discussed earlier: anything we are told goes straight into the belief system; it then requires effort, which is not always available or exercised, to remove it. So the distraction task had the effect of allowing the false material to stay in the belief box. Sperber and colleagues (2010) deny that everything we hear is initially believed; rather, we possess a mechanism of vigilance that keeps things out of the belief box, but operating it involves costs. So the mechanism is likely to be activated in situations of perceived risk and not in others. In particular, when the information is of no great personal relevance—as it was not in Gilbert's sentencing experiments—we would not expect there to be much vigilance displayed. Fictions that suggest or implicate real-world claims are not likely to have much vigilance lavished on them, unless they display relevance

---

[9] See Butler et al. (1995). See also above, Section 4.2.

[10] I note some convergence with a claim made by David Velleman (2003). He argues that narrative fails as a vehicle for knowledge because it imposes on us emotional transitions and a sense of closure that make us think we have caught on to a causal-explanatory process when all we have is our own 'sense of an ending'. Velleman has in mind the emotional 'cadence' of a narrative's overall structure; but the same idea could apply at the micro-level, where we consider, as we do in the case of Adam Verver in *The Golden Bowl*, a character's transition from thought to action. A writer can create an emotionally powerful effect that takes us across this mysterious divide, making us conclude that thinking that way really can help us act well—or equally, that thoughts with a certain quasi-aesthetic defect (the wrong image, maybe) will send us astray (see Nussbaum 1990: Chapter 5). But these ideas need better support than they get from our merely finding them emotionally or aesthetically satisfying.

[11] Gilbert et al. (1993). See above, Section 9.3.

to our personal circumstances.[12] If material is not very personally relevant—and so not likely to call our epistemic defences into play—*and* is emotionally charged through the use of expressive language or artfully arranged episodes of conflict and resolution, the chances of it getting through the defences of our belief system are quite high. And fictional material of superior quality often has both of these characteristics.

I said that Gilbert's subjects were influenced by the avowedly false material because they were distracted; this may lead us to question the relevance of his experiment to conclusions about the gullibility of fiction readers. It's true that fiction readers are not generally expected to carry out cognitively engaging tasks such as digital search while they are reading. But there are often serious claims on cognitive resources present when attending to the kinds of fictions we are focusing on here. Consider the tendency in high-end literature and drama to render language and other representational devices harder to process than they would be in less self-conscious projects, with complex sentences and strange tropes of narration.[13] These are elements of what we call style, and Sperber and Wilson have claimed that the function of style is to facilitate the discovery of relevance in communication. With epizeuxis, as in:

There's a fox, a fox in my garden,

we understand that the speaker was surprised or excited by the presence of the fox; the extra processing cost imposed by the repetition makes this relevant information available (Sperber and Wilson 1995: 219). But style may serve purposes that are the opposite of knowledge-enhancing. I suggest that one of the reasons we enjoy complexity in fiction—and hence one reason we find complexity in successful fiction—is that it provides the kind of distraction that lowers vigilance, helping thereby to generate an illusion of learning.[14] Paradoxically, the sheer complexity of great narrative art, so often taken as a sign of cognitive richness and subtlety, may increase its power to spread ignorance and error.[15]

---

[12] The implicatures are likely to be weak, in the sense of Sperber and Wilson (1995: 217–24). Discussing the unusually careful historical scholarship behind Gore Vidal's *Lincoln*, Stacie Friend gives an illuminating analysis both of the novel's capacity to enhance learning of factional knowledge through manipulation of point of view and the epistemic risks created by, among other things, reduced levels of scrutiny. She also emphasizes the extent to which judgements about the factual reliability of works of fiction depends on the particulars of the case and resist generalization (2006, especially 44).

[13] Murray Smith suggests that works of high-end literature may not be the place to go for examples of learning from literature 'for the good reason that their complexity obscures [their] basic narrative function' (2017: 190).

[14] This is not, as David Davies pointed out, the only reason we enjoy complexity; we enjoy complexity in situations where learning (in the sense relevant here) is not at issue, as with cryptic crosswords.

[15] Lowering the reader's level of epistemic vigilance might be one way of encouraging the sort of make-believe attitude to learning suggested in Section 6.4.

Why does style count for so little in science when it counts for so much in literature? In science we expect accuracy, simplicity, explanatory and predictive power. We don't demands that we be given theories that meet the constraints of the sonnet or *Bildungsroman* form; if we did we'd expect to get less accuracy and simplicity and to get, in consequence, less verisimilar theories. The demands of literature lead in another direction. Pasternak said of Shakespeare that 'Half his thought, and the words that verbalized them, were prompted by metre.'[16] What poets write is metrically constrained, and so is the thought they express. More than that, the demands of conformity to meter—or, if you are a novelist, the need to lay a trail of temporarily unanswered interesting questions—make everything more difficult, leaving fewer cognitive resources to think about truth. When you make it more difficult for people to do something, they are likely to do it less well.

There is another way in which the organizations of science and literature differ dramatically that is relevant to assessing literature's capacity for insight. Epistemic goals in science are met not simply by imposing rewards and punishments on the activity of creative individuals, but by facilitating *arguments* among them. One quite surprising result of the recent psychological study of rationality is the discovery of how fragile human reasoning seems to be; we are prone to errors of logic and statistical inference that, from a formal point of view, are simple and obvious, but which specialist training does little to protect us against. When we are thinking about epistemic goals, it is sensible to ask whether an institution— science, literature, or anything else—supports and enhances reasoning, helping to overcome its weaknesses. I suggest that there is something about the situation of the literary creator that militates against the effectiveness of their reasoning and contrasts dramatically with the situation in science.

I mean the *individuality* of creativity in the narrative arts. Occasionally, we find jointly authored fictions, but usually there are only two authors involved, and in those cases, it is often true that the work was largely divided between them. Certainly, the celebrated values of literature are those usually associated with an individual and highly idiosyncratic vision of the human situation. But there is some reason to think that the cognitive capacities necessary for the effective use of reason arc best exercised *interactively*. When people undertake reasoning tasks alone, their performance is surprisingly poor; as indicated above, even highly educated people are prone to fallacies that defeat their purposes time and time again. When the same tasks are undertaken by groups of about eight people working together, success is much higher. This apparently isn't because the group defers to someone who is obviously good at the task; rather, it is because the argumentative context, in which people listen to a proposed way of solving a problem and then criticize and improve on it, aids them in overcoming their

---

[16] Quoted in Gross (2002: 24).

individual tendencies toward error.[17] And studies show that people reason well in argumentative contexts and respond well to reasoning directed at them—much better than in isolation. Sperber and Mercier note that 'when people want to attack alternative views, they are very good at making use of *modus tollens* arguments... On the other hand, half of the people tested in standard reasoning tasks lacking an argumentative context fail on *modus tollens* tasks' (Sperber and Mercier 2012: 383). Even preschoolers do well in groups at spotting fallacies in argument, while late adolescents outside of an argumentative context perform not much better than chance.

Science helps to protect the creator from fallacies of reasoning by providing a richly argumentative environment. There are, it is true, notable instances of great scientific breakthroughs by individuals working in personal isolation. But they did not lack an *argumentative* context. Einstein, far from the centre of the physical universe (Berlin) was working in an intense intellectual environment characterized by Newton's absolutism about space and time, the null result of the Michelson-Morley experiment, Maxwell's electrodynamics, and the theories of Lorentz and Poincaré. Newton, isolated at Woolsthorpe, discovered the theory of gravitation and much else besides—but against the background of competing theories from Descartes, Huygens, Wren, and Hooke, and against which he was constantly testing his own theories. Newton's and Einstein's *argumentative* contexts were richly social ones.

Again, the contrast with literature is stark. I don't say writers never argue; sometimes they argue about their work. They are sometimes intensely social (but see Section 10.2 below) and their correspondence may be justly celebrated. But argument is not to them the professional requirement it is to the scientist. And while writers often discuss aspects of style, plot, and theme, it is much less usual for them to debate the empirical facts relating to human psychology, or the best way to make readers more empathic or otherwise better comprehenders of other people; at least I see little sign of this in the public aspects of this discourse of which, given the popularity of literary festivals and symposia, there is currently a good deal. While scientists on the whole do not concern themselves much with style or the creation of an individual voice, these are centrally important aspects of activity in the narrative arts, where convergence to a common view is not aimed at and the submergence of authorial voice not welcome.

How relevant to fiction-making is this discussion of reasoning? Surely novel writing is not a reasoning task. Of course such activities involve a great deal that

---

[17] Sperber and Mercier (2012) argue that this is because reasoning (inference at the personal level, generally accessible to consciousness) arose as a tool of social cognition; communicated information is highly likely to be deceptive, and so we developed a capacity to check for consistency between what is communicated and what we know or believe—that is our capacity to reason. For full development of the theory see Mercier and Sperber (2017).

is not reasoning. But the thoughtful construction of plot and character, the formulation of descriptions that invoke the right kinds of atmosphere and uncertainty, and—especially—the crafting of the narrative so as to suggest underlying serious themes: these are all activities that involve informal reasoning that matches ends to means. Reasoning in this context as in others rarely involves the construction of explicit inferences.

While we await serious empirical studies of the social epistemology of literature, my tentative conclusion is that literature has no significant institutional constraints that push its creative activity in the direct of truthfulness or impose realistic tests for truth on its outcomes. It has instead, and rather paradoxically, a set of institutional structures—prizes, critical commentary—whose representatives are given to making large and untested (perhaps untestable) claims about literature's capacity for insight. Literary creativity is strongly constrained in various ways, but not towards truthfulness. The real constraints on literary creativity are keyed to the development of arresting, emotionally engaging characters and plot, the artful creation of uncertainty, suspense, and the feeling that we, the audience, are being stretched and challenged by the work. All this may go along with the promise of psychological insight, and indeed with a genuine ambition on the author's part to be psychologically insightful. But the shared desire for psychological insight is not brought closer to fulfilment by the institutions of fiction. Would science produce highly explanatory theories if it was constrained merely to produce theories that people felt were explanatory? That is the way of magic and astrology.

Thus far I have run the argument in terms of truth. But, as I have said so often, we need to put learning from fiction on a much larger canvas. Do the institutions of fiction constrain its practitioners and audiences in ways which encourage learning skills, acquiring sensitivities or knowledge of what experiences are like? Not as far as I can see. What they may perhaps encourage is the inculcation in the audience of a belief that they are acquiring these things. We certainly see praise heaped on authors who, it is said, make us understand what it is like to undergo some experience, but no evidence is provided for the claim that the author has succeeded in this regard beyond the avowal, on the part of the subject, that they do understand. As I have said, understanding, of experiences, of mathematics, or of anything else, is not a transparent state. I may have thought that I understand tensor calculus but my complete failure in the exam tells me I do not. We don't have an examination that tests for understanding of experiences, but that does not make that kind of understanding any more self-validating.[18]

---

[18] See above, Section 6.2.

10.2 The creative personality

So far, I have put the problem in terms a social psychologist would find familiar if not agreeable, emphasizing the situational constraints on creativity in the arts versus those that prevail in the sciences. Might personal factors also play a part? Here we enter especially difficult territory. There is a mass of work on the psychology of creativity, and some on personality differences between creative people in the arts and elsewhere, not all of it tending in the same direction. Conclusions at this stage must be tentative, but what follows draws on a sustained and coherent thread in an admittedly more complex body of research.

Highly creative people are unusual simply by being highly creative, but they are often unusual in other ways. Some of these seem to be enabling conditions for the possession or development of extreme creativity. Extreme levels of creativity in any discipline are said to be accompanied by a significant capacity to be driven by one's own imaginings, rather than being dependent on external stimulus; a high level of responsiveness to one's own inner conceptions, projects, and standards of success, rather than being driven by the prospect of external reward; a high degree of immersion in and obsessive concern with one's own work; and a corresponding unwillingness to respond to personal and domestic responsibilities—a theme I will return to.

Not all creative people are unusual in the same way. Individual differences aside, there are differences according to the form that creativity takes. While it is said that creative writers share with scientists a degree of introversion and a tendency toward hostility and arrogance, they are less conforming and less socialized and more prone to intense affective experience than scientists generally are—bringing to mind a traditional picture of the literary artist as difficult, self-absorbed, and unstable. Other research gives some support to this last idea: Simonton (2014) distinguishes creative endeavor by degrees of unconventionality, drawing rough distinctions between 'normal' and 'revolutionary' scientific activity and between academic and avant-garde art; the less conventional the creative activity, the more proneness to psychopathology. Additionally, artistic creativity at any level tends to go with greater proneness to psychopathology than does scientific creativity. Thus we get a scale of increasing psychopathology along which we can progressively place normal science, revolutionary science, academic art, and avant-garde art. The creative people I am focusing on here would appear in the two most at-risk categories. Retrospective studies of notable creators—a genre with methodological problems that certainly make its results questionable—tend to support this.[19] In Post's study of fifty great writers, only one was

---

[19] The few studies there are of eminent writers—e.g. Claridge et al. (1998), Jamison (1993)—are often avowedly speculative, and it is hard to draw definite conclusions from them. In particular, their conclusions about the relation between creativity and madness (a favoured theme) may be confounded

considered free of psychopathology (Maupassant), and this group contained the highest proportion of individuals with severe psychopathology (nearly 50 per cent) compared with the other groups of creative people considered: scientists, political leaders, thinkers, artists, and composers.[20]

What kinds of psychopathology are in question here? Recent research into creativity has focused on two things: schizophrenia and affective or emotional disorders, notably bipolar disorder (BD). The relation between them is disputed, but some evidence supports the idea that they are aspects of a single underlying pathology.[21] However connected, there is evidence that both kinds of traits are disproportionately represented in highly creative groups.[22] Severe forms of both are too disabling to sustain creative work; creativity is promoted not by the disorders themselves but by possession of the 'underlying cognitive styles and personality traits' for these disorders.[23] This sometimes involves a life history in which psychotic episodes are interwoven with normal or relatively normal functioning.

What does this suggest about the credentials of creative writers when it comes to insight into the mind? Individual differences make generalizations hard, but I note emerging evidence that both schizophrenia and bipolar disorder are marked by difficulties in the area of understanding other people's minds—the area where we are apt to credit great literary artists with especially penetrative powers.[24] There are by now well-developed tests in this area. Sometimes called 'theory of mind tests,' many were developed in order to help us understand aspects of child development. It has subsequently been shown that these tests can reveal individual differences later in life, as well as point to situations in which people's normal ability to track the mental states of others is, with surprising ease, compromised (Mitchell et al. 1996). A large number of studies have now found impaired

by temporary cultural factors like romanticism that shift the boundaries of acceptable behaviour; see Sass (2001). It may also be that male dominance in these studies produces an unrepresentative profile for artistic creativity. Ludwig (1994) is a study of recent female writers.

[20] Post (1994). Another study looked at thirty creative writers and found 'a substantially higher [than normal] rate of mental illness, predominantly affective disorder, with a tendency toward the bipolar subtype' (Andreasen (1987: 1288)). For a contrary view see Schlesinger (2014).

[21] See, e.g. Claridge and Blakey (2009).

[22] For opposing views about the relative importance of these two for creativity, see Sass (2001) and Jamison (2000–2001). A 2013 review 'cautiously confirm[s] an association between creativity and both bipolar disorder and schizotypy' (Thys et al. 2014: 141).

[23] Glazer (2009: 756). 'The relationship is not between actual psychosis and creativity, but rather between "schizotypy" or "psychoticism" and creativity ... The putative link is with non-clinical expressions of schizotypal temperament and information processing style, along a personality dimension that leads from "normality" at one end, through differently weighted combinations of schizotypal traits, towards full-blown psychosis at the other end' (Brod 1997: 274).

[24] See Brüne (2005); Harrington et al. (2005); Sprong et al. (2007). I'm grateful to Peter Carruthers for drawing my attention to the last and most comprehensive of these studies. Recently data from an Asian population has become available, broadly in line with these conclusions: Charernboon and Patumanond (2017).

understanding of mental states in patients with schizophrenia. In the meta-analysis of Sprong et al. (2007), this correlation was shown to be strong, with patients on average one standard deviation below normal performance; mentalizing impairment in patients in remission was smaller but still significant.[25] Understanding of mental states is also impaired in people at risk for schizophrenia.[26] Thus the effect does not seem to be explicable wholly as a result of other symptoms such as thought disorganization; Sprong and colleagues hazard that 'mentalising impairment is a susceptibility indicator for schizophrenia and hence may be trait-dependent'.[27]

What about bipolar disorder? There is evidence here also of a connection with theory of mind deficits. One study found impaired performance on theory of mind tests for both depressed and manic patients, but not for patients in remission (Kerr et al. 2003). Another study examined bipolar patients currently in a normal mood state and found that they performed poorly when compared with controls on verbal theory of mind tests, but at a level comparable to controls on nonverbal tasks, though they were slower to respond (Olley et al. 2005). A third study of patients with unipolar or bipolar depression currently in remission concluded that they were impaired on a relatively complex theory of mind test, the second-order false belief test (Inoue et al. 2004). Finally, a report indicates that 'the bipolar patient group as a whole, as well as all three clinical subgroups [manic, depressed, and remitted], were impaired on all measures of ToM [theory of mind] relative to controls, but did not differ from each other in most ToM scores'.[28] So here, as with schizophrenia, there is some evidence that problems with mentalizing are connected to the underlying traits of the disorder and are not merely a product of the emotionally disturbed states that it manifests.

What all this suggests is that traits strongly associated with literary creativity include impairments in understanding mental states—contradicting our intuitive picture of the creative writer as an insightful observer of the human scene. Add to this the thought that creative writers often seem to be rather distanced from the reality of their subject—interpersonal relations: 'the creator rarely cares much for others' is the brutal summary of a survey in this area (Policastro and Gardner 1999: 222). It is striking that we tend to credit a certain group of individuals, who are apparently highly prone to mental disturbance, with a deep insight into human nature and conduct because of their imaginative depictions, and that we

---

[25] See also Herold et al. (2002).

[26] See Langdon and Coltheart (2004). Irani et al. (2006); Marjoram et al. (2006); Pickup (2006); Schiffman et al (2004); Wykes et al. (2001: 148).

[27] Sprong et al. (2007: 11). See also Bora et al. (2009). But see Pousa et al. (2008: 312).

[28] Assion et al. (2011). See also Mitchell and Young (2015: 17): 'there is convincing evidence that theory of mind is impaired in some way across the mood states, and into the supposedly asymptomatic state of euthymia. It may, therefore, be considered a trait rather than state impairment, i.e., one that is an enduring correlate of bipolar disorder.'

are not discouraged by the fact that many of them seem to have little experience of or even interest in the corresponding reality.

We must not take any of this too far. Not all authors, even great ones, are psychologically disturbed; fewer write effectively in a state of disturbance; some are no more socially incompetent than the rest of us. We certainly need better studies of the psychology of outstandingly creative people in all walks of life, a better understanding of how competence in mind-reading is distributed throughout normal and compromised populations, and good studies of the social epistemology of literature. And we must retain a critical attitude toward what psychologists tell us. My aim here is simply to urge the merits of a very moderate scepticism in dealing with claims about the insightful nature of literary creativity.

10.3 Authorship and expertise

Finally, let us consider an important assumption often made by those who assert the wisdom of the authors of great literary works. This is that there is such a thing as expertise in moral psychology: a discriminative, perhaps quasi-perceptual capacity to see what is morally relevant in a situation which is not dependent on the simple moral rules which are so often inadequate to the complexities of real life—something akin to the capacity of the chess expert to see the right move quickly. Surely, one might say, the rich detail of relationships between thinking and feeling agents that we find in the novelistic tradition effectively display the expertise of their authors and will be helpful in developing this kind of expertise in readers. On this view fiction enables a sort of moral and psychological apprentice system.

However, there is evidence that expertise—a genuine capacity to make better intuitive judgements than one would make by following simple rules—is, at least in many areas, an illusion. In a review of Nussbaum's *Love's Knowledge* Jesse Kalin posed the problem for the moral case:

> I am very poor in discerning the real motives and situations, as well as needs and cares, of people...I have been struck by how often, when I have allowed myself to try to make moral judgments in this way, I have gotten things quite wrong. It was both morally safer, and more morally correct, to stay within a moral context of rules and principles, of concern for rights and fairness and basic human welfare. Safer to act as a stranger among strangers than to seek to be a friend or someone closer to people I did not and could not know.   (Kalin 1992: 146)

Kalin is unusual in his recognition of his limitations as a moral expert, but all that we know about expertise in general suggests that the rest of us are in the same position. Following pioneering work by Paul Meehl sixty years ago, studies have shown that following simple rules—rules that take account of many fewer factors than a clinician or other expert would consider—does at least as well and generally better than relying on an expert's judgement.[29] This is true for the prediction of the future value of wine, the performance of baseball players, the health of newborn babies, a couple's prospects for marital stability, and in many other areas. Our aversion to algorithms and our respect for the idea of the diligent expert who insists on going further than the application of simple rules, combined with the strong but misplaced sense that experts have of their own indispensability, makes us resistant to this conclusion and we continue to rely on experts in these and other areas. But a review undertaken in 2004 of the evidence concerning clinical judgement since Meehl's work summarized the state of knowledge in this way:

> There may well be reasoning processes that clinicians sometimes use that a formula, table, or computer program cannot precisely mimic. However, whether such reasoning actually helps clinicians dependably outperform statistical formulas and computer programs is an empirical question with a clear, convincing answer: No, for prediction domains thus far studied.   (Grove and Lloyd 2006: 194)

Is the idea of moral expertise equally flawed? As far as I know this has not been tested directly, and one can easily see the difficulties of finding a reliable way of testing it; the problem of getting inter-tester agreement about what counts as the right moral choice is enough to sink the prospects for most testing regimes. It should be said that the evidence does point to the efficacy of expert judgement in certain domains. Daniel Kahneman and Richard Klein, researchers with opposing perspectives on this issue, agree in a recent joint article that failures of expert opinion are not due to cognitive incompetence but to the unpredictability of the environment (Kahneman and Klein 2009). Thus in what Kahneman and Klein call 'high-validity' environments expert judgement will often do better than reliance on algorithms; but where there are no stable relationships between objective cues and the outcomes of possible actions, reliance on algorithms is preferable. Is moral decision-making a high validity environment? Kahneman and Klein give as an example of low validity the case of decisions about personal loans—decisions which require judgements about people's honesty and reliability. This strikes me as a domain which calls on information at least overlapping with that required for sensible judgement in the moral psychological domain—judgement which often needs to take into account trustworthiness and honesty in order to work out what the right thing to do in a particular situation is. Perhaps moral decision-making is too various to be described as a single domain with a unique score on the validity

---

[29] See Meehl (1954). The issue is discussed in Chapter 21 of Kahneman (2011), where many studies illustrative of this thesis are cited.

scale. Perhaps we can find kinds of moral reasoning where experts trained partly by exposure to the fictional literature of complex moral choice do better than those who rely on simple moral rules of thumb. Perhaps. My point is not that the evidence from decision-making refutes the claim that moral expertise is a quality we should aspire to, but that it poses a challenge that needs to be met by anyone who seriously wants to press the case for moral expertise. Such a person needs to look very closely at the empirically informed psychological literature.

There are additional reasons for thinking it unlikely that literature has the capacity to create or improve moral expertise. Some are to do with the fragility of moral judgement itself. We know, for example, that such judgements are highly sensitive to the presence of morally irrelevant factors, such as the cleanliness or otherwise of the environment they are made in. We know that we are prone to judge people's character according to their appearance, and that we put a misplaced confidence in the consistency of people's moral behaviour across diverse circumstances.[30] Any project of creating moral expertise out of such low-base levels of competence surely faces difficulties. And while, in many areas, competence itself often does not improve to reliable levels, people's confidence in their judgement increases dramatically. So the possibility is that a project designed to improve moral expertise will lead not only to worse moral decisions but to more dogmatic ones.

Other reasons arise from what we know or suspect about the psychology of narrative fiction. Friends of the epistemic value of literature often emphasize its narrative form, suggesting that narrative is a vehicle particularly appropriate for understanding other people and ourselves.[31] While I don't suggest that narrative thought and utterance should be avoided in our interpersonal dealings (surely that's impossible) we should be alive to the tendency of narrative to encourage fallacious thinking, something that both philosophers and psychologists have noted. David Velleman (2003) suggests that the narrative form is defined by an 'arc of emotional cadence' in which events are brought to a satisfying conclusion: not a conclusion to events, but to our emotional response to events.[32] Oftentimes, he suggests, the audience is fooled by its own emotional resolution, induced by the narrative into an illusory sense of resolution to the events the narrative describes. And psychological research indicates that a good story seduces us into thinking of accidental outcomes as 'inevitable', of less probable events as more probable, of a jumble of events as spuriously coherent.[33] There is additionally evidence that narrative literature of the kind which occupies the current western cannon, and

---

[30] See Doris (2002) for a summary of this literature.
[31] See e.g. Nussbaum (1990: Introduction).   [32] See above, Section 10.1 n10.
[33] As Kahneman notes, the probability-defying judgements of people when presented with the famous Linda-the-feminist-bank-teller case suggest that, while 'Linda is a bank teller' seems odd given Linda's history of political commitment, 'Linda is a feminist bank teller' fits naturally into a story, so we rate the second more probable than the first (2011: 159). See also Currie and Jureidini (2004).

which often provides the examples used by defenders of the epistemic value of literature, encourages a false view of human motivation. Much of this literature emphasizes the role of character and character development in determining outcomes and explaining motivation. But the role of character in human psychology is deeply contested, with much evidence to support the proposition that people's situations play a significant but ill-recognized role in determining how they act.[34] Perhaps heroic efforts can overcome these error-inducing tendencies in the narrative form, but it seems odd to argue that narrative is especially well suited to the encouragement of epistemic virtue. That is a proposition for which we need a lot of evidence we don't currently have.

10.4 Conclusions

Excellence in creating narratives of fictional human lives is a rightly admired quality. Sometimes our admiration for one quality makes it tempting to attribute other qualities, such as wisdom or insightfulness, to the agent concerned—an instance of what is called the 'halo effect'.[35] I don't say wisdom and insight are never present in revered authors, only that we need to be careful in making these attributions, and mindful of ways in which the mind and the life of such a creator might not, after all, be conducive to wisdom or insightfulness. Beyond the halo effect, I found three specific reasons why we should be careful: the lack of support within the practices and institutions of fiction for the pursuit of truth, evidence that there is a degree of disconnection between literary creativity and a deep acquaintance with and understanding of moral psychology, and some quite general reasons to doubt the existence of expertise in this area.

The next and final chapter (Chapter 11) continues the policy of looking for ways that our optimism about learning from fiction should be tempered, this time in relation to the inculcation of empathy. As with this chapter, Chapter 11 seeks to provide at least some empirical support for the scenarios it conjures up.

---

[34] See my 2010b, Chapters 11–12.   [35] See e.g. Verhulst et al. (2010).

11

Fiction and empathy

A thought that has captured attention across the literary, philosophical, and psychological disciplines is this: fiction refines and enlarges our empathic sensitivities to morally charged situations, exposing us to exemplars—imaginary ones—of demanding, complex situations beyond those we are likely to encounter in daily life, expanding the circle of those we care about and our ability to help them. As Murray Smith puts the idea: 'Our ability to empathize is extended across a wide range of types of person and situation, and sustained and intensified by virtue of the artificial, "designed" environments created by narrative artefacts.'[1] As with all the arguments of this book I won't attempt a comprehensive refutation of this optimistic picture; rather I suggests that the pathway to learning of this kind is harder to travel and more prone to failure than the optimistic picture recognizes. I'll even suggest that the effect of fictive empathy may sometimes be to dampen or occasionally suppress its real-world counterpart. That must be understood if we are to gain an overall picture of the cognitive powers of fiction.

11.1 Empathy and representation

Empathy, like other emotions, can get things right. And that means it can get them wrong. Emotions, we saw in Chapter 4, represent people, things, and situations as fearful, lovable, guilty of transgression, worthy of admiration. Emotions get things right to the extent that their objects are as the emotion represents them. What is it that empathy needs to get right? Empathy represents another sentient being as feeling a certain way. It does that representing in virtue of its effect on the subject: I empathize with your sadness by feeling sad myself. But it is not enough that we both happen to feel sad, even sad in the same way. Nor is it enough that my sadness is caused by your sadness: that would not distinguish empathy from emotional contagion; your display of fear may cause me to be fearful without me empathizing with your fear.[2] Might an episode start as contagion and end as

---

[1] Smith (2017: 191). Smith refers here to narrative works generally but clearly means to include fictional ones. Psychologist Emy Koopman puts the claim like this: 'Through feeling for [characters], readers could generalize these feelings to the real world, becoming more sensitive to and gaining a better understanding of others' distress, and, perhaps, reacting more empathically to others' (2015: 64).
[2] On empathy and emotional contagion see Coplan (2004). But I disagree with Coplan when she says that 'cases of emotional contagion involve boundary confusion. When we "catch" the emotions of

Imagining and Knowing: The Shape of Fiction. Gregory Currie, Oxford University Press (2020). © Gregory Currie.
DOI: 10.1093/oso/9780199656615.001.0001

empathy? I 'catch' your feel, realize that we both fear fearful and then focus on what my own feeling of fearfulness tells me about the quality of your fear; I may finally do something with the intention of reducing your level of fearfulness. I doubt whether our common understanding of empathy (or better our practices of applying the word 'empathy') hold an answer to this and other questions that probe the boundaries between empathy and other emotions. Without seeking to define empathy I'll indicate the kinds of cases that we should focus on here, given that our interest is in the relation between empathy and fiction.

Simple illustrations of empathy often involve a direct perceptual encounter by one agent with another agent's display of affect, especially through facial expression. Such displays seem able to induce in the observer a similar affective state. Cinema, with its ability to focus on the details of facial expression, has long been said to be a powerful device for eliciting this kind of empathy, taking advantage of low-level psychological mechanisms that operate independently of belief; I know that the actor is not really sad or afraid, but my empathy-mechanism is triggered regardless. But it is a mistake to think that empathy is shielded from thought, or 'cognitively impenetrable'. Tania Singer and colleagues (2006), in a study of empathy for pain, found empathy to be modulated by the observer's judgements about the person in pain. Male but not female viewers' empathy was affected by whether the person in pain was perceived as having behaved unfairly in a prior game of iterated prisoner's dilemma. Males also showed an increase in experienced reward which was correlated with their expressed desire for revenge against the unfair player. In another study empathic response to pain was modulated by knowledge that the pain was caused in the process of curing a disorder.[3] The level and quality of empathic response is also influenced by people's beliefs about empathy itself. A study by Karina Schumann and colleagues found that people expended greater empathic effort in responding to someone with conflicting views and spent more time listening to the personal story of a racial outgroup member when they believed that empathy is capable of development than they did if they believed the contrary (Schumann et al. 2014). Section 11.2 will build on the thought that empathy is not merely a spontaneous and uncontrolled outburst of feeling but is susceptible to some degree of top-down influence.

It's the same with fiction, where empathy is affected by our understanding of and judgements about the characters and their situations. In literature it could not be otherwise, because we have no perceptual stimulus to draw on and must rely on

---

another, it is as though we fuse with the other, losing our separate identity' (145). I may acquire fear from you without being at all confused about our separate identities.

[3] Lamm et al. (2007). For arguments in favour of the responsiveness of empathy to belief, see de Vignemont and Singer (2006).

the thoughts that are conveyed by the narrative. If I misunderstand those thoughts I may end up empathizing with the wrong character. The same may happen in a non-fictional context, as when your account of a mutual friend's distress results in me empathizing with them; if your account got things wrong and our friend was delighted by the outcome my empathy will misfire. Recall now the distinction between emotional states which get things right by representing their objects as they are and cases of fictive or quasi-emotions where the conditions of rightness are given by how the character is represented in the story. My empathy, if I have any, with Anna Karenina's emotional state represents correctly when it represents her as feeling the way she feels *according to the story*.

Given what has been said about the rightness conditions for empathic states, the experiences we have in responding to fictional scenarios should be classed as 'quasi-empathic', for they are states which represent their objects correctly when they represent them *as they are represented by the fiction*.[4] But for ease of exposition I will simply talk, as everyone else does, of 'empathy for fictional characters'. As long as we remember that these are cases where representational correctness has this distinctive character, we shall not get into difficulty.

Here in summary form are what I take to be important features of the states I will be discussing under the heading of 'empathy' in this chapter. I take empathy to be:

1. a mental state involving affect;
2. a response to the (real or imagined) affect-involving state of another (the target),
3. in which you are (normally) aware that your state is a response to the state of the target,
4. which often presents itself as a way of understanding what the target's state feels like by presenting its affective component as *similar to* the affective state of the target,
5. which often involves having thoughts as well as feelings which mirror, or are presented as mirroring, the thoughts of the person you are empathizing with; in empathizing with your fear of the tiger I will have thoughts about tigers as well as anxious feelings,
6. which is not the same as sympathy; empathizing with someone may leave me devoid of sympathy; I might relish your suffering, and a powerful leader may exploit the emotions of others by having an empathic sense of their intensity and direction; conversely, my failure to empathize with your plight need not prohibit me from sympathizing, and taking steps to help you,

[4] For the relation between emotions and quasi-emotions see above Section 4.3.

7. but which may have, in normal circumstances and for psychologically normal subjects, a tendency to promote sympathy and may be an especially direct and effective mechanism for mobilizing helping behaviour,[5]

8. which seems to be cognitively penetrable, educable, and to some extent under the control of conscious will.

Points 7 and 8 are important for our purposes; they suggest both the possibility of a genuine place for fiction in motivating empathic effort and for empathy in affecting our moral behaviour. I take up this issue in the next section.

11.2 Reasons to be moral

Your plan to murder your neighbour failed yesterday: during the hour of opportunity you were immersed in reading *Crime and Punishment* and forgot to carry it out. This was a good effect of your engagement with the novel, but not the kind of evidence we look for when we wonder whether fiction is good for us. Fiction did not work in the right way in this case. Perhaps the problem is that your reading of *Crime and Punishment* did not provide you with a motivating reason to refrain from killing. You had, all along, a normative reason not to kill your neighbour—it would be wrong to do it. Unfortunately your morally inattentive reading failed to give you any vivid sense of this reason's force, and certainly did not motivate you to refrain from killing.[6]

Should we require that, when fiction produces morally desirable effects, it always does so by offering us reasons to be moral? No. We engineer schemes and institutions in order to improve behaviour without thereby giving anyone *reasons* for behaving differently. We try to shape urban environments that will reduce levels of aggression; we introduce opt-out pension schemes with a view to encouraging people to save. These are not reason-giving arrangements but we think (some of us) that they are worthy responses to the problem of reducing bad behaviour and encouraging a thoughtful approach to the future.[7] What we may celebrate in fiction's capacity to change us morally should extend beyond its

---

[5] The actual contribution of empathy to moral cognition and behaviour is disputed. Batson has argued for a close connection between empathy and altruistic behaviour (see e.g. Batson et al. (1991)); Jesse Prinz argues that empathy is not necessary for moral judgement, development, or motivation; he also questions whether we should cultivate moral systems based on empathy, and whether empathy is the 'key to a well functioning moral system' (2011a: 221). The answer might be no to both questions and yet it still be true that empathy has a role to play in mobilizing helping behaviour.

[6] On motivating and normative reasons see Smith (1994: Section 4.2).

[7] As well as trying to form habits in this way we may want such 'nudges' to go along with a public culture which encourages reflection and debate, which is reason-promoting in ways which will help subjects to exercise some control over the direction and strength of their habitual behaviour. See below, Section 11.4.

capacity to provide moral reasons. And importantly, empathy induced by fiction can work for us in both reason-based and non-reason-based ways. Fictions that help us empathize with groups outside our own may do so by revealing to us the status of such people as moral equals, as entitled to respect as anyone within our circle. But fictions may also simply nudge us in the direction of a more empathic response to people and their circumstances, operating more like exercise machines than arguments.

That at least is a combination of views about empathy and fiction often heard. And the idea that fictions may provoke better behaviour from outside the space of reasons is broadly in line with findings in other areas, notably sports science where the use of imagination in visual and motor modalities is common. In one study, golfers improved 30 per cent over baseline through imagined stroke play (Woolfolk et al. 1985). Other studies hint at even more welcome results: 'motor imagery may provide a valuable tool to access the motor network and improve outcome after stroke' (Sharma et. al. 2006: 1941). One concern about this from the point of view of fiction is that it surely matters a great deal that the imagined practice is correct in the sense of mirroring the conditions that would produce the desired real-world outcome; imagining taking a wild swing at the ball is unlikely to improve performance, even if one imagines, as in the study just mentioned, a successful outcome. It is not immediately clear how we would judge practice in empathetic understanding as correct or incorrect, but it is plausible to think that a requirement of correct practice in any area is that it be in response to ecologically realistic cues. And empathy exercised in response to fictional characters is generally a response to different cues from those available in the wild. In the fictional case we generally get a good deal of authorial input clarifying the character's situation and mental state; things much less easily available concerning real people. It should be a source of some concern to those who think that fiction improves empathic skills that the triggering conditions for fictional and for real cases are different in ways which, for all we know, matter to how facility with the one carries over to the other.[8]

The inculcation of skills and the provision of reasons need not be separable aspects of the cognitive work done by a fiction. Providing skills can itself be partly a matter of giving reasons: we give tennis players a reason to keep their eye focused on the point where ball and racket make contact when we say that this will help them control the subsequent direction of the ball. An increased capacity for empathy opens the way to motivating reasons. Sharing another's suffering makes you want to help, and knowing the quality of their suffering gives you a reason to do so.

[8] I made essentially this point in Section 8.4 above.

11.3 A complex picture

Any realistic account of the relations between fiction and empathy is bound to be messy. It's only ever some fictional works, in some contexts, for some readers, that promote this kind of cognitive change. Fiction can spread ignorance, prejudice, and insensitivity as effectively as it provides knowledge and openness. We know how easily we pick up false information from stories, and people's perception of risk is notoriously degraded by imagination. Risk perception is vulnerable, of course, to real but objectively improbable threats as when people continue to smoke while focusing their attention on the danger from rare pollutants. But we have seen evidence that we have only to imagine the danger from a non-existent psychiatric patient to want tighter controls on the mentally ill.[9] Nor is empathy always in the service of admirable results: empathy-inducing stories, fictional or not, of the wrongs done to one's ethnic group can fuel hatred against outsiders.[10] Reading a sustained and demanding literary work is a complex experience, some aspects of which may be empathy-friendly while others are its enemies, and the net moral effects of a given work for a given subject will be very hard to predict.

Current psychological research has yet to confront much of this complexity. Has it produced any evidence for the supposed effects of fiction on empathy? Reviewing work by now a decade old, Suzanne Keen judged the evidence weak at best.[11] Since then new studies have appeared, some of them claiming remarkable results. Below I comment on some of this work. But my main purpose in this chapter is to argue for two claims which may be of interest to those with a serious interest in the empirical study of literature and empathy. In brief: (i) It is one thing to show that literature makes us more empathic; another to show that it makes us more usefully discriminating empathizers; (ii) a serious study of the effects of literature on empathy should investigate possible ways that literature might compromise our empathic tendencies and not focus exclusively on good news stories.[12]

[9] See again above, Section 9.3. See also Gerrig and Prentice (1991: 2); Marsh et al. (2003).

[10] For this and other concerns about the partiality of empathy see Prinz (2011b). Others see an important role for empathy when reflectively constrained; Following Hume and Smith, Antti Kauppinen argues for the moral significance of an 'ideal-regulated empathy...a broadly affective response to another's perceived situation that is regulated by reference to an ideal perspective' (2014: 105). See also Driver (2011).

[11] See Keen (2007). As well as examining experimental studies Keen looked at suggestive commentary in the public domain and at the responses of her own students, finding similarly unsupportive results. Sarah Worth, more favourably disposed towards the idea of learning from fiction, concludes a later review of evidence with the belief that 'through the use of controlled experiments we *will* have some solid empirical evidence that reading fiction can increase empathy' (2017: Section 7.7, my emphasis).

[12] There is no inconsistency in supposing that fiction has both positive and negative effects on empathy; the same object may have both empathy-increasing and empathy-reducing features; the features may be activated in different circumstances or in the same circumstances; the features might affect different populations or the same one. If it's the same population in the same circumstances, the

Two further context-fixing points are worth making: First, I argued earlier that a fictional work's value as literature is not independent of the extent to which it contains, implies, or suggests truths of various kinds. It is a more difficult question, I think, as to whether a work's capacity to induce empathy is similarly connected to its literary value (if any). In fact I won't be concerned here with the question whether fiction's supposed capacity to enlarge empathy has consequences for how we should think about literary value in general or the literary value of particular works. What I say will be consistent with the view that a work's capacity to enlarge empathy makes no difference at all to its value as literature. Even people who hold that view may be interested in whether fiction is a valuable inducer of empathy; no one outside the circle of Dorian Grey thinks that artistic values are the only values worth having. Secondly, those who claim that literature's capacity to induce empathy contributes to personal growth, moral enlargement, helping behaviour, and the rest need not claim that this is the only mechanism by which literature has, or can have, these good outcomes. It might be claimed that literature calls forth non-empathic emotions and other states which independently contribute to these good outcomes. While some of the results I'll consider here may apply to these other states, I will limit my own discussion to empathy.

11.4 Monitoring the development and use of skills

Friends of fiction's moral significance have wanted to emphasize not merely its capacity to increase empathic sensitivity but its help in improving moral discrimination. For Nussbaum, following Henry James, the competent moral agent is 'finely aware and richly responsible', able to judge sensibly in a complex moral environment where available clues are subtle and potentially misleading.[13] Let us distinguish two kinds of purposes for which we work on our skills and capacities. Some skills quickly arrive at an adequate steady state, as with my bike-riding: barely passable, but able to get me to the village shop. With other purposes in mind a skill may require maintenance of higher-level control even though individual components of the action are performed so quickly as to be beyond rational deliberation, as with the piano playing of an aspirant concert artist. The pianist's behaviour never becomes automated in the way my bicycle-riding so obviously has. The pianist cannot let her mind wander; she must be constantly assessing and modulating her performance (Annas 2011).

positive and negative effects on a given individual would produce a net result for that individual, positive, negative, or null.

[13] Nussbaum (1990: Chapter 5). See above, Section 6.1.

This is a relevant distinction for us. Unconstrained, unreflective empathy often does not lead to desirable results. Helping behaviour produced by unreflective empathy tends to be arbitrarily disposed, favours those close to us with whom we empathize easily, and proceeds without regard to justice or economy of means; it makes us sensitive to the individual victim of a policy and indifferent to the anonymous many whose lives the policy saved.[14]

If reading literature simply magnifies our empathic responses without giving us the power to modulate and direct them it arguably does little good.[15] And some of the greatest literature seems vulnerable to the worry that it encourages sensitivity to irrelevant or distracting cues to the distribution of empathic concern. Tzachi Zamir points out that we care deeply about Cleopatra's death but rarely give thought to the deaths of Charmian and Iras whose speech is less memorable; their bodies lie on the stage unmourned.[16] What serious advocates of learning from literature surely hope for is that it will help us to be more thoughtful and discriminating empathizers, capable of putting our empathic capacities to good use by having moral reasoning in an oversight role. The internal demands of narrative coherence and the need to focus on interesting and atypical subjects do not make it easy for fictions at any level of quality to satisfy this goal. Nor does the currently available evidence, even on the most optimistic construal, support the idea that fiction does this. Experimentalists have found that, immediately after reading a short story, subjects were more willing to help someone pick up dropped pencils than were non-readers; other experiments have shown raised scores on tests of empathy such as 'Reading the Mind in the Eyes' in which subjects answer questions about the emotion expressed in a pictured face, and on self-reports of empathy.[17] While such tests may show elevated empathic tendencies they do not tell us much about the controlled, reflective, and discriminating use of empathy.[18]

---

[14] On the dampening of empathic responses to the suffering of out-group members see Cikara, Bruneau, and Saxe (2011). Paul Bloom writes, 'if a planet of billions is to survive, however, we'll need to take into consideration the welfare of people not yet harmed—and, even more, of people not yet born. They have no names, faces, or stories to grip our conscience or stir our fellow-feeling. Their prospects call, rather, for deliberation and calculation. Our hearts will always go out to the baby in the well; it's a measure of our humanity. But empathy will have to yield to reason if humanity is to have a future' (2013); see also Pappas (1997).

[15] Murray Smith gives special attention to fiction's capacity to 'intensify empathy' (2017: 192–3).

[16] Paper delivered at the Shakespeare and Philosophy conference, University of Hertfordshire, August 2014.

[17] Reading the Mind in the Eyes is a test of 'mentalizing' which is said to 'overlap' with empathy; see Baron-Cohen et al. (2001: 241).

[18] I do not suggest that the available tests are pointless; on the contrary they are to be welcomed as the beginning of a serious empirical investigation of a topic too long left to people's intuitive judgements.

11.5 Current evidence for the effects of fiction on empathy

What, in fact, do these tests show? Keith Oatley and colleagues at Toronto are pioneers in this field and have claimed that 'engaging in the simulative experiences of fiction literature can facilitate the understanding of others who are different from ourselves and can augment our capacity for empathy and social inference'.[19] The evidence they provide is somewhat weak. They say that reading a fictional narrative, as compared with reading an 'instructional text', led to the activation of more personal memories, and was engaged with for longer, and that, 'It is possible that these longer reading times reflected a more attentive approach to the text, which aids in producing a simulative experience when combined with certain text features such as metaphors and rich descriptions.'[20] Whether these factors do promote simulative activity and, if so, whether the resulting activity improves performance on empathy tasks is unclear. The same research group also claims a correlation between exposure to fiction and empathic abilities, though they say it would be difficult to see what the direction of causation is.[21] Another study (referred to in the Introduction) used the 'reading for the eyes' test, is ambitiously titled 'Reading Literary Fiction Improves Theory of Mind', and is popularly cited as having shown that fiction makes us better people.[22] The improvement in empathy performance was actually small, its durability was not examined, and the way of choosing reading materials—by the experimenters themselves and not by a neutral party—has been strongly criticized.[23] Another study found increased empathic tendencies a week after reading part of a Sherlock Holmes story, as measured by self-report, but only for readers who were highly emotionally involved in it ('transported' as psychologists say); readers who reported low emotional involvement were found to have reduced empathic tendencies after a week.[24] These results are somewhat difficult to interpret; taking them at face value

---

[19] Mar and Oatley (2008: 173). Uses of 'can' and 'it is possible that' make it unclear what they are claiming.

[20] Mar and Oatley (2008: 179). One problem here is that this research does not distinguish the effects of fiction from the effects of narrative; the contrast with an 'instructional text' creates a contrast between narrative and non-narrative discourse, not between fiction and non-fiction. This point is well made by Koopman (2015).

[21] Mar et al. 2006. Koopman found a correlation between exposure to literature and empathic responses but does not claim to have found a causal relation (2015: 76).

[22] Kidd and Castano (2013). For popular reaction to the study see, for example, 'Reading literary fiction improves empathy, study finds', *Guardian*, Tuesday 8 October 2013: 'New research shows works by writers such as Charles Dickens and Téa Obrecht sharpen our ability to understand others' emotions—more than thrillers or romance novels.' See also above, The Project, text to n13.

[23] For criticism see http://languagelog.ldc.upenn.edu/nll/?p=7715. This criticism applies to nearly all the available studies.

[24] Bal and Veltkamp (2013). In their second experiment in which readers read a fictional extract from Nobel Prize winner Jose Saramago the positive effect on empathy for those highly engaged by the story was not significant. The results of the first experiment were that people who were high in transportation into the Sherlock Holmes story increased their empathy from Time 1 to Time 3, but there was no significant change in empathy in those who read the newspaper extracts. In the second

one will worry that the overall impact of fiction-reading on empathy is negligible or negative, given that a good deal of our reading of fiction is not very emotionally involved; starting a novel and giving up because it is not very involving would then be a dangerous thing. It is also unclear whether substantial amounts of reading tend to reduce empathy (the exhaustion model) rather than raising it (the training model). van Lissa and colleagues (2016: 54) found that readers who had read the most fiction (novels) in the twelve months preceding the experiment experienced the least empathy with characters on a further reading. The idea that fiction-reading might suppress empathy will come up in Section 11.6.

Another concern is that the tests of empathy used in this experiment and in some others—self-report—did not demonstrate any change of behavioural disposition.[25] Another experiment (Johnson 2012) did probe for helping behaviour after the reading; a correlation was observed between those who helped and those who reported high levels of 'transportation' or imaginative engagement with the story. Since helping behaviour was manifested immediately after the reading it is unclear how long the effect lasted; we know that trivial events like finding a dime in a phone booth can lead to immediate and minor helping behaviour, without, presumably, leading to shifts in a person's outlook or dispositions (Isen and Levin 1972).

A question these studies have begun to address is the extent to which the 'literariness' of a fictional work contributes to its empathic effects. This question is crucial to some of the arguments that have been presented in favour of fiction's improving capacities; many have argued that the literary canon, or some revised version of it, is especially valuable in its capacity to illuminate obscure aspects of moral psychology—accepting at the same time that works less worthy in literary terms such as *Uncle Tom's Cabin* have made an historical difference to people's empathic connection to others. Some of the studies already mentioned have tried to get a handle on the effects of 'quality' fiction and on the responses of people who habitually read it. A recent study of this kind is by Emy Koopman (2015) who exposed subjects to three kinds of texts: literary and 'life' narratives, distinguished by the greater degree of foregrounding of language and style in the former, and non-narrative instructional texts. For readings of each of the two narrative texts subjects were divided into those who were told that the text was fiction and those who were told that it was non-fiction. The effect of reading on pro-social behaviour was measured by willingness to donate a small amount of money; results

experiment, people who were high in transportation into the story by Saramago increased their empathy somewhat from Time 1 to Time 3 but the increase was not significant, while people who were high in transportation into the newspaper extracts significantly decreased their empathy from Time 1 to Time 3. In both experiments, people who read the fictional stories but were not transported into them showed decreased empathy from Time 1 to Time 3.

[25] A recent review of studies of this kind notes that 'All the studies reviewed in this article avoid making claims about behavioral changes' (Caracciolo and Van Duuren 2015).

were inconclusive because few donated, but there was modest evidence that the life narrative was more effective than the literary one; it made no difference whether or not subjects were told they were reading fiction. Koopman concludes that 'reading single narrative fragments has limited effects on measures related to real-life empathy...when pro-social behaviour is triggered, this appears to be short-lived.'[26]

11.6 Doubts about the positive effects of fiction on empathy

Studies like those just outlined have contributed valuable methods and results to the debate over fiction's relations to empathy; that they leave the extent and even the existence of a positive causal relation in doubt is unsurprising at this early stage. Some studies hint at amplification effects, where reading precedes increased helping behaviour directed at available targets, and at increased self-estimations of empathy. A recent meta-analysis of fourteen studies (four unpublished) of the effect of fiction-reading on people's social cognition found that 'fiction reading marginally improves social cognition' (Dodell-Feder and Tamir 2018: 1722). To this modest conclusion two things need to be added. First, the marginal improvement found in this study (Table 3) is slightly reduced if we consider only experiments which compared reading fiction with reading non-fiction and leave out the results for comparisons between reading fiction and reading nothing; merely reading some narrative (fiction or non-fiction) accounts for part of the marginal improvement. Secondly, the authors noted that 'it is not clear whether improvements in social cognition from fiction-reading represent a short-term change, along the lines of a priming effect, versus an enduring change in social–cognitive ability' (1724), thus leaving open an extremely important issue for anyone concerned with the genuinely educative capacity of fiction.[27] In particular there is no evidence from available studies for fictions capacity to regulate empathy or make it the servant of a principled morality. Finding such evidence will not be easy.

Given the complexity and variety of literary fiction, the various circumstances in which we encounter it and the extent of variation between individual readers it is reasonable to expect that more sensitive studies will identify a range of effects, many specific to particular cases, including null effects and tendencies to reduce or misdirect empathy as well as cases where fiction boosts or refines it. With a view to extending our causal horizon, let's consider a range of deflationary assumptions

---

[26] Koopman (2015: 77). One might object, as David Davies did, that the effects of short narrative fragments (1,500 words) tell us little about the effects of sustained engagement with substantial fictions. I agree that little can be concluded either way from this and note the study mainly because it does use literary text samples rather than narratives constructed for experimental purposes.

[27] Empathy was a significant element in the battery of tests examined but not all the tests were of empathy. The most widely used test in the studies examined was the 'Reading the mind in the eyes' test.

we might make about the effects of fiction on moral cognition and moral behaviour. I divide them into two groups:

Empathy with fictional characters has no significant effect on helping behaviour
1. Empathizing with fictional characters has no significant effect on our tendency to empathize with real people, perhaps because the stimuli available in fictional cases, with direct access to the thoughts and feelings of the character, is so much richer than the stimuli available in real-life cases. Repeated responding to the richer stimulus does not make us more prone to respond to the weaker.[28]
2. Empathizing with fictional characters has a tendency to promote empathy for real people but little or no tendency to affect helping behaviour, because empathy and helping behaviour are in fact only weakly connected, if at all.[29]
3. Empathizing with fictional characters has a tendency to promote empathy and helping behaviour in the real world but only at very short time scales, perhaps because the empathizing with fictional characters merely primes us for empathizing with real people.
4. Empathizing with fictional characters is in fact a rare occurrence in the experience of reading fiction and so is largely irrelevant to our tendencies to real-world empathy and helping behaviour.[30]

Empathy with fictional characters has a significant but negative effect on helping behaviour
5. Empathizing with fictional characters eats into our empathy capital, leaving less empathic capacity for responding to real situations.[31]
6. Empathizing with fictional characters gives us a sense of having responded well, lessening our desire to be empathic to the real people we encounter when we put the book down; we have done enough empathizing for the day.
7. Empathizing with fictional characters, because it is not accompanied immediately by helping behaviour, weakens the psychological connection between empathy and helping behaviour. In general, the more one does A without then doing B, the less one is naturally inclined to do B after doing A.[32]

---

[28] Sklar (2009) found no correlation between empathy for fictional characters and real-world empathy, but van Lissa et al. (2016, especially p. 54) found a correlation in their study.

[29] If empathy does not promote helping behaviour, why has it evolved? One hypothesis is that it evolved as part of a more general capacity for mind-reading, not designed for helping but to aid in deceiving and avoiding deception. Alternatively, it might have evolved as part of a suite of capacities designed to promote social cohesion: empathy may help bring people's mental states into alignment.

[30] See Carroll (1997) and Kieran (2002). For a response to these claims see my 2004, Chapter 9; see also Gaut (2010).

[31] Josh Landy notes Diderot's ironic self-congratulation on reading *Clarissa* and wonders whether 'we are even *less* likely to make a positive contribution to society, having purged ourselves of all benevolent emotions in our favorite armchair' (2012: 32–3). I am indebted to Landy's discussion.

[32] Anna Laetitia Aiken wrote in 1773 that 'Nothing is more dangerous than to let any virtuous impressions of any kind pass through the mind without producing their proper effect' (quoted in Keen

8. Empathizing with fictional characters has a tendency to promote empathy for real people which then strongly affects helping behaviour, but in ways which lead to undesirable outcomes as often as to desirable ones. For empathy distorts our sense of justice and focuses us disproportionately on providing short-term help for those we happen to know.

I won't work through all eight scenarios: the list is there merely to illustrate the variety and richness of the set of strategies available to anyone who wants to pour cold or at least cooling water on the enthusiasm of some for the literature/empathy connection. I have said something briefly about 8. I will focus now on 6. It alerts us to the possibility that, as well as amplifying our empathic responses fiction may sometimes depress them.

11.7 Self-licensing

Recent psychological work on what is called moral self-licensing claims to identify a system governing conscientious behaviour, mediated by subjects' perception of their own status as just and rational beings.[33] The relevance of this literature was suggested to me by Catarina Dutilh Novaes, to whom I am very grateful. Here are some examples:

> Participants in one study reported events at random intervals during their daily lives; people who performed good deeds early in a day typically performed fewer good deeds and more bad deeds later that day . . . Other researchers found that an intervention that reduced water usage among homeowners ironically increased electricity usage, suggesting that feeling virtuous about conserving water may have licensed homeowners to conserve less electricity . . . Licensing may also occur at the organizational level . . . an archival study of 49 Fortune-500 companies found that corporate social responsibility efforts predicted subsequent corporate social irresponsibility.   (Effron and Conway 2015: 32–3)

The hypothesis is that the prior behaviour enhances a sense of self-worth which in turn gives people the feeling of being licensed to behave less well or less sensibly thereafter. This suggests that the experience of empathizing with fictional characters might actually reduce our tendency to exercise empathy in response to the plights of other, real people.

2007: 47). But Aiken turns out to be making a slightly different suggestion than the one above: that virtuous feeling itself grows progressively weaker if not accompanied by action.

[33] For a review of current research in this area see Merritt et al. (2010).

It is worth noting that self-licensing does not seem to be the product of the admitted fact that people have limited capacities for empathy or other energy-consuming activities, leading to a decline in worthy behaviours in a given time period.[34] For one thing, we can easily produce what we might call the mirror-image phenomenon: when people perceive their actions to be lazy, indulgent, or otherwise unworthy they are, it turns out, more inclined to engage in subsequently worthy action. Researchers into self-licensing tend to assume that the process in either direction is a homeostatic one, mediated by self-image. This means that a boost to your self-image licenses a relaxation of standards, while a threat to it posed by perceived transgression calls forth compensating good behaviour.[35]

An assumption here is that empathizing with others does increase our sense of self-worth. Is that true? I don't know of any direct tests of the proposition but it is something that we should expect if we think that empathy is valuable, on the general grounds that engaging in activities we think of as worthy is a likely route to feelings of self-worth. Available studies of self-licensing explain observed behaviour in cases where, for example, people make a pro-egalitarian or environmentally sensitive choice by attributing an increased sense of self-worth to subjects.[36] It would then want some special reason to refrain from making the same attribution in cases of empathic behaviour. I don't rule out there being such a reason but present knowledge does not provide one.

It is important also to understand what the hypothesis of self-licensing is not claiming. The idea is not that a good act is always or even usually followed by a compensating bad or negligent one; people are capable of extraordinarily sustained tendencies to helpfulness, charity, and responsible behaviour. Self-licensing is but one factor in a vastly complex mix of potential causes of behaviour which include differences in circumstances, personality, levels of self-control, and habituation to certain courses of action. But that self-licensing is one of these factors is strongly suggested not only by the experimental studies here cited but—for what it's worth—a sense that many of us (I'm one and I have asked others) have that having behaved well does at least provide a temptation to behave less well in the immediately following period—without, generally speaking, pushing us so far as to rob the next pensioner we see of their life savings.[37]

---

[34] One (fictional) social worker's experience seems to exemplify this—Clare Barker (played by Sally Phillips): 'My engine runs on empathy all day. By the time I get home there are only fumes left' (*Clare in the Community*, BBC Radio 4, series 11, 2016). But given Clare's established tendency to self-deception, this could well be self-licensing.

[35] As we might expect, factors impacting on self-conception can affect behaviour without their being a record of good/bad prior behaviour; simply framing an action in terms which make the self salient ('Don't be a cheater' vs. 'Don't cheat') makes it less likely that people will perform the bad act (Bryan et al. 2013).

[36] See e.g. Dütschke et al. 2018.

[37] A meta-analysis of ninety-one studies concluded that self-licensing has a 'small to moderate' effect on behaviour (Cohen's $d = 0.31$). The authors note that 'The effect is somewhat smaller than

In all this it is important to remember the dialectical situation: many people claim, without much evidential support, that:

R.   Reading fiction makes us more likely to experience empathy and to behave empathically towards real people.

That may be true in some circumstances. My points are that (i) an opposing tendency may also exist, that (ii) its existence is no less well evidenced than the tendency described in R, and (iii) this opposing tendency may, for the following reason, be apt to win out in the contest of opposed forces: empathizing with fictional characters is very low-cost, since there is nothing we can do to help them. It therefore has an attraction that its real-world counterpart, with its close association to committing scarce resources, lacks. I propose therefore that we give at least as much attention, in terms of conceptual elaboration and evidence-gathering, to this opposing tendency as we do to R.

Now a little more on self-image and its relation to self-licensing. How, first, does self-image mediate this process of self-licensing? Not, presumably, by providing a reason for the subsequent behaviour; you could not justify apparently unworthy behaviour produced by such a mechanism by saying that you were feeling sufficiently good about yourself to warrant behaving badly.[38] If self-image mediates in these cases it is more likely that it does so via something more akin to emotion than to judgement. I don't think we commonly recognize an emotion triggered by fluctuations in self-worth, though we do speak of 'feeling good (bad) about ourselves'. Still, something rather emotion-like seems to operate here. Just as fear may disincline you to walk on a solid glass floor above a ravine without your judging that there is any danger, you may be demotivated from carrying out good deeds by comfortable feelings of self-worth, without thinking of this as justifying your behaviour.[39]

I said that feelings of self-worth partially control but do not justify cessation of such worthy activities as smoking less, being vigilant about racist attitudes, and empathizing with others. I don't however mean that such feelings are simply brute causes of the cessation. Things are a little more complicated. Discussing the way

other typical effects in social psychology...but also relatively small effects can have large societal implications' (Blanken et al. 2015: 556).

[38] Though thinking badly of yourself would be an acceptable reason, if one is wanted, for doing good.

[39] That said, some of the behaviours recorded in the self-licensing literature may have a more strategic motivation: in one experiment subjects were told they would, a day later, chose between a white and a black candidate for a job. Before reporting their decision, subjects were asked whether certain behaviours (a police officer stops a black man whose appearance matches the description of a suspect) were racist. When the white applicant was more qualified, participants were more inclined to judge these behaviours as racist, perhaps in anticipation of the suspicion that their choice would itself be thought racially biased (Merritt et al. 2012).

stereotype threat leads to a loss of access to knowledge and hence to poor performance on a test, Tamar Gendler makes a distinction which is likely to apply here also. I'll use Gendler's words to suggest that moral self licensing

> isn't just the result of something straightforwardly causal like bumping your head and getting a concussion...nor is it the result of something straightforwardly reason-based like reading a revisionist textbook or thinking through a Brain-in-a-Vat scenario...Rather, it's the result of something...I'll provisionally call an eason...something that is not sufficiently well-conceptualized to call a reason, but that (in a way in between a reasony and a causy fashion) *eases* us towards a certain outlook on the world.   (Gendler (2011: 51))

In the cases we are considering, a feeling of self-worth whispers permission to be less good.

A similar point needs to be made about another aspect of my account. Self-licensing is a two-stage process, and we have been looking at the second stage, the transition from feelings of self-worth to cessation or reduction of good behaviour.[40] But the first stage is from good behaviour to feelings of self-worth, and here the relation looks to be conventionally justifying. I'm right, aren't I, to think of myself as a good person when I do good things? There are worries here about the competing roles of situation and character in determining action and the possibility of a general scepticism about characterological assessments. But putting these controversial and arcane considerations aside, folk psychology seems to endorse the idea that good behaviour justifies feelings of self-worth, while recognizing that such feelings can be excessive. But if that is how self-licensing works, how can it apply to fictional cases? Beatrice, who spends her day counselling people in difficult situations, is entitled to all the feelings of self-worth she allows herself; Eugenie, who spends her days reading Tolstoy and empathizing energetically with Anna Karenina surely isn't.[41]

What I suggest in response is that stage one of the process is governed as little by rational processes as is stage two. We are familiar with situations in which mental processes which normally provide some kind of justificatory warrant are vulnerable to illusions of warrant created by merely imagined experience or activity. If I had been watching a serious documentary about the danger from vampires lurking in dark places I would have some reason to think twice before taking the short but dark-alley-involving way home. Watching an avowedly fictional movie on the same topic would provide no such justification, but it

---

[40] Or from feelings of lack of self-worth to increased demonstrations of goodness; given the topic of this chapter, I am focusing on the other disjunct but it must not be forgotten that both kinds of transition are, on current thinking, aspects of the same, homeostatic phenomenon.

[41] Which is not to say that there is anything wrong with such an activity.

might still cause me to avoid the dark alley.[42] In the light of the feelings, the alley-avoiding behaviour can surely seem to the agent appropriate in some admittedly rather shallow sense; certain feelings unambiguously suggest to us certain courses of action, and we are naturally and for good evolutionary reasons prone to respond to those promptings, without waiting for further justification.[43] Similarly, the *Anna Karenina*-induced feelings of personal effort, accomplishment, and sensitivity might seem to legitimize (and not merely be a cause of) subsequently reduced levels of effort when it comes to empathizing with family, friends, and those real but distant people in desperate need. Indeed there is evidence that self-licensing operates across the imaginary-real divide. Half the subjects in one experiment were asked to imagine volunteering for community service; those who did so subsequently rated themselves higher than the rest in terms of warmth, helpfulness, sympathy, and compassion; the imagined volunteering seems to have improved self image though imagining yourself doing something worthy is little reason to raise your assessment of your actual worth (Khan and Dhar 2006). There is also evidence that describing how well you would behave in ideal circumstances, which very likely produces an imagining of behaving well, makes people report less creditable and more realistic intentions to actually do things (Tanner and Carlson 2008). Again, the process here is not merely causal even though it is not properly justificatory; imagining volunteering eases us, as Gendler puts it, towards a better self-image; imagining acting ideally eases us subsequently to acknowledge our limitations.

11.8 Conclusions

It is certainly plausible that exposure to fiction has consequences for empathy: for the intensity and the amount of empathy a person displays on occasion. Some fictions, sometimes and for some people, will result in increased empathy; sometimes the effect could well be a decrease. It may even be that the same fiction, on the same occasion and for the same person has effects in both directions, with the net effect being something like a resultant of forces. Beyond this there is little we can say with confidence given the present state of evidence and argument.

*

[42] One can ask awkward questions about the justification provided by the documentary; perhaps, like many representations of risk, the effect on people's behaviour would be disproportionate to the real probability of vampire attack (perhaps vampires are actually rather rare and the probability of one being in this alley is vanishingly small). Still, relative to the generally poor sensitivity to probabilities among humans, disinclination to walk down the alley would have some justification in the circumstances described above.

[43] Advice on avoiding dangerous situations often emphasizes the importance of responding to one's feelings of danger even when unaccompanied by grounds one could give for the danger's existence.

It is important, once again, to say what this chapter and the others in Part III have tried to do. None have aimed at showing that we cannot learn from fiction in general, from certain kinds of fiction, or from particular works of fiction. Instead, each chapter has emphasized the ways in which engagement with a work of fiction that shows promise of resulting in learning of some kind may instead result in ignorance, error, or a blunted sensibility. We always knew that, you may say, and in a sense we probably did; no sensible person ever claimed that every engagement with fiction results in learning, and it is a commonplace that much fiction is an unrealistic fantasy. What I have tried to do is to map out some previously unrecognized pathways to epistemic failure that ought to make us a little more hesitant in our claims.

Where we are

I began this book by saying that it would be an inquiry into the role of fiction in our lives and in particular into two things we care about a great deal and expend a lot of energy on: imagining and knowing. Fiction, I have argued, has a happier, deeper, and more stable relation to imagination than it does to knowledge. Understanding the concept of fiction (a very stable concept I have argued) depends on appreciating what it is to communicate something with the intention that it be imagined: armed with that and a general sense of the overarching purpose the maker of a text has and the ways that avowedly fictional material can be seen to serve some more important non-fictional purpose (and vice versa) we can often come to reasoned judgements that this work is fiction and that one non-fiction: judgments that don't deviate much from the judgements of common readers, librarians, and booksellers. Later chapters in Part I sought to extend the varieties of imagination we see as involved in our engagements with fiction, and getting these varieties in place is important if we are to understand how imaginative engagement, broadly understood, can make fiction a source of learning.

In moving from imagination to knowledge, or what I more guardedly called learning, I emphasized the role of imagination in the formation of conditional beliefs and from thence to its role in thought experiments. I argued that the successes, such as they are, of thought experiments in philosophy and the sciences don't give us much reason for thinking that fictions in the shape of novels, plays, and movies are thought experiments with comparable epistemic potential. I suggested that, while there are circumstances in which we can acquire reliable factual beliefs from fictions, reliability drops off badly when we start to consider the sorts of evaluative or partly evaluative propositions fictions are sometimes celebrated for conveying. I offered three general reasons why we should be wary of thinking that authors of admired fictions can be relied on for their wisdom or insight. I argued that fiction's role in promoting empathy is apt to be over-rated if we ignore the distinction between how easily we respond empathically, and how intelligently we do so. Finally, I suggested that in some situations empathizing with fictions and their characters may suppress rather than encourage empathy.

Is there anything more here than a deeply boring message: sometimes we learn from fiction, sometimes we don't? There is. It's not interesting to be told we can go wrong in our thinking; it can be interesting to be told how. I have tried to find some specific ways we can go wrong in seeking to learn from fiction, some of which look superficially like ways very likely to go right. That is not all. I have

Imagining and Knowing: The Shape of Fiction. Gregory Currie, Oxford University Press (2020). © Gregory Currie.
DOI: 10.1093/oso/9780199656615.001.0001

argued for certain general propositions—about the inefficacy of highly elaborated thought experiments, the absence of epistemically benign institutions of fiction, a tendency towards disengagement with other minds on the part of very talented authors, the illusory nature of moral-psychological expertise—that ought at least to moderate our optimism about learning from fiction. And I suggested that much of our talk about learning from fiction is a kind of largely unwitting pretence in which we claim results without doing the hard work necessary to get them. Putting all this together justifies, I think, a suspicion of claims that we learn from fiction, though an attitude of suspicion towards a class of propositions is not the same as taking all of them to be false. These claims ought, if seriously meant, to come with some pretty substantial backing before they can be taken seriously. That is the reorientation my arguments require, if they are sound.

At the beginning of this book I likened my activity to that of a look-out for icebergs. That's a person everyone on the *Titanic* was happy to see in action, however optimistic they were about reaching their destination. But the idea that our journey is one towards a place neatly marked 'fiction teaches us stuff' needs to be abandoned. Our destination is more like a vast archipelago with a confusingly diverse geography and fauna, some bits delightfully habitable, some intensely hostile, and everything in between. Roughly mapping that territory is the best we can hope for. There surely are ways that fiction teaches, and lots of people are working hard to find them. Very likely, there are ways fiction creates error and ignorance, apathy and excessive self-confidence, illusions of knowledge, understanding, and of wisdom. A map of the territory that's worth anything will have to subsume both perspectives.

References

Adolphs, R., D. Tranel, and A. R. Damasio. 2003. 'Dissociable Neural Systems for Recognizing Emotions'. *Brain and Cognition*, 52 (1): pp. 61–9.

Alchourrón, C., P. Gärdenfors, and D. Makinson. 1985. 'On the Logic of Theory Change: Partial Meet Contraction and Revision Functions'. *Journal of Symbolic Logic*, 50 (2): pp. 510–30.

Altschuler, E., A. S. Calude, A. Meade, and M. Pagel. 2013. 'Linguistic Evidence Supports Date for Homeric Epics', *Bioessays*, 35: pp. 417–20.

Andreasen, N. 1987. 'Creativity and Mental Illness: Prevalence Rates in Writers and their First-Degree Relatives'. *American Journal of Psychiatry*, 144 (10): pp. 1288–92.

Annas, J. 2011. 'Practical Expertise'. In *Knowing How*, edited by J. Bengson and M. A. Moffett, pp. 101–12. Oxford: Oxford University Press.

Armour, P. 1971. 'Galileo and the Crisis of Italian literature'. In *Collected Essays on Italian Language and Literature Presented to Kathleen Speight*, edited by G. Aquilecchia, S. Cristea, and S. Ralphs, pp. 143–71. New York: Barnes & Noble.

Assion, H.-J., F. Wolf, and M. Brüne. 2011. 'Theory of Mind and Neurocognitive Functioning in Patients with Bipolar Disorder'. *European Psychiatry*, 26 (S1): p. 191.

Atran, S., and J. Henrich. 2010. 'The Evolution of Religion: How Cognitive By-Products, Adaptive Learning Heuristics, Ritual Displays, and Group Competition Generate Deep Commitments to Prosocial Religions'. *Biological Theory*, 5 (1): pp.18–30.

Baier, A. 1986. 'Trust and Antitrust'. *Ethics*, 96 (2): pp. 231–60.

Baker, R. 2008. 'Defamation and the Moral Community'. *Deakin Law Review*, 13 (1): pp. 1–35.

Bal, P. M., and M. Veltkamp. 2013. How Does Fiction Reading Influence Empathy? An Experimental Investigation on the Role of Emotional Transportation. *Plos One.* doi.org/10.1371/journal.pone.0055341.

Baron-Cohen, S., S. Wheelwright, J. Hill, Y. Raste, and I. Plumb. 2001. 'The "Reading the Mind in the Eyes" Test Revised Version: A Study with Normal Adults, and Adults with Asperger Syndrome or High-functioning Autism'. *Journal of Child Psychology and Psychiatry*, 42 (2): pp. 241–451.

Barrett, J., and F. Keil. 1996. 'Conceptualizing a Non-Natural Entity: Anthropomorphism in God Concepts'. *Cognitive Psychology*, 31: pp. 219–47.

Bartlett, R. 2011. *Tolstoy: A Russian Life.* Boston: Houghton Mifflin Harcourt.

Batson, D., J. G. Batson, J. K. Slingsby, K. L. Harrell, H. M. Peekna, and M. R. Todd. 1991. 'Empathic Joy and the Empathy-Altruism Hypothesis'. *Journal of Personality and Social Psychology*, 61 (3): pp. 413–26.

Bechara, A., A. R. Damasio, H. Damasio, and S. W. Anderson. 1994. 'Insensitivity to Future Consequences Following Damage to Human Prefrontal Cortex'. *Cognition*, 50 (1): pp. 7–15.

Beistegui, M. de. 2012. *Proust as Philosopher: The Art of Metaphor.* Abingdon: Routledge.

Bennett, J. 1988. 'Farewell to the Phlogiston Theory of Conditionals'. *Mind*, 97 (338): pp. 509–27.

Blackburn, S. 2010. 'Some Remarks about Value as a Work of Literature'. *British Journal of Aesthetics*, 50 (1): pp. 85–8.

Blanken, I., N. van de Ven, and M. Zeelenberg. 2015. 'A Meta-Analytic Review of Moral Licensing', *Personality and Social Psychology Bulletin*, 41 (4): pp. 540–58.

Bloom, P. 2007. 'Water as an Artifact Kind'. In *Creations of the Mind: Theories of Artifacts and their Representation*, edited by E. Margolis and S. Laurence, pp. 150–6. Oxford: Oxford University Press.

Bloom, P. 2013. 'The Baby in the Well', *New Yorker*, http://www.newyorker.com/magazine/2013/05/20/the-baby-in-the-well.

Bond, C., and B. DePaulo. 2006. 'Accuracy of Deception Judgments', *Personality and Social Psychology Review*, 10 (3): pp. 214–34.

BonJour, L. 2002. 'Internalism and Externalism'. In *The Oxford Handbook of Epistemology*, edited by P. K. Moser, pp. 234–63. Oxford: Oxford University Press.

Booth, W. C. 1988. *The Company We Keep: An Ethics of Fiction*. Los Angeles: University of California Press.

Bora, E., M. Yucel, and C. Pantelis. 2009. 'Theory of Mind Impairment in Schizophrenia: Meta-Analysis'. *Schizophrenia Research*, 109: pp. 1–9.

Boyd, B. 2006. 'Fiction and Theory of Mind'. *Philosophy and Literature*, 30 (2): pp. 590–600.

Boyd, B. 2009. *On the Origin of Stories: Evolution, Cognition, and Fiction*. Cambridge, MA: Harvard University Press.

Bradley, A. C. 1904. *Shakespearean Tragedy*. London: Macmillan and Co.

Brod, J. 1997. 'Creativity and Schizotypy'. In *Schizotypy: Implications for Illness and Health*, edited by G. Claridge, pp. 276–98. Oxford: Oxford University Press.

Brodie, M., U. Foehr, V. Rideout, N. Baer, C. Miller, R. Flournoy, and D. Altman. 2001. 'Communicating Health Information through the Entertainment Media: A Study of the Television Drama ER Lends Support to the Notion that Americans Pick up Information While Being Entertained'. *Health Affairs*, 20 (1): pp. 192–9.

Brown, J. R. (2004). 'Why Thought Experiments Transcend Empiricism'. In *Contemporary Debates in the Philosophy of Science*, edited by C. Hitchcock, pp. 23–44. Malden, MA: Blackwell.

Brüne, M. 2005. '"Theory of Mind" in Schizophrenia: A Review of the Literature'. *Schizophrenia Bulletin*, 31 (1): pp. 21–42.

Bryan, C., G. Adams, and B. Monin. 2013. 'When Cheating Would Make You a Cheater: Implicating the Self Prevents Unethical Behaviour'. *Journal of Experimental Psychology: General*, 142 (4): pp. 1001–5.

Buckwalter, W., and K. Tullmann. 2017. 'The Genuine Attitude View of Fictional Belief'. In *Art and Belief*, edited by H. Bradley, E. Sullivan-Bissett, and P. Noordhof, pp. 194–209. Oxford: Oxford University Press.

Burge, T. 2003. 'Perceptual Entitlement', *Philosophy and Phenomenological Research*, 67 (3): pp. 503–48.

Butler, L., C. Koopman, and P. G. Zimbardo. 1995. 'The Psychological Impact of Viewing the Film "JFK"', *Political Psychology*, 16 (2): pp. 237–57.

Byrne, A. 2007. 'Possibility and Imagination'. *Philosophical Perspectives*, 21 (1): pp. 125–44.

Cappelen, H. 2012. *Philosophy without Intuitions*. Oxford: Oxford University Press.

Cappelen, H. 2018. *Fixing Language: An Essay on Conceptual Engineering*. Oxford: Oxford University Press.

Caracciolo, M., and T. Van Duuren. 2015. 'Changed by Literature? A Critical Review of Psychological Research on the Effects of Reading Fiction'. *Interdisciplinary Literary Studies*, 17 (4): pp. 517–39.

Carroll, J. 2011. *Reading Human Nature: Literary Darwinism in Theory and Practice*. New York: SUNY Press.

Carroll, N. 1997. 'Simulation, Emotion and Morality'. In *Emotions in Postmodernism*, edited by G. Hoffmann and A. Hornung, pp. 383–401. Heidelberg: C. Winter.

Carroll, N. 1998. 'Art, Narrative and Moral Understanding'. In *Aesthetics and Ethics: Essays at the Intersection*, edited by J. Levinson, pp. 126–61. Cambridge: Cambridge University Press.

Carroll, N. 2002. 'The Wheel of Virtue: Art, Literature, and Moral Knowledge'. *Journal of Aesthetics and Art Criticism*, 60 (1): pp. 3–26.

Carroll, N. 2010. *Art in Three Dimensions*. Oxford: Oxford University Press.

Carruthers, P. 2006. *The Architecture of Mind*. Oxford: Oxford University Press.

Carruthers, P. 2011. *The Opacity of Mind: An Integrative Theory of Self-Knowledge*. Oxford: Oxford University Press.

Carruthers, P. 2015. 'Perceiving Mental States'. *Consciousness and Cognition*, 36: pp. 498–507.

Carston, R. 2002a. 'Explicature and Semantics'. In *Semantics: A Reader*, edited by S. Davies and B. Gillon, pp. 817–45. Oxford: Oxford University Press.

Carston, R. 2002b. *Thoughts and Utterances*. Malden, MA: Blackwell.

Chabris, C., P. Heck, J. Mandart, D. Benjamin, and D. Simons. 2019. 'Two Failures to Replicate Williams and Bargh (2008): No Evidence That Experiencing Physical Warmth Promotes Interpersonal Warmth'. *Social Psychology*, 50: pp. 127–32.

Chan, T. (ed.) 2013. *The Aim of Belief*. Oxford: Oxford University Press.

Charernboon, T., and J. Patumanoud. 2017. 'Social Cognition in Schizophrenia'. *Mental Illness*, 9. doi: 10.4081/mi.2017.7054.

Chiou, W.-B., C.-S. Wan, W.-H. Wu, and K.-T. Lee. 2011. 'A Randomized Experiment to Examine Unintended Consequences of Dietary Supplement Use among Daily Smokers: Taking Supplements Reduces Self-regulation of Smoking'. *Addiction*, 106 (12): pp. 2221–8.

Cikara, M., E. G. Bruneau, and R. R. Saxe. 2011. 'Us and Them: Intergroup Failures of Empathy. *Current Directions in Psychological Science*, 20 (3): pp.149–53.

Cixous, H. 1974. 'The Character of "Character"'. *New Literary History*, 5 (2): pp. 383–402.

Claridge, G. 1993. 'When Is Psychoticism? And How Does It Really Relate to Creativity?' *Psychological Inquiry*, 4 (3): pp. 184–8.

Claridge, G., and S. Blakey. 2009. 'Schizotypy and Affective Temperament: Relationships with Divergent Thinking and Creativity Styles'. *Personality and Individual Differences*, 46 (8): 820–6.

Claridge, G., R. Pryor, and G. Watkins. 1998. *Sounds from the Bell Jar: Ten Psychotic Authors*. Los Altos, CA: Malor Books.

Clark, H. 2016. 'Depicting as a Method of Communication'. *Psychological Review*, 123 (3): 324–47.

Clore, G., and K. Gasper. 2000. 'Feeling Is Believing'. In *Emotions and Beliefs: How Feelings Influence Thought*, edited by A. Manstead, N. Frijda, and S. Bem, pp. 10–44. Cambridge: Cambridge University Press.

Coady, C. A. J. 1992. *Testimony: A Philosophical Study*. Oxford: Oxford University Press.

Conee, E. 1994. 'Phenomenal Knowledge'. *Australasian Journal of Philosophy*, 72 (2): 136–50.

Coplan, A. 2004. 'Empathic Engagement with Narrative Fictions'. *The Journal of Aesthetics and Art Criticism*, 62 (2): 141–152.

Craig, E. 1990. *Knowledge and the State of Nature*. Oxford: Oxford University Press.

Crosby, E. 1906. *Tolstoy on Shakespeare: A Critical Essay on Shakespeare*. New York: Funk & Wagnalls Company.

Currie, G. 1990. *The Nature of Fiction*. Cambridge: Cambridge University Press.

Currie, G. 1995. The Moral Psychology of Fiction, *Australian Journal of Philosophy*, 73: 250–59.

Currie, G. 1998. Realism of Character and the Value of Fiction, in J. Levinson (ed.) *Aesthetics and Ethics. Essays at the Intersection*, pp.161–181. Cambridge: Cambridge University Press.

Currie, G. 2000. 'Imagination, Delusion and Hallucinations'. *Mind and Language*, 15 (1): pp. 168–83.

Currie, G. 2004. 'Anne Bronte and the Uses of Narrative'. In *Arts and Minds*, pp. 173–88. Oxford: Oxford University Press.

Currie, G. 2006. 'Rationality and Pretend Play: The Case of Animals'. In *Rational Animals*, edited by S. Hurley and M. Nudds, pp. 275–93. Oxford: Oxford University Press.

Currie, G. 2010a. 'Agency and Repentance in *The Winter's Tale*'. In *Shakespeare and Moral Agency*, edited by M. Bristol, pp. 171–84. London: Continuum.

Currie, G. 2010b. *Narratives and Narrators: A Philosophy of Stories*. Oxford: Oxford University Press.

Currie, G. 2010c. 'Tragedy'. *Analysis*, 70 (4): pp. 1–7.

Currie, G. 2014. 'Standing in the Last Ditch: On the Communicative Intentions of Fiction Makers'. *Journal of Aesthetics and Art Criticism*, 72 (4): pp. 351–63.

Currie, G. 2016. 'Models as Fictions and Fictions as Models'. *Monist*, 99 (3): 296–310.

Currie, G., and A. Ichino. 2010. 'Aliefs Do Not Exist'. *Analysis*, 72 (4): pp. 788–98.

Currie, G., and A. Ichino. 2017. 'Truth and Trust in Fiction'. In *Art and Belief*, edited by H. Bradley, E. Sullivan-Bissett, and P. Noordhof, pp. 63–85. Oxford: Oxford University Press.

Currie, G., and J. Jureidini. 2003. 'Art and Delusion'. *Monist*, 86 (4): 556–78.

Currie, G., and J. Jureidini. 2004. 'Narrative and Coherence'. *Mind and Language*, 19 (4): pp. 409–27.

Currie, G., and I. Ravenscroft. 2002. *Recreative Minds: Imagination in Philosophy and Psychology*. Oxford: Oxford University Press.

Currie, G., and K. Sterelny. 2000. 'How to Think about the Modularity of Mind-Reading'. *Philosophical Quarterly*, 50 (199): pp. 145–60.

Dadlez, E. 2009. *Mirrors to Each Other*. Oxford: Wiley-Blackwell.

Dal Cin, S., M. Zanna, and G. Fong. 2004. 'Narrative Persuasion and Overcoming Resistance'. In *Resistance and Persuasion*, edited by E. Knowles and J. Lin, pp. 175–91. Mahwah, NJ: Lawrence Erlbaum Associates Publishers.

Damasio, A. 1994. *Descartes' Error*. New York: G P Putnam's Sons.

Dancy, J. 1996. 'In Defense of Thick Concepts'. *Midwest Studies in Philosophy*, 20 (1): pp. 263–79.

Darley, J., and C. D. Batson. 1973. 'From Jerusalem to Jericho: A Study of Situational and Dispositional Variables in Helping Behavior'. *Journal of Personality and Social Psychology*, 27 (1): pp. 100–8.

Davies, D. 2007. *Aesthetics and Literature*. London: Continuum Press.

Davies, D. 2010. 'Learning through Fictional Narratives in Art and Science'. In *Beyond Mimesis and Convention*, edited by R. Frigg and M. Hunter, pp. 51–71. Berlin: Springer.

Davison, W. P. 1983. 'The Third-Person Effect in Communication'. *Public Opinion Quarterly*, 47 (1): 1–15.

de Sousa, R. 1987. *The Rationality of Emotion*. London: MIT Press.

de Vignemont, F., and T. Singer. (2006). 'The Empathic Brain: How, When and Why?' *Trends in Cognitive Science*, 10 (10): pp. 435–41.

Decety, J., M. Jeannerod, and C. Prablanc. 1989. 'The Timing of Mentally Represented Actions'. *Behavioural Brain Research*, 34 (1–2): pp. 35–42.

Del Mar, M. 2018. 'Common Virtue and the Perspectival Imagination: Adam Smith and Common Law Reasoning'. *Jurisprudence*, 9 (1): pp. 58–70.

Dennett, D. 1978. 'Beliefs about Beliefs'. *Behavioural and Brain Sciences*, 1 (4): pp. 568–70.

Dennett, D. 1995. 'Intuition Pumps'. In *The Third Culture*, edited by J. Brockman, pp. 181–91. New York: Simon & Schuster.

Descartes, R. 1999. *Discourse on Method*, translated by D. A. Cress, Indianapolis, IN: Hackett Publishing.

Devitt, M. 2011. 'Methodology and the Nature of Knowing How'. *Journal of Philosophy*, 108 (4): pp. 205–18.

Dodell-Feder, D., and D. Tamir. 2018. 'Fiction Reading Has a Small Positive Impact on Social Cognition: A Meta-Analysis'. *Journal of Experimental Psychology: General*, 147 (11): pp. 1713–27.

Doggett, T., and A. Egan. 2007. 'Wanting Things You Don't Want', *Philosophers' Imprint* 7: pp. 1–17.

Doggett, T., and A. Egan. 2012. 'How We Feel About Terrible, Non-existent Mafiosi'. *Philosophy and Phenomenological Research*, 84 (2): pp. 277–306.

Döring, S. 2007. 'Seeing What to Do: Affective Perception and Rational Motivation'. *Dialectica*, 61: pp. 363–94.

Doris, J. 2002. *Lack of Character: Personality and Moral Behavior*. Cambridge: Cambridge University Press.

Doris, J. 2015. *Talking to Ourselves*. Oxford: Oxford University Press.

Driver, J. 2011. 'The Secret Chain'. *Southern Journal of Philosophy*, 49 (1): pp. 234–8.

Dunn, B., T. Dalgleish, and A. Lawrence. 2006. 'The Somatic Marker Hypothesis: A Critical Evaluation'. *Neuroscience and Biobehavioral Reviews*, 30: pp. 239–71.

Dunning, D., C. Heath, and J. Suls. 2004. 'Flawed Self-assessment'. *Psychological Sciences in the Public Interest*, 5: pp. 69–106.

Dütschke, E., M. Frondel, J. Schleich, and C. Vance. 2018. Moral Licensing—Another Source of Rebound? *Frontiers in Energy Research*, doi:10.4419/86788867.

Eaton, A. W. 2007. 'A Sensible Antiporn Feminism'. *Ethics*, 117 (4): pp. 674–715.

Effron, D., and P. Conway. 2015. 'When Virtue Leads to Villainy: Advances in Research on Moral Self-licensing'. *Current Opinion in Psychology*, 6: pp. 32–5.

Egan, D. 2016. 'Literature and Thought Experiments'. *Journal of Aesthetics and Art Criticism*, 74 (2): pp. 139–50.

Egginton, W. 2016. *The Man Who Invented Fiction: How Cervantes Ushered in the Modern World*. London: Bloomsbury.

Elgin, C. 2007. 'The Laboratory of the Mind'. In *A Sense of the World: Essays on Fiction, Narrative, and Knowledge*, edited by J. Gibson, W. Huemer, and L. Pocci. London: Routledge.

Elster, J. 2000. *Ulysses Unbound*. Cambridge: Cambridge University Press.

Emerson, R. W. 1850/1996. *Representative Men: Seven Lectures*. Cambridge, MA: Harvard University Press.

Empson, W. 1951. *The Structure of Complex Words*. London: Chatto & Windus.

Engel, P. 2016. 'Literature and Practical Knowledge'. *Argumenta*, 2 (1): pp. 55–71.

Felski, R. 2011. Editorial, special issue of *New Literary History* on 'Character,' 42(2).

Flavell, J. 1979. 'Metacognition and Cognitive Monitoring: A New Area of Psychological Inquiry'. *American Psychologist*, 34 (10): pp. 906–11.

Flynn, F., and G. Adams. 2009. 'Money Can't Buy Love: Asymmetric Beliefs about Gift Price and Feelings of Appreciation'. *Journal of Experimental Social Psychology*, 45 (2): pp. 404–9.

Fodor, J. 1983. *The Modularity of Mind*. Cambridge, MA: MIT Press.

Foot, P. 1978. 'The Problem of Abortion and the Doctrine of the Double Effect'. In her *Virtues and Vices*, pp. 19–32. Oxford: Basil Blackwell.

Frankfurt, H. 1988. *The Importance of What We Care about*. Cambridge: Cambridge University Press.

Fricker, E. 1994. 'Against Gullibility'. In *Knowing from Words*, edited by B. Matilal and A. Chakrabarti, pp. 125–63. London: Springer.

Friend, S. 2003. 'How I Really Feel about JFK'. In *Imagination, Philosophy and the Arts*, edited by M. Kieran and D. Lopes, pp. 35–54. London: Routledge.

Friend, S. 2006. 'Narrating the Truth'. In *Knowing Art: Essays in Aesthetics and Epistemology*, edited by M. Kieran and D. Lopes, pp. 35–49. London: Springer.

Friend, S. 2011. 'Fictive Utterance and Imagining II'. *Proceedings of the Aristotelian Society Supplementary Volume*, 85 (1):163–180.

Friend, S. 2012. 'Fiction as a Genre'. *Proceedings of the Aristotelian Society*, 112 (2): pp. 179–209.

Friend, S. 2014. 'Believing in Stories'. In *Aesthetics and the Sciences of Mind*, edited by G. Currie, M. Kieran, A. Meskin, and J. Robson, pp. 227–49. Oxford: Oxford University Press.

Gal, D. 2006. 'A Psychological Law of Inertia and the Illusion of Loss Aversion'. *Judgment and Decision Making*, 1 (1): pp. 23–32.

Gallagher, C. 2006. The rise of fictionality. In *The Novel, Volume 1*, edited by Franco Moretti, pp. 336–63. Princeton: Princeton University Press.

Gallagher, S. 2004. 'Understanding Interpersonal Problems in Autism: Interaction Theory as an Alternative to Theory of Mind'. *Philosophy, Psychiatry, & Psychology*, 11 (3): pp. 199–217.

Gallagher, S. 2008. 'Inference or Interaction: Social Cognition without Precursors'. *Philosophical Explorations*, 11 (3): 163–74.

Gallagher, S. 2015. 'The New Hybrids: Continuing Debates on Social Perception'. *Consciousness and Cognition*, 36: pp. 452–65.

Gallagher, S., and D. Hutto. 2008. 'Understanding Others through Primary Interaction and Narrative Practice'. In *The Shared Mind: Perspectives on Intersubjectivity*, edited by J. Zlatev, T. P. Racine, C. Sinha, and E. Itkonen, pp. 17–38. London: John Benjamins.

García-Carpintero, M. 2013. 'Norms of Fiction-Making'. *British Journal of Aesthetics*, 53 (3): pp. 339–57.

Garry, M., C. Manning, E. Loftus and S. Sherman. 1996. 'Imagination Inflation: Imagining a Childhood Event Inflates Confidence That It Occurred'. *Psychonomic Bulletin & Review*, 3 (2): pp. 208–14.

Gaskin, R. 2013. *Language, Truth, and Literature: A Defence of Literary Humanism*. Oxford: Oxford University Press.

Gaut, B. 2007. *Art, Emotion, and Ethics*. Oxford: Oxford University Press.

Gaut, B. 2010. 'Empathy and Identification in Cinema'. *Midwest Studies in Philosophy*, 34 (1): pp. 136–57.

Gendler, T. S. 2010. *Intuition, Imagination, and Philosophical Methodology*. Oxford: Oxford University Press.

Gendler, T. S. 2011. 'On the Epistemic Costs of Implicit Bias'. *Philosophical Studies*, 156 (1): pp. 33–63.

George, A. 2003a. *The Epic of Gilgamesh,* revised edition. London: Penguin Classics.

George, A. 2003b. *The Babylonian Gilgamesh Epic, Volume 1,* Oxford: Oxford University Press.

Gerrig, R. 1993. *Experiencing Narrative Worlds: On the Psychological Activities of Reading.* New Haven, CT: Yale University Press.

Gerrig, R., and D. Prentice. 1991. 'The Representation of Fictional Information'. *Psychological Science,* 2 (5): pp. 336–40.

Gettier, E. 1963. 'Is Justified True Belief Knowledge?' *Analysis,* 23 (6): pp. 121–3.

Gibbard, A. 1990. *Wise Choices, Apt Feelings.* Cambridge, MA: Harvard University Press.

Gibson, J. 2007. *Fiction and the Weave of Life.* Oxford: Oxford University Press.

Gigerenzer, G., and W. Gaissmaier. 2011. 'Heuristic Decision Making'. *Annual Review of Psychology,* 62 (1): pp. 451–82.

Gilbert, D., and T. Wilson. 2007. 'Prospection: Experiencing the Future'. *Science,* 317 (5843): pp. 1351–4.

Gilbert, D., R. Tafarodi, and P. S. Malone. 1993. 'You Can't Not Believe Everything You Read'. *Journal of Personality and Social Psychology,* 65 (2): pp. 221–33.

Gilmore, J. 2011. 'Aptness of Emotions for Fictions and Imaginings'. *Pacific Philosophical Quarterly,* 92 (4): 468–89.

Gino, F., and F. Flynn. 2011. 'Give Them What They Want: The Benefits of Explicitness in Gift Exchange'. *Journal of Experimental Social Psychology,* 47 (5): pp. 915–22.

Glazer, E. 2009. 'Rephrasing the Madness and Creativity Debate: What Is the Nature of the Creativity Construct?' *Personality and Individual Differences,* 46: pp. 755–64.

Godfrey-Smith, P. 1991. 'Signal, Detection, Action'. *Journal of Philosophy,* 88 (12): pp. 709–22.

Goethals, G. R. 1986. 'Fabricating and Ignoring Social Reality: Self-serving Estimates of Consensus'. In *Relative Deprivation and Social Comparison: The Ontario Symposium, Volume 4,* edited by J. M. Olson, C. P. Herman, and M. P. Zanna, pp. 135–57. Hillsdale, NJ: Erlbaum.

Goldman, A. I. 1976. 'Discrimination and Perceptual Knowledge'. *Journal of Philosophy,* 73: pp. 771–91.

Goldman, A. I. 1979. 'What Is Justified Belief?' In *Justification and Knowledge,* edited by G. Pappas, pp. 1–25. Boston: D. Reidel.

Gottschall, J., and Wilson, D. S. (eds.) 2005. *The Literary Animal.* Evanston: Northwestern University Press.

Green, D. 2002. *The Beginnings of Mediaeval Romance: Fact and Fiction, 1150–1220.* Cambridge: Cambridge University Press.

Green, Melanie, and T. Brock. 2000. 'The Role of Transportation in the Persuasiveness of Public Narratives'. *Journal of Personality and Social Psychology,* 79 (5): pp. 701–21.

Green, Mitchell. 2017. 'Narrative Fiction as a Source of Knowledge'. In *Narration as Argument,* edited by Paula Olmos, pp. 47–67. Cham, Switzerland: Springer.

Grice, P. 1989. *Studies in the Way of Words,* Cambridge, MA: Harvard University Press.

Griffiths, P. E. 2004. 'Is Emotion a Natural Kind?' In *Thinking about Feeling: Contemporary Philosophers on Emotion,* edited by R. C. Solomon, pp. 233–50. Oxford: Oxford University Press.

Gross, J. (ed.) 2002. *After Shakespeare: An Anthology.* Oxford: Oxford University Press.

Grove, W., and M. Lloyd. 2006. 'Meehl's Contribution to Clinical Versus Statistical Prediction'. *Journal of Abnormal Psychology,* 115 (2): pp. 192–4.

Gurney, O. 1956. 'The Sultantepe Tablets (Continued). V. The Tale of the Poor Man of Nippur'. *Anatolian Studies,* 6: pp. 145–64.

Haidt, J. 2001. 'The Emotional Dog and its Rational Tail: A Social Intuitionist Approach to Moral Judgment'. *Psychological Review*, 108 (4): pp. 814–34.

Hakemulder, F. 2000. *The Moral Laboratory: Experiments Examining the Effects of Reading Literature on Social Perception and Moral Self-knowledge*. Amsterdam: John Benjamins Publishing Company.

Harcourt, E. 2010. 'Truth and the 'Work' of Literary Fiction'. *British Journal of Aesthetics*, 50 (1): pp. 93–7.

Harold, J. 2005. 'Infected by Evil'. *Philosophical Explorations*, 8 (2): 173–87.

Harrington, L., R. Siegert, and J. McClure. 2005. 'Theory of Mind in Schizophrenia: A Critical Review'. *Cognitive Neuropsychiatry*, 10 (4): pp. 249–86.

Harris, P. L. (nd) 'Early Constraints on the Imagination: The Realism of Young Children'. Unpublished MS.

Hawley, K. 2003. 'Success and Knowledge-How'. *American Philosophical Quarterly*, 40 (1): pp. 19–31.

Hazlett, A. (2017). 'Imagination that Amounts to Knowledge from Fiction'. In *Art and Belief*, edited by H. Bradley, E. Sullivan-Bissett, and P. Noordhof, pp. 119–35. Oxford: Oxford University Press.

Heal, J. 2003. *Mind, Reason and Imagination: Selected Essays in Philosophy of Mind and Language*. Cambridge: Cambridge University Press.

Herold, R., T. Tényi, K. Lénárd, and M. Trixler. 2002. 'Theory of Mind Deficit in People with Schizophrenia during Remission'. *Psychological Medicine*, 32: pp. 1125–9.

Hetherington, S. 2008. 'Knowing-That, Knowing-How, and Knowing Philosophically'. *Grazer Philosophische Studien*, 77 (1): pp. 307–24.

Hills, A. 2009. 'Moral Testimony and Moral Epistemology'. *Ethics*, 120 (1): pp. 94–127.

Hochman, B. 2011. *Uncle Tom's Cabin and the Reading Revolution: Race, Literacy, Childhood, and Fiction, 1851–1911*. Amherst, MA: University of Massachusetts Press.

Hoefer, C. and G. Martí. 2019. 'Water Has a Microstructural Essence After All'. *European Journal for Philosophy of Science*, 9 (12), https://doi.org/10.1007/s13194-018-0236-2.

Holton, R. 1994. 'Deciding to Trust, Coming to Believe'. *Australasian Journal of Philosophy*, 72 (1): pp. 63–76.

Hornsby, J. 2011. 'Ryle's Knowing-How, and Knowing How to Act'. In *Know How*, edited by J. Bengson and M. Moffett, pp. 80–101. Oxford: Oxford University Press.

Hospers, J. 1960. 'Implied Truths in Literature'. *Journal of Aesthetics and Art Criticism*, 19 (1): pp. 37–46.

Hume, D. (1748/1999). *Enquiry Concerning Human Understanding*. Oxford: Oxford University Press.

Hume, D. (1777/2008). 'Of Tragedy'. In *Selected Essays*, edited by S. Copley, pp. 126–33. Oxford: Oxford University Press.

Hurley, S. 2006. 'Bypassing Conscious Control: Media Violence, Unconscious Imitation, and Freedom of Speech'. In *Does Consciousness Cause Behavior? An Investigation of the Nature of Volition*, edited by S. Pockett, W. Banks, and S. Gallagher, pp. 301–39. Cambridge, MA: MIT Press.

Hutto, D. 2008. *Folk Psychological Narratives: The Sociocultural Basis of Understanding Reasons*. Cambridge, MA: MIT Press.

Ichino, A. 2018. Superstitious confabulations, *Topoi*, https://doi.org/10.1007/s11245-018-9620-y

Inoue, Y., Y. Tonooka, K. Yamada, and S. Kanba. 2004. 'Deficiency of Theory of Mind in Patients with Remitted Mood Disorder'. *Journal of Affective Disorders*, 82 (3): pp. 403–9.

Irani, F., et al. 2006. 'Self-face Recognition and Theory of Mind in Patients with Schizophrenia and First-degree Relatives'. *Schizophrenia Research*, 88 (1–3): pp. 151–60.

Isen, A., and P. Levin. 1972. 'Effect of Feeling Good on Helping'. *Journal of Personality and Social Psychology*, 21 (3): pp. 384–8.

Jackson, F. 1982. 'Epiphenomenal Qualia'. *Philosophical Quarterly*, 32 (127): pp. 127–36.

Jackson, F. 2011. 'Mind and Illusion'. In *Minds and Persons. Royal Institute of Philosophy Supplements*, edited by A. O'Hear, pp. 251–73. Cambridge: Cambridge University Press.

James, H. 1907–9. Preface to *The Lesson of the Master*, volume 15 of the *New York Edition of the Novels and Tales of Henry James*. New York: Schribner.

Jamison, K. R. 1993. *Touched by Fire: Manic-depressive Illness and the Artistic Temperament*. New York: Free Press.

Jamison, K. R. 2000–2001. 'Reply to Louis Sass'. *Creativity Research Journal*, 13 (1): pp. 75–6.

Johnson, D. 2012. 'Transportation into a Story Increases Empathy, Prosocial Behaviour, and Perceptual Bias toward Fearful Expressions'. *Personality and Individual Differences*, 52 (2): pp. 150–5.

Johnson, S. 1765. *Preface to the Plays of William Shakespeare*, reprinted by Scholar Press, Menston, 1969.

Jones, K. 1996. 'Trust as an Affective Attitude'. *Ethics*, 107 (1): pp. 4–25.

Jones, K. 2006. 'Quick and Smart? Modularity and the Pro-emotion Consensus'. *Canadian Journal of Philosophy*, 36: pp. 2–27.

Kahneman, D. 2011. *Thinking Fast and Slow*. London: Penguin.

Kahneman, D., and G. Klein. 2009. 'Conditions for Intuitive Expertise: A Failure to Disagree'. *American Psychologist*, 64 (6): pp. 515–26.

Kahneman, D., and A. Tversky. 1984. 'Choices, Values, and Frames', *American Psychologist*, 39: pp. 341–50.

Kalin, J. 1992. 'Knowing Novels: Nussbaum on Fiction and Moral Theory'. *Ethics*, 103 (1): pp. 135–51.

Karttunen, L. 1977. 'Syntax and Semantics of Questions'. *Linguistics and Philosophy*, 1 (1): pp. 3–44.

Kauppinen, A. 2014. 'Empathy, Emotion Regulation, and Moral Judgment'. In *Empathy and Morality*, edited by H. Maibom, pp. 97–122. Oxford: Oxford University Press.

Keen, S. 2007. *Empathy and the Novel*. Oxford: Oxford University Press.

Kermode, F. 2001. 'Review of McEwan's Atonement', *London Review of Books*, 4 October, 23(19): pp. 8–9.

Kerr, N., R. Dunbar, and R. Bentall. 2003. 'Theory of Mind Deficits in Bipolar Affective Disorder'. *Journal of Affective Disorders*, 73 (3): pp. 253–9.

Khan, U., and R. Dhar. 2006. 'Licensing Effect in Consumer Choice'. *Journal of Marketing Research*, 43: pp. 259–66.

Kidd, D., and E. Castano. 2013. 'Reading Literary Fiction Improves Theory of Mind'. *Science*, 342 (6156): pp. 377–80.

Kidd, D., and E. Castano. 2017. Panero et al. (2016): Failure to Replicate Methods Caused the Failure to Replicate Results'. *Journal of Personality and Social Psychology*, 112 (3): 1–4.

Kidd, D., and E. Castano. 2018. 'Reading Literary Fiction and Theory of Mind: Three Preregistered Replications and Extensions of Kidd and Castano (2013)'. *Social Psychological and Personality Science*, 10. https://doi.org/10.1177/1948550618775410

Kieran, M. 2002. 'In Search of a Narrative'. In *Art and Imagination*, edited by M. Kieran and D. Lopes, pp. 69–89. London: Routledge.

Kieren, M. 2013. 'Comedy and Tragedy'. *Ethical Perspectives*, 20 (3): pp. 427–50.

Kim, M., and Y. Yuan. 2015. 'No Cross-cultural Differences in the Gettier Car Case Intuition: A Replication Study of Weinberg et al. 2001'. *Episteme*, 12: pp. 355–61.

Kind, A. 2001. 'Putting the Image Back in Imagination'. *Philosophy and Phenomenological Research*, 62 (1): pp. 85–110.

Kind, A. 2016. 'Imagining under Constraints.' In *Knowledge through Imagination*, edited by Amy Kind and Peter Kung, pp. 145–159. Oxford: Oxford University Press.

King, B. 1999. 'The Rhetoric of the Victim: Odysseus in the Swineherd's Hut'. *Classical Antiquity*, 18 (1): pp. 74–93.

King, J. C. 2014. 'What Role Do Propositions Play in our Theories?' In *New Thinking about Propositions*, J. C. King, S. Soames, and J. Speaks, pp. 5–9. Oxford: Oxford University Press.

Kiverstein, J. 2011. 'Social Understanding without Mentalizing'. *Philosophical Topics*, 39 (1): pp. 41–65.

Kivy, P. 1997. *Philosophies of Arts: An Essay in Differences*. Cambridge: Cambridge University Press.

Koethe, J. 2002. 'Stanley and Williamson on Knowing How'. *The Journal of Philosophy*, 99 (4): pp. 325–8.

Koopman, E. 2015. 'Empathic Reactions after Reading: The Role of Genre, Personal Factors and Affective Responses'. *Poetics*, 50: pp. 62–79.

Kripke, S. 1980. *Naming and Necessity*. Oxford: Basil Blackwell.

Kripke, S. 2013. *Reference and Existence: The John Locke Lectures*. Oxford: Oxford University Press.

Kumkale, G. T. and D. Albarracín. 2004. 'The Sleeper Effect in Persuasion: A Meta-analytic Review'. *Psychological Bulletin*, 130 (1): pp. 143–72.

Lamarque, P. 2010. 'Replies to Attridge, Blackburn, Feagin, and Harcourt'. *British Journal of Aesthetics*, 50 (1): pp. 99–106.

Lamarque, P. 2014. *The Opacity of Narrative*. London: Rowman & Littlefield International.

Lamarque, P., and S. H. Olsen. 1994. *Truth, Fiction, and Literature*. Oxford: Clarendon Press.

Lamm, C. C., D. Batson, and J. Decety. 2007. 'The Neural Substrate of Human Empathy: Effects of Perspective Taking and Emotion Regulation'. *Journal of Cognitive Neuroscience*, 19 (1): 42–58.

Landy, J. 2012. *How to Do Things with Fictions*. Oxford: Oxford University Press.

Langdon, R., and M. Coltheart. 2004. 'Recognition of Metaphor and Irony in Young Adults: The Impact of Schizotypal Personality Traits'. *Psychiatry Research*, 125 (1): pp. 9–20.

Langland-Hassan, P. 2012. 'Pretense, Imagination, and Belief: The Single Attitude Theory'. *Philosophical Studies*, 159 (2): pp. 155–79.

Langland-Hassan, P. 2016. 'On Choosing What to Imagine'. In *Knowledge through Imagination*, edited by A. Kind and P. Kung, pp. 61–84. Oxford: Oxford University Press.

Leavis, F. R. 1948. *The Great Tradition*. London: Chatto & Windus.

Leslie, A. M. 1994. 'Pretending and Believing: Issues in the Theory of ToMM'. *Cognition*, 50 (1–3): pp. 211–38.

Leverage, P., H. Mancing, R. Schweickert, and J. M. Williams (eds) 2010. *Theory of Mind and Literature*. West Lafayette: Purdue University Press.

Levine, J. 2009. 'Leonard's System: Why Doesn't it Work?' In *Memento*, edited by A. Kania, pp. 45–65. New York: Routledge.

Levine, T. R. 2010. 'A Few Transparent Liars: Explaining 54% Accuracy in Deception Detection Experiments'. *Annals of the International Communication Association*, 34 (1): pp. 41–61.

Lewis, D. K. 1978. Truth in Fiction. *American Philosophical Quarterly*, 15: 37–46. Reprinted in his *Philosophical Papers*, Volume 1, pp. 261–275. Oxford: Oxford University Press, 1983.

Lewis, D. K. 1983a. 'Postcript to "Mad Pain and Martian Pain"'. In his *Philosophical Papers*, Volume 1, pp. 130–2. Oxford: Oxford University Press.

Lewis, D. K. 1983b. 'Postscript to "Truth in Fiction"'. In his *Philosophical Papers*, Volume 1, pp. 276–80. Oxford: Oxford University Press.

Liao, S., and T. Doggett. 2014. 'The Imagination Box'. *Journal of Philosophy*, 111 (5): pp. 259–75.

Lillard, A., M. Lerner, E. J. Hopkins, R. A. Dore, E. D. Smith, and C. Palmquist. 2013. 'The Impact of Pretend Play on Children's Development: A Review of the Evidence'. *Psychological Bulletin*, 139 (1): pp. 1–34.

Linquist, S., and J. Bartol. 2013. 'Two Myths about Somatic Markers'. *British Journal for the Philosophy of Science*, 64 (3), pp. 455–84.

Livingston, P. 2006. 'Theses on Cinema as Philosophy'. *Journal of Aesthetics and Art Criticism*, 64: pp. 11–18.

Livingston, P. 2009. *Cinema, Philosophy, Bergman: On Film as Philosophy*. Oxford: Oxford University Press.

Livingston, P., and A. Mele. 1997. 'Evaluating Emotional Responses to Fiction'. In *Emotion and the Arts*, edited by M. Hjort and S. Lavers. Oxford: Oxford University Press.

Ludwig, A. M. 1994. 'Mental Illness and Creative Activity in Female Writers'. *American Journal of Psychiatry*, 151: pp. 1650–6.

Ludwig, A. M. 1995. *The Price of Greatness: Resolving the Creativity and Madness Controversy*. New York: Guilford Press.

Macdonald, D. 1958. 'By Cozzens Possessed—A Review of Reviews'. *Commentary*, https://www.commentarymagazine.com/articles/by-cozzens-possesseda-review-of-reviews/.

Mach, E. 1905/1976. *Knowledge and Error: Sketches on the Psychology of Enquiry*. London: Springer.

Mach, E. 1919. *The Science of Mechanics*, 4th edition. La Salle: Open Court.

Machery, E. 2017. *Philosophy within its Proper Bounds*. Oxford: Oxford University Press.

Mack, M. 2012. *How Literature Changes the Way We Think*. London: Continuum.

Mar, R., and K. Oatley. 2008. 'The Function of Fiction Is the Abstraction and Simulation of Social Experience'. *Perspectives on Psychological Science*, 3 (3): pp. 173–92.

Mar, R., K. Oatley, J. Hirsh, J. dela Paz, and J. B. Peterson. 2006. 'Bookworms versus Nerds: Exposure to Fiction versus Non-fiction, Divergent Associations with Social Ability, and the Simulation of Fictional Social Worlds'. *Journal of Research in Personality*, 40 (5): pp. 694–712.

Marjoram, D., P. Miller, A. M. McIntosh, D. G. Cunningham-Owens, E. C. Johnstone, and S. Lawrie. 2006. 'A Neuropsychological Investigation into "Theory of Mind" and Enhanced Risk of Schizophrenia'. *Psychiatry Research*, 144 (1): pp. 29–37.

Marsh, E., and L. K. Fazio. 2006. 'Learning Errors from Fiction: Difficulties in Reducing Reliance on Fictional Stories'. *Memory & Cognition*, 34 (5): pp. 1140–9.

Marsh, E., M. L. Meade, and H. L. Roediger. 2003. 'Learning Facts from Fiction'. *Journal of Memory & Language*, 49 (4): pp. 519–36.

Matravers, D. 2014. *Fiction and Narrative*. Oxford: Oxford University Press.

McCormick, I., F. Walkley, and D. Green. 1986. 'Comparative Perceptions of Driver Ability—A Confirmation and Expansion'. *Accident Analysis & Prevention*, 18 (3): pp. 331–50.

McDowell, J. 1979. 'Virtue and Reason'. *The Monist*, 62 (3): pp. 331–50.

McGinn, C. 2004. *Mindsight: Image, Dream, Meaning*. Cambridge, MA: Harvard University Press.

Meehl, P. 1954. *Clinical vs. Statistical Prediction: A Theoretical Analysis and a Review of the Evidence*. Minneapolis: University of Minnesota Press.

Mercier, H., and D. Sperber. 2017. *The Enigma of Reason: A New Theory of Human Understanding*. Cambridge, MA: Harvard University Press.

Merritt, A., D. A. Effron, S. Fein, K. K. Savitsky, D. M. Tuller, and B. Monin. 2012. 'The Strategic Pursuit of Moral Credentials'. *Journal of Experimental Social Psychology*, 48 (3): pp. 774–7.

Merritt, A., D. A. Effron, and B. Monin. 2010. 'Moral Self-licensing: When Being Good Frees Us to Be Bad'. *Social and Personality Psychology Compass*, 4 (5): pp. 344–57.

Meyer, J., and G. Shean. 2006. 'Social-Cognitive Functioning and Schizotypal Characteristics'. *Journal of Psychology*, 140 (3): pp. 199–207.

Mikkonen, J. 2010. 'Implicit Assertions in Literary Fiction'. *Proceedings of the European Society for Aesthetics*, 2: pp. 312–30.

Miller, R. W. 1998. 'Three Versions of Objectivity: Aesthetic, Moral, and Scientific'. In *Aesthetics and Ethics: Essays at the Intersection*, edited by J. Levinson, pp. 26–59. Cambridge: Cambridge University Press.

Mitchell, P., G. Currie, and F. Ziegler. 2009. 'Two Routes to Perspective: Simulation and Rule-Use as Approaches to Mentalizing'. *British Journal of Developmental Psychology*, 27 (3): pp. 513–43.

Mitchell, P., E. Robinson, J. Isaacs, and R. Nye. 1996. 'Contamination in Reasoning about False Belief: An Instance of Realist Bias in Adults but Not Children'. *Cognition*, 59: 1–2.

Mitchell, R., and A. H. Young. 2015. 'Theory of Mind in Bipolar Disorder, with Comparison to the Impairments Observed in Schizophrenia'. *Frontiers of Psychiatry*, 6. Article ID 188. http://dx.doi.org/10.3389/fpsyt.2015.00188.

Monin, B., and D. Miller. 2001. 'Moral Credentials and the Expression of Prejudice'. *Journal of Personality and Social Psychology*, 81: 33–43.

Moran, R. 1994. 'The Expression of Feeling in Imagination'. *Philosophical Review*, 103 (1): pp. 75–106.

Morris, M. 2012. 'The Meaning of Music'. *The Monist*, 95: 556–86.

Morton, A. 1996. 'Folk Psychology Is Not a Predictive Device'. *Mind*, 105 (4): pp. 119–37.

Mulhall, S. 2001. *On Film*. London: Routledge.

Murdoch, I. 1998. *Existentialists and Mystics: Writings on Philosophy and Literature*. Allen Lane/the Penguin Press.

Mutz, D. C., and L. Nir. 2010. 'Not Necessarily the News: Does Fictional Television Influence Real-world Policy Preferences?' *Mass Communication and Society*, 13 (2): pp. 196–217.

Nagel, J. 2016. 'Knowledge and Reliability'. In *Alvin Goldman and his Critics*, edited by H. Kornblith and B. P. McLaughlin, pp. 239–59. Oxford: Blackwell.

Nagel, J. 2017. 'Factive and Nonfactive Mental State Attribution'. *Mind and Language*, 32 (5): pp. 525–44.

Nemirow, L. 1980. 'Review of Nagel's *Mortal Questions*'. *Philosophical Review*, 89 (3): pp. 473–7.

Noggle, R. 2016. 'Belief, Quasi-belief, and Obsessive–Compulsive Disorder'. *Philosophical Psychology*, 29 (5): pp. 654–68.

Norton, J. D. 2004. 'On Thought Experiments: Is There More to the Argument?' *Philosophy of Science*, 71 (5): pp. 1139–51.

Novitz, D. 1987. *Knowledge, Fiction, and Imagination*. Philadelphia: Temple University Press.

Nunning, V. 2015. 'Narrative Fiction and Cognition: Why We Should Read Fiction'. *Forum for World Literature Studies*, 7 (1): pp. 41–61.

Nussbaum, M. C. 1990. *Love's Knowledge*. Oxford: Oxford University.

Nussbaum, M. C. 1994. 'The Ascent of Love: Plato, Spinoza, Proust'. *New Literary History*, 25 (4): pp. 925–49.

Nussbaum, M. C. 2001. *Upheavals of Thought: The Intelligence of Emotions*. Cambridge: Cambridge University Press.

Oatley, K. 1999. 'Why Fiction May Be Twice as True as Fact: Fiction as Cognitive and Emotional Simulation'. *Review of General Psychology*, 3 (2): pp. 101–17.

Oddie, G. 2014. 'Truthlikeness'. *The Stanford Encyclopaedia of Philosophy*. http://plato.stanford.edu/archives/sum2014/entries/truthlikeness/.

Olley, A., G. S. Malhi, J. Bachelor, C. M. Cahill, P. B. Mitchell, and M. Berk. 2005. 'Executive Functioning and Theory of Mind in Euthymic Bipolar Disorder'. *Bipolar Disorders*, 7 (5): pp. 43–52.

Origgi, G., and D. Sperber. 2000. 'Evolution, Communication and the Proper Function of Language'. In *Evolution and the Human Mind: Language, Modularity and Social Cognition*, edited by P. Carruthers and A. Chamberlain, pp. 140–70. Cambridge: Cambridge University Press.

Orosz, G., P. Krekó, B. Paskuj, I. Tóth-Királyl, B. Bőthe, and C. Roland-Lévy. 2016. 'Changing Conspiracy Beliefs through Rationality and Ridiculing'. *Frontiers in Psychology* 7, https://doi.org/10.3389/fpsyg.2016.01525.

Owens, D. 2006. 'Testimony and Assertion'. *Philosophical Studies*, 130 (1): pp. 105–29.

Palmer, F. 1992. *Literature and Moral Understanding: A Philosophical Essay on Ethics, Aesthetics, Education, and Culture*. Oxford: Clarendon Press.

Panero, M. E., D. Weisberg, J. Black, T. R. Goldstein, J. L. Barnes, H. Brown, and E. Winner. 2016. 'Does Reading a Single Passage of Literary Fiction Really Improve Theory of Mind? An Attempt at Replication'. *Journal of Personality and Social Psychology*, 111 (5): pp. 46–64.

Papineau, D. 2005. 'Social Learning and the Baldwin Effect'. In *Evolution, Rationality, and Cognition: A Cognitive Science for the Twenty-First Century*, edited by A. Zilhão, pp. 40–61. New York: Routledge.

Pappas, N. 1997. 'Fancy Justice: Martha Nussbaum on the Political Value of the Novel'. *Pacific Philosophical Quarterly*, 78 (3): pp. 278–96.

Pashler, H., and E.-J. Wagenmakers. 2012. 'Special Section on Replicability in Psychological Science: A Crisis in Confidence?' *Perspectives on Psychological Science*, 7 (6): 528–687.

Paul, L. A. 2014. *Transformative Experiences*. Oxford: Oxford University Press.

Pavese, C. 2015. 'Practical Senses'. *Philosophers' Imprint*, 15.

Perry, J. 1979. 'The Problem of the Essential Indexicals'. *Noûs*, 13 (1): pp. 3–21.

Pettersson, A. 2012. 'Review of Mack 2012'. *Notre Dame Philosophical Reviews*, 2012. https://ndpr.nd.edu/news/how-literature-changes-the-way-we-think/.

Pettit, P. 1995. 'The Cunning of Trust'. *Philosophy and Public Affairs*, 24 (3): pp. 202–25.

Pickup, G. 2006. 'Theory of Mind and its Relation to Schizotypy'. *Cognitive Neuropsychiatry*, 11 (2): pp. 177–92.

Pippin, R. B. 2001. *Henry James and Modern Moral Life*. Cambridge: Cambridge University Press.

Policastro, E., and H. Gardner. 1999. 'From Case Studies to Robust Generalizations: An Approach to the Study of Creativity'. In *Handbook of Creativity*, edited by R. J. Sternberg, pp. 213–26. Cambridge: Cambridge University Press.

Popper, K. 1976. 'A Note on Verisimilitude'. *British Journal for the Philosophy of Science*, 27 (2): pp. 147–59.

Post, F. 1994. 'Creativity and Psychopathology: A Study of 291 World-famous Men'. *British Journal of Psychiatry*, 165 (1): pp. 22–34.

Pousa, E., A. I. Ruiz, and A. S. David. 2008. 'Mentalising Impairment as a Trait Marker of Schizophrenia?' *British Journal of Psychiatry*, 192 (4): p. 312.

Premack, D., and G. Woodruff. 1978. 'Does the Chimpanzee Have a Theory of Mind?' *Behavioral and Brain Sciences*, 1 (4): pp. 515–26.

Prentice, D. A., and R. J. Gerrig. 1999. 'Exploring the Boundary between Fiction and Reality'. In *Dual-Process Theories in Social Psychology*, edited by S. Chaiken and Y. Trope, pp. 529–74. New York: Guilford.

Prinz, J. J. 2011a. 'Is Empathy Necessary for Morality?' In *Empathy: Philosophical and Psychological Perspectives*, edited by A. Coplan and P. Goldie, pp. 211–30. Oxford: Oxford University Press.

Prinz, J. J. 2011b. 'Against Empathy', *Southern Journal of Philosophy*, 49 (1): pp. 214–233.

Pritchard, D. 2005. *Epistemic Luck*. Oxford: Oxford University Press.

Putnam, H. 1978. *Meaning and the Moral Sciences*. London: Routledge.

Proust, M. 1992. *Time Regained*, revised translation by D. J. Enright of *Le Temps Retrouvé*, 1927. London: Chatto and Windus.

Quine, W. V. O. 1976. *Ways of Paradox and Other Essays*. Cambridge, MA: Harvard University Press.

Radford, C. 1975. 'How Can We Be Moved by the Fate of Anna Karenina?' *Aristotelian Society Supplementary Volume*, 49 (1): pp. 67–93.

Ramsey, F. P. (1929/1990). 'Law and Causality'. In *Philosophical Papers*, edited by H. Mellor, pp. 140–63. Cambridge: Cambridge University Press.

Ratcliffe, M. 2007. *Rethinking Commonsense Psychology: A Critique of Folk Psychology, Theory of Mind and Simulation*. London: Palgrave Macmillan.

Ratcliffe, M., and D. Hutto. 2007. 'Introduction'. In *Folk Psychology Reassessed*, edited by D. Hutto and M. Ratcliffe, pp. 1–25. Dordrecht: Springer.

Rey, G. (2007). 'Meta-atheism: Religious Avowal as Self-Deception'. In *Philosophers without Gods: Meditations on Atheism and the Secular Life*, edited by L. M. Anthony, pp. 243–66. Oxford: Oxford University Press.

Ryle, G. 1949. *The Concept of Mind*. London: Hutchinson.

Rymer, T. (1970/1693). *A Short View of Tragedy*. Menston: Scolar Press.

Salis, F. 2016. 'The Problem of Satisfaction Conditions and the Dispensability of i-Desire'. *Erkenntnis*, 81 (1): pp. 105–18.

Sass, L. A. 2001. 'Schizophrenia, Modernism, and the "Creative Imagination": On Creativity and Psychopathology'. *Creativity Research Journal*, 13 (1): pp. 55–74.

Schellenberg, S. 2013. 'Belief and Desire in Imagination and Immersion'. *Journal of Philosophy*, 110 (9): pp. 497–517.

Schier, F. 1983. 'Tragedy and the Community of Sentiment'. In *Philosophy and Fiction: Essays in Literary Aesthetics*, edited by P. Lamarque, pp. 73–92. Aberdeen: Aberdeen University Press.

Schiffman, J., C. W. Lam, T. Jiwatram, and M. Ekstrom. 2004. 'Perspective-taking Deficits in People with Schizophrenia Spectrum Disorders: A Prospective Investigation'. *Psychological Medicine*, 34 (8): pp. 1581–6.

Schlesinger, J. 2014. 'Building Connections on Sand: The Cautionary Chapter'. In *Creativity and Mental Illness*, edited by J. C. Kaufman, pp. 60–75. Cambridge: Cambridge University Press.

Schrenk, M. A. 2004. 'Galileo vs Aristotle on Freely-falling Bodies'. *Logical Analysis and History of Philosophy*, 7: pp. 1–11.

Schumann, K., J. Zaki, and C. S. Dweck. 2014. 'Addressing the Empathy Deficit: Beliefs about the Malleability of Empathy Predict Effortful Responses When Empathy Is Challenging'. *Journal of Personality and Social Psychology*, 107 (3): pp. 475–93.

Schwarz, N., and G. Clore. 1983. 'Mood, Misattribution, and Judgments of Well-Being: Informative and Directive Functions of Affective States'. *Journal of Personality and Social Psychology*, 45 (3): pp. 513–23.

Schwitzgebel, E. 2001. 'In-between Believing'. *Philosophical Quarterly*, 51 (202): pp. 76–82.

Scruton, R. 1974. *Art and Imagination: A Study in the Philosophy of Mind*. London: Methuen.

Seamon, J., M. Philbin, and L. Harrison. 2006. 'Do You Remember Proposing Marriage to the Pepsi Machine? False Recollections from a Campus Walk'. *Psychonomic Bulletin & Review*, 13 (5): pp. 752–6.

Searle, J. 1975. 'The Logical Status of Fictional Discourse'. *New Literary History*, 6 (2): pp. 319–32.

Sedikides, C., R. Meek, M. Alicke, and S. Taylor. 2014. 'Behind Bars But above the Bar: Prisoners Consider Themselves More Prosocial than Non-prisoners'. *British Journal of Social Psychology*, 53: pp. 396–403.

Sharma, N., V. M. Pomeroy, & J. Baron. 2006, 'Motor imagery: A Back Door to the Motor System after Stroke?' *Stroke*, 37, pp.1941–1952.

Shrum, L. J., R. S. Wyer, Jr, and T. C. O'Guinn. 1998. 'The Effects of Television Consumption on Social Perceptions'. *Journal of Consumer Research*, 24 (4): pp. 447–58.

Simonton, D. 2014. 'Hierarchies of Creative Domains'. In *The Philosophy of Creativity*, edited by E. S. Paul and S. B. Kaufman, pp. 247–61. New York: Oxford University Press.

Singer, P. 1997. 'The Drowning Child and the Expanding Circle'. *New Internationalist*, 289: 28–30.

Singer, P. 2011. *Practical Ethics*. Cambridge: Cambridge University Press.

Singer, T., B. Seymour, J. P. O'Doherty, K. E. Stephan, R. J. Dolan, and C. D. Frith. 2006. 'Empathic Neural Responses Are Modulated by the Perceived Fairness of Others'. *Nature*, 439: pp. 466–9.

Sklar, H. 2009. 'Narrative Structuring of Sympathetic Response'. *Poetics Today*, 30 (3): pp. 561–607.

Skow, B. 2009. 'Preferentialism and the Paradox of Desire'. *Journal of Ethics and Social Philosophy*, 3 (3): pp. 1–16.

Smith, Michael. 1994. *The Moral Problem*. London: Blackwell.

Smith, Murray. 2006. 'Film Art, Argument, and Ambiguity'. *Journal of Aesthetics and Art Criticism*, 64 (1): pp. 33–42.

Smith, M. 2017. *Film, Art, and the Third Culture*. Oxford: Oxford University Press.

Smuts, A. 2009. 'Film as Philosophy: In Defense of a Bold Thesis'. *Journal of Aesthetics and Art Criticism*, 67 (3): pp. 409–20.

Snowdon, P. 2003. 'Knowing How and Knowing That: a Distinction Reconsidered'. *Proceedings of the Aristotelian Society*, 104 (1): pp. 1–29.

Sober, E. 1984. *The Nature of Selection: Evolutionary Theory in Philosophical Focus.* Chicago, IL: University of Chicago Press.

Sodian, B., and U. Frith. 1992. 'Deception and Sabotage in Autistic, Retarded, and Normal Children'. *Journal of Child Psychology and Psychiatry*, 33 (3): pp. 591–605.

Sosa, E. 2001. 'Human Knowledge, Animal and Reflective'. *Philosophical Studies*, 106 (3): pp. 193–6.

Sosa, E. 2009. *Reflective Knowledge: Apt Belief and Reflective Knowledge*, Volume II, Oxford: Oxford University Press.

Spaulding, S. 2015. 'On Direct Social Perception'. *Consciousness and Cognition*, 36: pp. 472–82.

Sperber, D., F. Clément, C. Heintz, O. Mascaro, H. Mercier, G. Origgi, and D. Wilson. 2010. 'Epistemic Vigilance'. *Mind & Language*, 25 (4): 359–93.

Sperber, D., and H. Mercier. 2012. 'Reasoning as a Social Competence'. In *Collective Wisdom: Principles and Mechanisms*, edited by H. Landemore and J. Elster, pp. 368–93. Cambridge: Cambridge University Press.

Sperber, D., and D. Wilson. 1995. *Relevance: Communication, and Cognition*, 2nd edition. Oxford: Blackwell.

Sprong, M., P. Schothorst, E. Vos, J. Hox, and H. van Engeland. 2007. 'Theory of Mind in Schizophrenia: Meta-analysis'. *British Journal of Psychiatry*, 191 (1): pp. 5–13.

Stanley, J., and T. Williamson. 2001. 'Knowing How'. *Journal of Philosophy*, 98 (8): pp. 411–44.

Sterelny, K. 2012. *The Evolved Apprentice: How Evolution Made Humans Unique.* Cambridge, MA: MIT Press.

Stock, K. 2006. 'Fiction and Psychological Insight'. In *Knowing Art*, edited by M. Kieran and D. Lopes, pp. 51–67. London: Springer.

Stock, K. 2017. *Only Imagine: Fiction, Interpretation and Imagination.* Oxford: Oxford University Press.

Stolnitz, J. 1992. 'On the Cognitive Triviality of Art'. *British Journal of Aesthetics*, 32 (3): pp. 191–200.

Sugiyama, M. S. 2017. 'Oral Storytelling as Evidence of Pedagogy in Forager Societies'. *Frontiers in Psychology*, 8: 471. doi: 10.3389/fpsyg.2017.00471.

Sullivan-Bissett, E., and L. Bortolotti. 2017. 'Fictional Persuasion, Transparency, and the Aim of Belief'. In *Art and Belief*, edited by H. Bradley, E. Sullivan-Bissett, and P. Noordhof, pp. 153–74. Oxford: Oxford University Press.

Tang, W. H. 2016. 'Reliability Theories of Justified Credence'. *Mind*, 125 (497): pp. 63–94.

Tanner, R., and K. Carlson. 2008. 'Unrealistically Optimistic Consumers: A Selective Hypothesis Testing Account for Optimism in Predictions of Future Behaviour'. *Journal of Consumer Research*, 35 (5): pp. 810–22.

ten Brinke, L., D. Stimson, and D. R. Carney. 2014. 'Some Evidence for Unconscious Lie Detection'. *Psychological Science*, 25 (5): pp. 1098–105.

Thomasson, A. 1999. *Fiction and Metaphysics.* Cambridge: Cambridge University Press.

Thomson, J. J. 1971. 'A Defense of Abortion'. *Philosophy and Public Affairs*, 1 (1): pp. 47–66.

Thys, E., B. Sabbe and M. De Hert. 2014. 'Creativity and Psychopathology: A Systematic Review'. *Psychopathology*, 47: 141–7.

Tversky, A., and D. Kahneman. 1973. 'Availability: A Heuristic for Judging Frequency and Probability'. *Cognitive Psychology*, 5: 207–33.

Unger, P. 1996. *Living High and Letting Die.* New York: Oxford University Press.

van Laer, T., K. de Ruyter, L. M. Visconti, and M. Wetzels. 2014. 'The Extended Transportation–Imagery Model: A Meta-analysis of the Antecedents and Consequences of Consumers' Narrative Transportation'. *Journal of Consumer Research*, 40 (5): 797–817.

van Leeuwen, N. 2014. 'Religious Credence Is Not Factual Belief'. *Cognition*, 133 (3): pp. 698–715.

van Leeuwen, N. 2016. 'Beyond Fakers and Fanatics: A Reply to Maarten Boudry and Jerry Coyne'. *Philosophical Psychology*, 29 (4): pp. 1–6.

van Leeuwen, N. 2017. 'Two Paradigms for Religious Representation: The Physicist and the Playground'. *Cognition*, 164: pp. 206–11.

van Lissa, C., M. Caracciolo, B. Van Leuveren, and T. Van Duuren. 2016. 'Difficult Empathy'. *Diegesis*, 5 (1): pp. 43–63.

Velleman, J. D. 2000. *The Possibility of Practical Reason*. Oxford: Oxford University Press.

Velleman, J. D. 2003. 'Narrative Explanation'. *Philosophical Review*, 112 (1): pp. 1–25.

Verhulst, B., M. Lodge, and H. Lavine. 2010. 'The Attractiveness Halo: Why Some Candidates Are Perceived More Favourably Than Others'. *Journal of Nonverbal Behaviour*, 34 (2): pp. 111–117.

Vermazen, B. 1986. 'Expression as Expression'. *Pacific Philosophical Quarterly*, 67 (3): pp. 196–224.

Vermeule, B. 2010. *Why Do We Care about Literary Characters?* Baltimore, MD: Johns Hopkins University Press.

Verpooten, J. 2011. 'Brian Boyd's Evolutionary Account of Art: Fiction or Future?' *Biological Theory*, 6 (2): pp. 176–83.

Walsh, D. 1969. *Literature and Knowledge*. Middletown, CT: Wesleyan University Press.

Walton, K. L. 1970. 'Categories of Art'. *Philosophical Review*, 79 (3): pp. 334–67.

Walton, K. L. 1978. 'Fearing Fictions'. *Journal of Philosophy* 75, (1): pp. 5–27.

Walton, K. L. 1990. *Mimesis as Make-Believe*. Cambridge, MA: Harvard University Press.

Walton, K. L. 1994. 'Morals in Fiction and Fictional Morality (I)'. *Proceedings of the Aristotelian Society*, 68: 27–50.

Wartenberg, T. E. 2006. 'Beyond Mere Illustration: How Films Can Be Philosophy'. *Journal of Aesthetics and Art Criticism*, 64 (1): pp. 19–32.

Wartenberg, T. E. 2007. *Thinking on Screen*. London: Routledge.

Weinberg, J. M., S. Nichols, and S. Stich. 2001. 'Normativity and Epistemic Intuitions'. *Philosophical Topics*, 29 (1–2): pp. 429–60.

Wilkes, K. V. 1988. *Real People: Personal Identity without Thought Experiments*. Oxford: Oxford University Press.

Williams, B. 1973. *Problems of the Self*. Cambridge: Cambridge University Press.

Williams, B. 1989. 'Review of Rorty, *Contingency, Irony and Solidarity*'. *London Review of Books*, 11: 3–5.

Williams, B. 1993. *Shame and Necessity*, Los Angeles: University of California Press.

Williams, L. E., and J. A. Bargh. 2008. 'Experiencing Physical Warmth Promotes Interpersonal Warmth'. *Science*, 322: 606–7.

Williamson, T. 2000. *Knowledge and its Limits*. Oxford: Oxford University Press.

Williamson, T. 2016. 'Knowing by Imagining'. In *Knowledge through Imagination*, edited by A. Kind and P. Kung, pp. 113–24. Oxford: Oxford University Press.

Wilson, D., and D. Sperber. 2002. 'Truthfulness and Relevance'. *Mind*, 111 (443): pp. 583–632.

Wilson, G. 2011. *Seeing Fictions in Film: The Epistemology of Movies*. Oxford: Oxford University Press.

Woolfolk, R., M. W. Parrish, and S. M. Murphy. 1985. 'The Effects of Positive and Negative Imagery on Motor Skill Performance'. *Cognitive Therapy and Research*, 9 (3): pp. 335–41.

Worth, S. 2017. *In Defense of Reading*. Lanham: Rowman & Littlefield International.

Wright, J. L. 2007. 'The Role of Moral Perception in Mature Moral Agency'. In *Moral Perception*, edited by J. Wisnewski, pp. 1–25. Newcastle: Cambridge Scholars Publishing.

Wykes, T., S. Hamid, and K. Wagstaff. 2001. 'Theory of Mind and Executive Functions in the Non-psychotic Siblings of Patients with Schizophrenia'. *Schizophrenia Research*, 49 (Suppl.): 148.

Wynn, T. 2002. 'Archaeology and Cognitive Evolution'. *Behavioral and Brain Sciences*, 25: 389–438.

Young, J. O. 2001. *Art and Knowledge*. London: Routledge.

Young, J. O. 2017. Literary Fiction and True Beliefs. In *Art and Belief*, edited by Helen Bradley, Ema Sullivan-Bissett, and Paul Noordhof, pp. 85–100. Oxford: Oxford University Press.

Zagzebski, L. 1996. *Virtues of the Mind: An Inquiry into the Nature of Virtue and the Ethical Foundations of Knowledge*. Cambridge: Cambridge University Press.

Zunshine, L. 2006. *Why We Read Fiction: Theory of Mind and the Novel*. Columbus, OH: Ohio State University Press.

Zunshine, L. 2012. *Getting inside your Head*. Baltimore, MD: Johns Hopkins University Press.

Zunshine, L. (ed.) 2015. *The Oxford Handbook of Cognitive Literary Studies*. Oxford: Oxford University Press.

Index

For the benefit of digital users, indexed terms that span two pages (e.g., 52–53) may, on occasion, appear on only one of those pages.